DATE DUE

OE 3 97			

DEMCO 38-296

Shakespeare, Philosophy, and Literature

New Studies in Aesthetics

Robert Ginsberg
General Editor

Vol. 10

PETER LANG
New York • Washington, D.C./Baltimore • San Francisco
Bern • Frankfurt am Main • Berlin • Vienna • Paris

Morris Weitz

Shakespeare, Philosophy, and Literature

Essays

Edited by
Margaret Collins Weitz

Introduction by Harry Levin

PETER LANG
New York • Washington, D.C./Baltimore • San Francisco
Bern • Frankfurt am Main • Berlin • Vienna • Paris

loging-in-Publication Data

Morris.
Shakespeare, philosophy, and literature: essays/by Morris Weitz;
Margaret Collins Weitz, editor.
p. cm. — (New studies in aesthetics; vol. 10)
Selection of previously published essays from 1962 on.
Includes bibliographical references.
1. Shakespeare, William, 1564–1616—Philosophy. 2. Literature—
History and criticism—Theory, etc. 3. Philosophy in literature.
4. Literature—Philosophy. 5. Poetics. I. Weitz, Margaret Collins.
II. Title. III. Series.
PR3001.W45   822.3'3—dc20   93-29764
ISBN 0-8204-1679-7
ISSN 0893-6005

Die Deutsche Bibliothek-CIP-Einheitsaufnahme

Weitz, Morris:
Shakespeare, philosophy, and literature: essays / by Morris Weitz. Margaret
Collins Weitz, ed.—New York; San Francisco; Bern; Baltimore; Frankfurt am
Main; Berlin; Wien; Paris: Lang.
(New studies in aesthetics; Vol. 10)
ISBN 0-8204-1679-7
NE: GT

Cover design by James F. Brisson.

The paper in this book meets the guidelines for permanence and durability of
the Committee on Production Guidelines for Book Longevity of the Council of
Library Resources.

© 1995 Peter Lang Publishing, Inc., New York

Printed in the United States of America.

Dedicated to the Memory of Harry Levin

TABLE OF CONTENTS

ACKNOWLEDGMENTS

This collection of selected essays of Morris Weitz would not have been possible without the generosity of the following presses which allowed inclusion of those essays which had been previously published. I am most pleased to acknowledge this generosity in chronological sequence. Wayne State University Press granted permission to reprint "*Hamlet*: Philosophy the Intruder," from *Philosophy in Literature*, by Morris Weitz, 1963, Wayne State University Press. The University of Chicago Press granted permission to reprint "Poetics," from *Hamlet and the Philosophy of Literary Criticism* by Morris Weitz, 1964, the University of Chicago Press. "Reasons in Criticism" first appeared in *The Journal of Aesthetics and Art Criticism*, vol. xx, no. 4, 1962. Permission to reprint this essay was extended by the American Society for Aesthetics, which holds the copyright. "Tragedy," appeared in *The Encyclopedia of Philosophy*, Paul Edwards editor-in-chief, and published by the Macmillan Company, 1967, Macmillan Inc. "Genre and Style" appeared in *Perspectives in Education, Religion, and the Arts*, edited by Howard E. Kiefer and Milton K. Munitz, published by the State University Press of New York, Albany, in 1970. "The Coinage of Man: *King Lear* and Camus's *L'Étranger*" appeared in *The Modern Language Review*, vol. 66, 1971. Cambridge University Press published "Literature Without Philosophy: *Antony and Cleopatra*" in *Shakespeare Survey*, no. 28, Cambridge University Press, 1975. "Literature and Philosophy: Sense and Nonsense," appeared in the *Yearbook of Comparative Criticism*, Pennsylvania State University Press, 1983 (© Margaret Collins Weitz).

It is also a pleasure to acknowledge the contribution of those who helped in seeing this volume to press. Firstly to my mentor, Harry Levin, who so graciously agreed to write the introduction and made editorial "suggestions". Michael R. Ronayne, Dean of the College of Liberal Arts and Sciences of Suffolk University offered encouragement and support from the beginning. Andrea Ortisi, also of Suffolk University, provided much needed assistance. The computer wizardry of my secretary, John Mulrooney, played a large role in making the appearance of this book possible. It remains for me to offer sincere thanks to Robert Ginsberg of Peter Lang for his meticulous editing.

M. C. W.

PREFACE

This volume brings together a group of essays that examine the relationship between philosophy and literature, focusing primarily on the plays of Shakespeare. There is also a related article exploring the use of the term *"Maniera."* Most of these essays have been previously published in philosophy or literary journals, in Britain or the United States. These articles have been brought together at the suggestion of Morris Weitz's colleagues and friends. They felt that this was a much more appropriate vehicle than the *Festschrift* to commemorate a lifetime devoted to reflection on the problem of the relationship between philosophy and literature—disciplines that have been opposed as often as they have been combined.

Weitz initially started to focus on history. After completing his B. A. at Wayne State University, he started graduate work in French History at the University of Chicago. There he met Bertrand Russell. This meeting changed the direction of his studies. He decided to focus on philosophy. He completed his Ph.D. at the University of Michigan with a dissertation on "The Method of Analysis in the Philosophy of Bertrand Russell." The topic was suggested, indirectly to be sure, by Russell's lectures on semantics. Weitz examined the method Russell used to determine the sort of doctrines that he advocated—an examination that he was to extend to the arts.

After a year teaching at the University of Washington, Weitz moved to Vassar College, where he spent nine years. At Vassar his intellectual enquiry extended to aesthetics, in addition to analytical philosophy. His first major book, *Philosophy of the Arts* (1950), is generally recognized as the first work to apply the theory of meaning and logical analysis to contemporary problems in the arts and aesthetics. Critics noted his close acquaintance with the arts themselves: literature, painting, sculpture, architecture, music, dance, and film.

Weitz spent the 1959-60 academic year at Oxford as a Fulbright Senior Scholar. This year was enriching, both professionally and personally. In addition to seeing Russell frequently, he made what were to be lifetime friendships with the philosophers of Oxford: Ryle, Hart, and Berlin, amongst others. His monograph, "Oxford Philosophy" (1953), is credited with introducing the then developing Oxford school of philosophy to the American public.

Everett J. Nelson (Chairman of Philosophy when Weitz spent a year at the University of Washington) was instrumental in persuading him to accept a Full Professorship at the Ohio State University where Nelson now chaired the Department of Philosophy. Nelson was a colleague who shared his passion for philosophical discussions. While at Ohio State Weitz continued to publish extensively and to lecture and participate in symposia in the United States and abroad, including Cérisy, the Aspen Institute, and Lincoln Center. He married Margaret Collins; they had three children: Richard, David and, Catherine.

During the course of his academic career Weitz held visiting appointments at Columbia, Harvard, and Oxford. Among his many honors and awards were Guggenheim and National Endowment for the Humanities fellowships, the Matchette prize, and the Best Teacher award of the College of Arts and Sciences at Ohio State. He felt particularly honored to be the first philosopher invited to join the Shakespeare Institute of Stratford-upon-Avon.

After turning down a number of posts, Weitz chose to accept the Richard Koret Professorship at Brandeis University in 1969. He thought that the intellectual and artistic resources of the greater Boston area would enhance his professional work and provide a stimulating environment for his family. A year later he assumed chairmanship of the Brandeis Department of Philosophy.

In 1972 Weitz underwent the first in a series of operations for cancer. During a lengthy reprieve, he concentrated on his teaching and on writing the two books which were to summarize his life's work: *The Opening Mind* (1977) and *Theories of Concepts* (1988). In the late 1970's his health deteriorated. He had more surgery and painful treatments. Nevertheless, he continued his commitment to teaching (his sabbatical leave coincided with his final five months) and wrote up to the end. His last, lengthy article, "Literature and Philosophy: Sense and Nonsense" (included here) was dedicated to all the nurses who had cared for him. Morris Weitz died on February 1, 1981.

As one of his graduate students noted, wherever Morris happened to be and with whomever he happened to be—students, colleagues, friends, or medical students—he was on fire with ideas and passion. I can only hope that some of this commitment is conveyed by these essays.

Margaret Collins Weitz
Suffolk University

INTRODUCTION

The relationship between philosophy and the arts, as Plato warned, has never been an easy one; and yet, as two of the uppermost concerns of the human mind, they have continued to seek each other's company. During the eighteenth century they were brought together within a new branch of philosophy, namely aesthetics. Twentieth-century views of that provocative subject are lucidly discussed in Morris Weitz's first book, *Philosophy of the Arts* (1950). Literary criticism, on the other hand, has been more occasional in its philosophizing: Coleridge stands out as a man of letters who pursued the imaginative process into the spheres of systematic abstraction. Recent critics, concerned with questions of meaning that have too often been taken for granted in the past, have at least been demonstrating their need for an ampler philosophical background. In their quest for more theoretical approaches, they might profitably turn to Morris Weitz's prize essay, much reprinted and anthologized, "The Role of Theory in Aesthetics" (1956).

Dedicated teacher and cogent thinker, Morris Weitz (1916-1981) has left us a substantial bibliography, out of which the following key articles—representing his central combination of interests—have been collected and published together here. A graduate of Wayne State University who received his doctorate from the University of Michigan, Professor Weitz taught philosophy and the history of ideas at Vassar College, Ohio State University, and Brandeis Universities. Designated for awards and fellowships, welcomed for lectures elsewhere, he was a regular and respected summer visitor at Stratford-upon-Avon, where he took equal pleasure in its theatrical performances and in the more academic sessions of its Shakespeare Institute. Some of his early writings had dealt with the outlook of Bertrand Russell, with the positions of the Oxford School, and with what was becoming the logical and analytic mainstream of Anglo-American philosophy in our time. Thus he could bring an analytical rigor and an empirical insight to the aesthetic issues he chose to examine.

Theory must be grounded in and tested by practice, which in turn it elucidates and illuminates. Morris Weitz was especially drawn toward Shakespeare, as the most articulate of artistic practitioners, and he centered a whole volume upon Shakespeare's most speculative play, *Hamlet and the*

Philosophy of Literature (1964). "Hamlet: Philosophy the Intruder," a chapter from the earlier *Philosophy in Literature: Shakespeare, Voltaire, Tolstoy and Proust* (1963) included here, indicates how far this commentator stood from those who would superimpose their own speculations. It is not indeed the critic's business to resolve the problems that made Hamlet's dilemma so problematic. And if the essence of that drama lies in the heart of its mystery, Shakespeare moves on to make something out of the nothingness in *King Lear*. Here the royal divestiture is underlined by an existential contrast with the "unaccommodated man" of Albert Camus's novel, *L'Etranger*. The essay on *Antony and Cleopatra* owes its titular disclaimer, "Literature without Philosophy," to its highly exceptional protagonists; yet if it lays down no controlling thesis, it sounds many incidental themes.

It should be very clear from these essays that Shakespeare was not writing in the modern vein of the "problem-play"—or what the French have, even more pointedly, termed the *pièce à thèse*. G. B. Shaw, who gloried in that hortatory vein, mistook openmindedness for a lack of ideas; hence his pontifical put-down: "I despise Shakespear /sic/ when I measure my mind against his." T. S. Eliot condescendingly argued that poets did not really think, but rather gave us "the emotional equivalent of thought," and that Shakespeare borrowed his thoughts at second hand from the second-rate ethical code of the Stoic philosophers. Such reductive and self-serving comments fall by the wayside of the more serious and objective train of discussion before us. Aristotle, after all, had specified thought (*dianoia*) along with more formal elements, when he sketched the outlines of tragedy. And those first words of his, as we shall be seeing, were quite distant and different from many later ones on the tragic form.

Terms not only need to be defined, but may be redefined by continuing discourse; and Morris Weitz is not only adept at such formulation, but invariably helpful in guiding us away from the all-too-frequent pitfalls of obfuscating terminology. In evoking, quoting, or restating some of the major texts from Plato to Wittgenstein, he reminds us that the critical function—if not always progressive—is ultimately cumulative in its historical scope. Literature, as the most explicit of the arts, depending like philosophy upon words, claims his fullest attention: most centrally the drama, but also such preeminent novels as those of Tolstoy and Proust (and he has written discerningly of Eliot's poetry). However, his observations would not have reached their high level of general application, if he had not been so well versed in the other aesthetic media. His considerations on "Genre and Style," though they can be much more widely applied, are concretely based upon a well-informed survey of the techniques and concepts of Mannerist painting.

In those border regions between art itself and our awareness of its principles—an area where "Sense and Nonsense" readily cohabit, and individual works can be obscured by overarching generalizations—it is salutary to watch common sense prevailing over all the impressionistic small-talk. When these evaluations are validated, when these interpretations lead to understanding, it is through a philosopher's heedful search for "Reasons in Criticism." We may confidently place ourselves in his hands because he respects the complexities of our basic subject-matter, and shows himself to be modest as well as rigorous, precise as well as open, knowledgeable as well as skeptical. To have attended his classes must have been an inviting and rewarding experience. Having missed that opportunity, we are now fortunate in being enabled to draw upon so lively and solid a printed record. It should help us to sharpen our perceptions, to appreciate the artistry that has quickened them, and to think more clearly about the interaction.

Harry Levin
Harvard University

Chapter One

TRAGEDY

Philosophers from Aristotle to the present day are almost unanimous in subscribing to the doctrine that the term "tragedy" denotes a class of works of art, distinguishable from all other classes, whose members possess certain common properties by virtue of which they are tragic, and, hence, that these properties are necessary and sufficient, essential, or defining properties of tragedy; that without a definition of tragedy, critical discourse about particular tragedies cannot be shown to be either intelligible or true; and, consequently that the major task of a philosophy of tragedy is to provide such a theory. Literary critics and writers of dramatic tragedies who theorize about tragedy, such as Dryden, Corneille, Racine, and Arthur Miller, concur with philosophers in this doctrine.

Is there a theory (a poetics, true statement, or real definition) of tragedy? Can there be such a theory? Need there be such a theory in order to guarantee the intelligibility of critical talk about why X is tragic or whether X is tragic? These shall be our focal questions in examining the major historical theories of tragedy.

Aristotle. "Tragedy, then, is an imitation of an action that is serious, complete, and of a certain magnitude; in language embellished with each kind of artistic ornament, the several kinds being found in separate parts of the play; in the form of action, not of narrative; with incidents arousing pity and fear effecting the proper purgation of these emotions" (*Poetics*, 1449B; Butcher translation).

Aristotle's definition is the most famous ever given, and the major part of the *Poetics* is an explication of it. First, Aristotle states that tragedy is a mode or species of imitation which differs from the other modes of poetic imitation (comedy, epic, dithyramb, and music) in that it imitates the action of men who are better than or like us, and that it imitates by means of language, rhythm, and harmony, in the medium of representation.

Aristotle, however, does not define "imitation" (*mimesis*), which is the genus of tragedy. Exegetes of Aristotle dispute its meaning: "replica," "reproduction," "ideal representation," "re-creation," among others, have been suggested. But the only meaning, vague as it is, which seems warranted by *Poetics*, especially by the discussion of the origin of poetry in man's instinct to imitate, is that imitation is the creation of a likeness which is not necessarily an exact copy.

"Action" is not defined either. All that seems clear is that it implies personal agents with distinctive qualities of character and thought, and that it has to do with what men do and suffer. By "serious action" Aristotle means a passage, which is necessary or probable, from happiness to misery and which is worth while; it is not an action that necessarily ends unhappily or in death.

"Action" leads to "plot," which is one of the central concepts of the *Poetics*, yet one that is not even articulated in Aristotle's explicit definition of "tragedy." By "plot" Aristotle means the arrangement of the incidents of the story. Fundamentally, plot is an imitation of the action. As such, it is central to tragedy, more important than the other qualitative or formative elements: characters, thought, diction, melody, and spectacle. According to Aristotle, plot is the most important element of tragedy because (1) it imitates what in life is most important for tragedy, namely, the actions of men or the passage from happiness to misery; (2) because it induces pity and fear and the tragic effect, purgation; and (3) because it may contain (as the best tragedies do) the most powerful elements of emotional interest in tragedy, namely, reversal of the situation (*peripeteia*) and recognition (*anagnorisis*).

Neither "pity" nor "fear" is defined. All Aristotle says is that pity is aroused by unmerited misfortune, and fear by the misfortune of one like ourselves. "Reversal of the situation" denotes a change of the action to its opposite, as in *Oedipus Rex*, in which the messenger attempts to cheer Oedipus and instead produces the opposite effect by revealing who Oedipus really is. "Recognition" refers to the change from ignorance to knowledge. The best form of recognition is one that coincides with a reversal of the situation, as in *Oedipus Rex*. Further, there are various kinds of recognition, ranging from "recognition by signs," such as scars or tokens (the least artistic), to "recognition...from the incidents themselves" (the most artistic), as is also exemplified in *Oedipus Rex*.

"Purgation" (*katharsis*) is the most debated term in the Poetics. Explanations of the term range from expulsion of harmful emotions to purification of them. F. L. Lucas suggests that purgation is the partial removal of excess humors, and thereby the restitution of the passions to a healthy balance which effects the pleasure of emotion relieved (*Tragedy*, pp. 38 ff.). Whatever the exact meaning the term has for Aristotle, the effect of tragedy upon its audience, and hence the function of tragedy, is an intrinsic part of its definition.

The best tragic plots are complete, whole, and of a certain magnitude. Briefly, this means that a good plot has a causally related beginning, middle, and end, and a length that allows the hero to pass, by a series of probable or necessary stages, from happiness to misfortune, or vice versa. Good plots also possess unity—a unity of action, not of the hero and not of time and place. Aristotle says nothing about unity of place, insofar as time is concerned, he says only that tragedy, unlike epic, tends to confine itself within or nearly within the period of 24 hours. Further, good plots can indicate what may happen as well as what did happen. Indeed, this concern for the possible (provided the possible is probable or necessary) distinguishes poetry from history, making poetry more philosophical and elevated than history. For the statements of poetry are universal, that is, they are about what A or B will probably or necessarily do, rather than about what A or B did do. Finally, the worst plots are episodic, that is, they are plots in which the sequence are not probable or necessary.

Character is subordinate to plot. Indeed, tragic plots determine their chief characters. Characters should manifest good moral purpose, act appropriately (for example, men, but not women, should be valorous), be true to life, and be consistent. But in order that the tragedy, may achieve the tragic effect, the tragic hero must also be highly renowned and prosperous, although not eminently good or just, and in fact must display some error of judgement or fault (*hamartia*) that causes his misfortune; however, he need not have any vice or depravity as the cause of his downfall. Hence, the tragic plot cannot present a virtuous man brought from prosperity to adversity, nor a bad man proceeding from adversity to prosperity, nor an utter villain being defeated, for none of these inspires pity or fear.

As his explication reveals, Aristotle offers two definitions of tragedy, which he subdivides into tragedy and good tragedy. Every tragedy is an imitation of the passage from happiness to misery and contains the requisite pity and fear, *hamartia*, purgation, thought melody, representation, and spectacle. Every good tragedy is characterized by all these but has reversal and recognition (together); unity of action; good, appropriate, true, and consistent characters; and a fine use of language, especially metaphor. That Aristotle does offer these two definitions, and hence two sets of criteria for tragedy, can be seen in the fact that, for him, a certain vehicle may be a tragedy even though it has no reversal, but it cannot be a tragedy if it has no pity and fear.

Is Aristotle's theory true? Does it cover all tragedies, or even the Greek ones? Philosophers and critics after Aristotle challenge his description of Greek tragedy and of tragedy altogether. Critics (for example, H. D. F. Kitto, in *Greek Tragedy*) point out that *hamartia* does not characterize Oedipus or Medea, as it does Creon in *Antigone*, and that awe rather than pity or fear is inspired by *Agamemnon*. Some critics question the priority of plot, the subordination of plot, the subordination of character to plot, and the denigration of spectacle. They also challenge the concept that *hamartia*, purgation, and the tragic hero as a relatively good man are necessary properties or even members of a disjunctive set of sufficient properties of tragedy, for there are tragedies without *hamartia* or purgation, and tragedies with a wicked hero or an eminently just one. Many critics and philosophers argue that Aristotle's list of formative elements leaves out the essential property of the hero's *areté* (excellence), as well as the elements of conflict, doom, regeneration, spiritual waste, and a just punishment, without which there can be no tragedy. Contemporary writers of tragedy, for example, Samuel Beckett and Eugene Ionesco, perhaps echoing the views of Schopenhauer, even go so far as to suggest through their work that tragedy need have no hero, plot, or imitation of a serious action, but only the bare presentation of the underlying "absurdity" of life.

Aristotle seems to be on safer ground with his list of evaluative criteria. In the sense in which *hamartia*, purgation, the tragic hero, and so forth are challengeable properties of tragedy, Aristotle's criteria of great tragedy—the unity of action, wholeness, completeness and magnitude of plot, consistency of character, and the coincidence of reversal of the situation with recognition—remain intact. "*Oedipus Rex* is a great tragedy because of (among other reasons) its relentless unity of action and plot and its messenger scene of reversal and recognition" is unchallengeable in the way that "*Oedipus Rex* is a tragedy because Oedipus is a relatively good man whose error or frailty leads to his downfall, which induces pity and fear and their purgation" is not unchallengeable. Nevertheless, Aristotle's list of evaluative criteria, brilliant as it is, cannot be said to sum up a real or true definition of great tragedy; his criteria are neither necessary nor sufficient for great tragedy.

Medieval, Renaissance, and Neoclassic Themes. A. C. Bradley, in his celebrated essay "Hegel's Theory of Tragedy" (in *Oxford Lectures on Poetry*), writes, "Since Aristotle dealt with tragedy and, as usual, drew the main features of his subject with those sure and simple strokes which no later hand has rivalled, the only philosopher who has treated it in a manner both original and searching is Hegel." Accurate as this assessment of Hegel may be, it would be wrong to infer from it that there is little or nothing of philosophical interest written about tragedy from Aristotle to Hegel. For there are original ideas about tragedy in the medieval period as well as ideas derived from the Poetics during the Renaissance and neoclassic periods which, because they represent variant uses of the concept of tragedy, are extremely important for philosophy.

The great medieval contribution to the theory of tragedy is the tradition that is reflected in the writings of Boccaccio, Chaucer, and later medieval authors, according to which tragedies are nondramatic narratives such as those in *De Casibus Illustrium Vitorum*—stories of the falls of illustrious men. Central in these tales is a total reverse of fortune that comes upon a man of high degree who is in apparent prosperity. Chaucer's monk sums up this medieval notion of the tragic in the *Canterbury Tales*. A tragedy is a story

> Of him that stood in greet prosperitee
> And is y—fallen out of heigh degree
> Into miserie, and endeth wrecchedly.
>
> (*Canterbury Tales* B, 3165-3167)

Scholarly views about the significance of the fall differ. Lily Campbell, for instance, argues (in *Shakespeare's Tragic Heroes*) that these medieval tales function as *exempla* which, by pointing out man's uncertainty in and possible fall from prosperity, warn all men of the fickleness of fortune, and by ascribing the cause of the fall to vice, of divine justice in the world. Consequently, for her, medieval tragedy, like all tragedy, not only presents evil but explains it. English Renaissance tragedy, including that of Shakespeare, incorporates this medieval view but also constitutes a shift from the mere presentation of the fall of princes to the justification of evil in the retribution of God against those who bring evil upon themselves in their exercise of passion. Tragedies thus become *exempla* of moral philosophy, admonishing men to attend to the lessons of the consequences of evil in order to avoid ruin and misery. Renaissance theorists of tragedy fused the medieval notion of tragedies as *exempla* with the Aristotelian doctrine of drama as lively imitation, the latter teaching us (delightfully) how not to live.

But Willard Farnham, in *The Medieval Heritage of Elizabethan Tragedy*, interprets the significance of the fall differently. Without acceptance of the world, he claims, there can be no tragedy, only surrender. In spite of their scorn for the world, these medieval tales of the fall of illustrious princes transcend moralizing about man's evil to become absorbed emotionally and sympathetically in the sufferings of these princes. According to Farnham, affirmation of the grandeur of man, not denigration of him, is central to these tales of woe, and it is this affirmation that also characterizes Elizabethan tragedy, as indeed it does all tragedy. Thus, for Farnham, neither medieval nor Renaissance tragedy is an explanation or justification of evil; it is an espousal of life in spite of evil.

Shakespearean and French classical tragedy, along with the ancient Greek, are universally acknowledged as the great moments in the history of dramatic tragedy. Shakespearean tragedy derives in part from the medieval type. The tragedies of Corneille and Racine, however, are partly rooted in Greek drama (and Roman, which was modeled on the Greek) and in an extensive interpretation (or misinterpretation) of Aristotle's *Poetics*.

The *Poetics* was not known in the West until the Italian Renaissance. The first critical edition with a commentary was Francisco Robortello's (1548). From the time of Robortello to that of Coleridge (and later, too) certain views about tragedy, either Aristotelian or those attributed to Aristotle, were vehemently debated. The most notorious issue, of course, concerned the three unities. But imitation, purgation, probability, and necessity, and action also figured prominently in the long discussion.

J. C. Scaliger first formulated the three unities of action, time, and place. L. Castelvetro and others repeated them as being necessary for tragedy. But it was the French theorists, and especially, Corneille (after *Le Cid*) and Racine, who codified the unities and rendered them sacrosanct in their tragedies. They based the concept that the action of a tragedy must coincide temporally with the performance itself and that it must occur in one place on an interpretation of Aristotle's notions of probability and necessity as verisimilitude—that is, on the way things are likely to work in nature. To create and preserve belief in the action on the stage, strict limitations of time and place must be preserved. The audience cannot be expected to retain belief in the action if it covers years or occurs in many different places.

According to French classical theory, however, the three unities are not the main requirement of tragedy. The stress was laid on imitation of a serious action, which was conceived of as a representation of human action during a particular crisis of duty or honor versus love, or of passion versus will or reason (as in Racine's masterpiece, *Phèdre*). The tragic hero is not so much renowned and prosperous as he is noble, in the quite literal sense of belonging to the nobility. The action is confined to the crisis; no complicated or double plots are tolerated, and no mixture of the serious and the comic is allowed. Nor can there be scenes of violence on the stage. The action also inspires pity and fear and their purgation, which effects pleasure and moral instruction. Finally, insofar as Aristotle's linguistic embellishments are concerned, only verse, with no prose, can be present.

The fact that these characteristics were considered to be defining properties of all tragedy, and not simply of French or Greek tragedy, can be seen in Voltaire's indictment of the tragedies of Shakespeare—especially *Hamlet*, which Voltaire castigated as a "monstrous farce."

Dryden, Johnson, and Coleridge answered the French theorists by challenging, in effect, their restrictive defining criteria in order to force an enlargement of the concept of tragedy so that it would include Shakespeare. In his *Essay of Dramatic Poesy* (1668), Dryden first paid tribute to the three unities, not because they produce verisimilitude but because they effect an aesthetic unity; then he rejected the three unities, as well as the French conception of serious action, in favor of Shakespearean tragedy, with all its irregularities, mixture of the comic and serious, use of prose, and violation of the rules, on the ground that Shakespearean tragedy possesses a variety whose liveliness pleases as the French, in all its rigidity, does not. Johnson supplemented Dryden's attack by dismissing credibility as being basic to verisimilitude and the two unities of time and place, and argued that delusion, not belief, governs our response to the drama; and in order to justify Shakespeare's irregularities, he substituted truth to nature ("just representations of general nature") for truth to conventional rules. Coleridge ended the debate by rejecting both the French insistence upon the rules and Johnson's notion of delusion. Shakespeare's dramas, he argued at length, have their own unity, which is organic, not mechanical like that of the French tragedies. We respond to these dramas, as we do to all poetry, not with belief or disbelief (delusion) but with the suspension of disbelief that constitutes poetic faith. With Coleridge, the tragedies of Shakespeare enter among the paradigms of tragedy.

Hegel, Schopenhauer, and Nietzsche. Before Hegel, German critics and philosophers theorized about the nature of tragedy. Lessing conceived of tragedy as fundamentally a revelation and justification of the divine order in the universe, whereas Schiller contended that moral resistance to suffering, not ysuffering by itself, is primary in tragedy. F. Schlegel emphasized the struggle in tragedy between man and fate which results in man's physical defeat, yet also his moral victory, and A.W. Schlegel insisted upon the ultimately inexplicable character of the tragic in the world. Goethe's brilliant insight that catharsis is best understood as expiation and reconciliation on the part of the hero rather than as purgation on the part of the public should also be noted.

Hegel, Schopenhauer, and Nietzsche proclaimed metaphysical theories of tragedy. Unlike Aristotle, who did not subscribe to any tragic event in the world which is imitated by dramatic tragedy but only to the passage in human affairs from happiness to misery, these three philosophers concur in their basic doctrine that dramatic tragedy depicts and rests upon some tragic fact in the world. For Aristotle, tragedy existed only in art, whereas for these three philosophers, there is tragic art primarily because there is tragedy in life. Hegel makes this explicit in his assessment of the life and trial of Socrates:

> In what is truly tragic there must be valid moral powers on both sides which come into collision; this was so with Socrates . . . . Two opposed rights come into collision, and the one destroys the other. Thus both suffer loss and yet both are mutually justified . . . . The one power is the divine right, the natural morality . . . objective freedom. The other . . . is the right . . . of subjective freedom . . . . It is these two principles which we see coming into opposition in the life and philosophy of Socrates. (*Lectures on the History of Philosophy*.)

Hegel. In his most important work on tragedy, *The Philosophy of Fine Art*, Hegel singles out *Antigone* as the best illustration of the dramatic representation of the tragic fact of collision and reconciliation. Two great forces are present in the play: public law and order, and familial love and duty. Both are good, both are integral aspects of a moral society (hence of absolute justice), and both are recognized to be such by Creon and Antigone. But both forces are pushed to their extremes by the protagonists so that they negate each other, thereby violating the absolute nature of justice. And because of this violation, both Creon and Antigone are condemned. Only absolute justice is vindicated.

For Hegel the tragic hero, in drama as in life, is identical with the finite force he represents. Indeed, his tragic flaw consists in this identification, since it renders him one—sided and hence incompatible with the demands of absolute justice. His one—sidedness makes his action and condemnation inevitable.

Dramatic tragedy intensifies, unifies, and embellishes upon the tragic fact, through plot, character, language, and scenic representation. It also produces the requisite pity, fear, and purgation. But, Hegel argues, dramatic tragedy excites and purifies us by more than the sufferings of the hero, for our fear and pity are directed ultimately toward the might of absolute justice that rules the world, the comprehension of which brings us the feeling of reconciliation—according to Hegel, the true tragic effect.

All dramatic tragedies share the basic elements of collision and reconciliation. Ancient dramatic tragedy, however, differs from modern tragedy in regard to the modes of conflict and resolution. Because character is subordinate to ethical forces in ancient dramatic tragedy, the conflict is always of two ethical principles, even in *Oedipus Rex*, in which, Hegel strainingly (and obscurely) suggests, the conflict is between what one consciously wants to do and what one unconsciously has done. Resolution, and with it triumphant vindication of the ethical absolute, is achieved either by the downfall of the hero, as in *Antigone*; the surrender or sacrifice of the hero, as in *Oedipus Rex*; the harmonization of interests, as in *Eumenides*; or the reconciliation in the soul of the hero, as in *Oedipus at Colonus*. In modern dramatic tragedy, in which the ethical forces are at work, and the subjectivity of character is paramount, the conflict centers in the hero himself. He is inwardly torn and thereby destroys himself. *Hamlet*, for example, is tragic not because Hamlet violates morality but because his noble nature prevents him from acting, and this, together with external circumstances, brings about his doom. Pure reconciliation is also played down or eliminated altogether in much modern tragedy. It is present in *Hamlet*, but not in *Richard III*, where it is replaced by "criminal justice;" nor is it to be found in many social tragedies, which create only sadness at misfortune and hence, for Hegel, are not really tragic at all.

Schopenhauer. For Schopenhauer, the tragic fact in the world that is represented by dramatic tragedy, and without which there could be no such art form, is the terrible side of life—"the unspeakable pain, the wail of humanity, the triumph of evil, the scornful mastery of chance, and the irretrievable fall of the just and innocent (*The World As Will and Idea*, Book III)." It is this fact that hints at the nature of the world, the ceaseless and futile strife of the irrational will; it also hints at the only way to escape from the struggle, namely, by the complete renunciation of the will. Man, thus, can overcome the tragedy involved in volition not, as Hegel claims, by a mastery of the dialectic of negotiation but only by a total surrender of the will to live.

Dramatic tragedy mirrors the tragic fact of life and at the same time projects the way out. By centering on the real tragic flaw, which is not the individual sin of the tragic hero but the original sin of being born at all, it demonstrates that "the representation of a great misfortune is alone essential to tragedy."

Great misfortune is represented in three ways: by a character of extraordinary wickedness, such as Richard III, Iago, Shylock, or Creon in *Antigone*, who authors his own misery; by blind fate, such as that which permeates *Oedipus Rex* or *Romeo and Juliet*, in which chance and error dominate man; and by ordinary, decent characters in ordinary circumstances who hurt each other simply through the ways in which they are juxtaposed with one another. This third kind, exemplified best by Goëthe's *Clavigo*, is the geatest dramatic tragedy because it depicts the tragic fact of life as it threatens or is actually experienced by most of us, who are neither monstrous nor placed in extraordinary circumstances. This type of tragedy, Schopenhauer concludes, leaves us shuddering as "we feel ourselves already in the midst of hell."

Nietzsche. For Nietzsche, too, human suffering is basic to tragedy, but in his view it yields neither despair nor resignation, as it did for Schopenhauer, nor can it be overcome by reason and knowledge, as Socrates maintained. It can be transcended, but only by an affirmation of the life force that lies behind it, the belief that "despite every phenomenal change, life is at bottom joyful and powerful" (*The Birth of Tragedy*, vii). It is this affirmation that constitutes the "tragic myth," the fundamental truth about man, without which dramatic tragedy is impossible.

Suffering and affirmation derive from more fundamental forces in the world, (namely the Dionysian and Apollonian), for nature rests upon the duality of "intoxication" and "dream," of "individuality" and "unification." The world is a constant struggle between the irrational, absurd, and ecstatic, on the one hand, and the rational, intelligible, and harmonious on the other. Dramatic tragedy joins these two forces, and in this process the tragic hero, in spite of his terrible suffering and his fall, affirms his annihilation by accepting his consequent unification with the Dionysian forces.

Thus, dramatic tragedy is a ritualistic affirmation of life. The horrors of human experience are rendered palatable by the principles of artistic order and beauty, as well as triumphant through the necessary destruction of human individuality. In Greek tragedy both the chorus and the hero represent this fusion of the Dionysian and the Apollonian. Apollo is the artistic victor, but Dionysus is the metaphysical one. The serenity traditionally attributed to Greek tragedy, consequently, must give way to the orgiastic joy of man's identification with nature, which is the hidden reality of Greek tragedy.

Dramatic tragedy, as myth and ritual, also includes the spectator. He, too, is part of the pattern of unification with the Dionysian forces. Like the hero and the chorus, he shares in the affirmation of life that is presented in the annihilation of the hero. The tragic effect, therefore, is not purgation, purification, resignation, or detachment but joyful participation in the tragic ritual, which alone offers "metaphysical solace" for our existence in an absurd world.

Some Contemporary Theories. Theories of tragedy abound in modern thought. Among the influential ones are those of A. C. Bradley, J. W. Krutch, F. L. Lucas, E. M. W. Tillyard and Una Ellis-Fermor. For Bradley, the essence of tragedy, both human and dramatic, is the irretrievable self—waste or destruction of value in the conflict of spiritual forces in the world. Dramatic tragedy involved the requisite action or conflict: a hero need not be morally good but must be touched by human excellence and who, because of his one—sidedness (tragic flaw), is responsible for his inevitable suffering and fall; and the tragic effect, which includes awe and admiration, as well as pity and fear. But plot, character, and, of course, dialogue and spectacle are tragic because they entail or are entailed by the essential self—waste of good, a loss that cannot be ultimately justified or explained.

Krutch, in his jeremiad *The Modern Temper*, denies the possibility of tragedy except in those ages (for example, the Periclean and Elizabethan) when man accepts as real his own nobility and importance in the universe. Tragedy, thus, is not a representation of noble actions but of actions considered to be noble. Without this projection—"the tragic fallacy"—there can be no tragedy. Tragedy may contain calamity, but it must show man's greatness in overcoming it. When calamity becomes an end in itself, thereby inducing misery and despair, as it does in modern tragedy (especially in Ibsen), the term "tragedy" loses its correct meaning, for tragedy cannot denigrate man; it must exalt him.

Lucas defines tragedy as a "representation of human unhappiness which pleases us notwithstanding, by the truth with which it is seen and the fineness with which it is communicated . . . . Tragedy, in fine, is man's answer to this universe that crushes him so pitilessly. Destiny scowls upon him: his answer is to sit down and paint her where she stands" (*Tragedy*, p. 78).

Tillyard distinguishes between three types of tragedies: those of suffering, sacrifice, and regeneration. The tragedy of suffering (such as Webster's *The Duchess of Malfi*) involves the suffering of a strong character who is not greatly responsible for his plight and who protests against it as he reflects upon it and its place in the universe. The tragedy of sacrifice, which is rooted in religion, has for its characters a god, a victim, a killer, and an audience, and for its aim the riddance of a taint on the social organism (as in *Oedipus Rex*). The tragedy of regeneration (such as Aeschylus' *Oresteia*) is one of spiritual renewal after disintegration; it symbolizes the life cycle from birth to destruction which leads to re-creation, and it is the "centrally tragic" (*Shakespeare's Problem Plays*, p. 14).

Una Ellis-Fermor, in *The Frontiers of Drama*, describes tragedy as an interim reading of life between religion, on the one hand, and Satanism, or pressimistic materialism, on the other. Basic to tragedy is the equilibrium of the evil that is observed and the good that is guessed at. Dramatic tragedy includes the great strength of emotion, revealed through character, action, and thought, directness of presentation, and catastrophe. What is central, however, is the balance between and intense awareness of pain or evil, which is clearly revealed, and an intuitive apprehension of a transcendent realm of values. This balance is achieved by the chorus and outer action, as in *Agamemnon*; by inner and outer action, as in *Hamlet*; or by form and action, as in *Oedipus Rex*. In each case evil is affirmed, but it is transcended by a higher good which induces exultation, not despair or faith. The balance is destroyed when evil is denied, as in Milton's *Samson Agonistes*; or is seen as remedial, as in Elmer Rice's *The Adding Machine*; or is affirmed as ultimate, as in Marlowe's *Dr. Faustus*. These dramas, therefore, are not really tragedies.

Finally, Peter Alexander, in *Hamlet: Father and Son*, rejects the traditional conception according to which tragedy includes *hamartia* and purgation, and defines tragedy instead as the dramatization and celebration of the virtues of men—their glory, achieved through affliction and calamity. *Areté*, not *hamartia*, therefore, is central. Tragedy includes suffering and calamity, but these need not be created and sustained by human frailty or wickedness. Love, honor, and duty can also effect suffering and catastrophe. Thus, *hamartia* as the tragic flaw that justifies the hero's fall and punishment is not basic or even necessary in tragedy. Nor is catharsis the rational acceptance of the fall of the hero as a result of his tragic flaw; rather, catharsis is an active mastery over life's pain, which is intelligible only if tragedy glorifies human virtues.

Is there, then, a true theory of tragedy? Do any of the critics or philosophers provide a true statement of the necessary and sufficient properties of all tragedies, their common, essential nature, by virtue of which all of them are tragic? Does any formula cover all tragedies—Greek, Elizabethan, French, and modern—without leaving out any of their tragic properties?

The fundamental disagreements among the theorists themselves about the nature of tragedy seriously call into question such a formula, for, as we have amply seen, the theorists disagree not only about the essence of tragedy but even about its necessary properties. Do all tragedies have a hero? Do all tragic heroes possess the tragic flaw? Are all tragic heroes responsible for their fate? Do all of them suffer terribly, fall, and die? Are all touched by greatness? Do all get their just desserts? Do all tragedies commemorate human excellence? Do all end unhappily? Do all stir us deeply? Is the action in all of them inevitable? Are there collision and conflict in all? Do all induce catharsis in any of its numerous senses, purgation, purification, moderation, redemption, active mastery of pain, reconciliation, and so forth—or do all produce any other uniform reaction in their spectators? There is much basic disagreement over all these properties.

Perhaps, as all the theorists imply, the disagreements can be resolved by further examination of dramatic tragedies and of the human situation. But neither of these yields a true theory of tragedy. Research into all existing dramatic tragedies and the probing of their shared properties reveal no essences. What, for example, do *Oedipus Rex*, *Oedipus at Colonus*, *Medea*,

Hamlet, *Phèdre*, *Hedda Gabler*, *The Weavers*, and *The Three Sisters*, to mention only a very few tragedies, have in common that makes them tragic and distinguishable from other works of art? Perhaps they share some similarities, but no set of necessary and sufficient properties is common to all. Nor will further examination of the human situation furnish us with a theory of tragedy, because there is no tragic fact in the world about which a theory of tragedy could be true or which would corroborate such a theory. There may be spiritual waste, loss of greatness, suffering, struggle, defeat, *areté*, regeneration, explicable or inexplicable evil, and catharsis. But whether any of these, or a collection of them, is tragic cannot be determined by any investigation. In spite of the enormous effort expended by the great theorists, one cannot but conclude that there is no established true theory of tragedy.

Can there be a true theory of tragedy? It seems that there cannot be, for underlying every theory of tragedy is the assumption that tragedy has a set of necessary and sufficient properties. This assumption is equivalent to the doctrine that the concept of tragedy or the term "tragedy" and its adjectival derivatives have a set of necessary and sufficient conditions for their correct, intelligible use, and this doctrine is false. That it is false has already been disclosed by the logical behavior of the concept of tragedy, whose use has not and cannot have a set of essential conditions of employment.

It is the disagreements among the theorists about the necessary and sufficient properties of tragedy that furnish the clue to the logical behavior of the concept of tragedy and the consequent impossibility of a theory, for these disagreements are not primarily over the application of accepted criteria for the correct use of the concept but over the very criteria themselves. What is central in the disagreements about the theories of tragedy are the debates over which criteria shall determine the correct use of the concept of tragedy.

Tragedy is not definable (in the theory sense of a true, real definition) for another reason, namely, that its use must allow for the ever present possibility of new conditions. It is simply a historical fact that the concept, as we know and use it, has continuously accommodated new cases of tragedy, and, more important, the new properties of these new cases. One cannot state the necessary and sufficient conditions for the correct use of a concept whose very use entails the requirement that the concept be applicable to new conditions.

Each theory of tragedy expresses an honorific redefinition of tragedy that restricts the use of the term to a selection from its multiple criteria. It is this selection that gives point and value to all the theories of tragedy, for each serves, through its specific selection, as a recommendation to concentrate upon certain preferred criteria or properties of tragedy that are neglected, distorted, or omitted by other theories. If we attend to these criteria or properties instead of to the unsuccessful attempts of essentialist definitions, we shall have much to learn from the individual theories about what to look for in tragedies as well as how to look at them.

Does criticism need a theory of tragedy in order to give intelligible reasons for any particular drama's being tragic? If so, then discourse about the tragic is unintelligible, since there is not and cannot be such a theory. But such discourse is intelligible; hence, the reasons for describing something as tragic must depend upon something other than a theory. The critic, for example, says, "*Hamlet* is tragic because it has P," whatever P may be; "because it has P" is intelligible not because P is necessary or sufficient for tragedy but because P is a member of an open set of acknowledged (yet debatable) traditional properties or of argued—for 'new' properties of the tragic. The reasons require properties, but none of these properties need be necessary or sufficient; hence, none need depend for its cogency upon a theory of tragedy.

14

Bibliography

Alexander, Peter. *Hamlet: Father and Son*. Oxford, 1955.

Aristotle. *The Poetics*, translated with a commentary by S. H. Butcher. London, 1911.

Bradley, A. C. *Shakespearean Tragedy*. London, 1904.

Bradley, A. C. *Oxford Lectures on Poetry*. London, 1909.

Campbell, Lily B. *Shakespeare's Tragic Heroes: Slaves of Passion*. Cambridge, 1930.

Castelvetro, Lodovico. *Poetics d'Aristotele vulgarizzata ed esposta*, 1570.

Coleridge, S. T. *Coleridge's Shakespearean Criticism*, T. Raysor, ed. 2 vols. Cambridge, 1930.

Corneille, Pierre. *Examens* and *Discours*, 1660.

Dixon, W. Macneile. *Tragedy*. London, 1929.

Dryden, John. *Essays of John Dryden*, W. P. Ker, ed., 2 vols. Oxford, 1926.

Ellis-Fermor, Una. *The Frontiers of Drama*. London, 1945.

Farnham, Willard. *The Medieval Heritage of Elizabethan Tragedy*. Oxford, 1956.

Goethe, J. W. von, *Nachlese zu Aristoteles Poetik*, 1827.

Harrison, Jane. *Themis*. Cambridge, 1912.

Harrison, Jane. *Ancient Art and Ritual*. New York, 1913.

Hegel, G. W. F. *The Philosophy of Fine Art*, translated by F. P. B. Osmaston, 4 vols. London, 1920.

Henn, T. R. *The Harvest of Tragedy*. London, 1956. Contains good summaries of classical theories of tragedy as well as an excellent bibliography.

Johnson, Samuel. *Johnson on Shakespeare*, W. Raleigh, ed. Oxford, 1908.

Kitto, H. D. F. *Greek Tragedy*. London, 1950.

Krutch, J. W. *The Modern Temper*. New York, 1929.

Lessing, G. E. *Hamburgische Dramaturgie*. Hamburg, 1767—1769. Translated by H. Zimmern, with introduction by V. Lange, as *Hamburg Dramaturgy*. New York, 1962.

Lucas, F. L. *Tragedy*. rev. ed. London, 1957.

Margoliouth. D. S. *The Poetics of Aristotle*. London, 1911.

Murray, Gilbert. *The Classical Tradition in Poetry*. Cambridge, 1927.

Nietzsche, Friedrich. *The Birth of Tragedy*, translated by F. Golffing. New York, 1956.

Quinton, A. *"Tragedy."* PAS, Supp. Vol. 34 (1960).

Raphael, D. D. *The Paradox of Tragedy*. Bloomington, Ind., 1960.

Schiller, Friedrich. *Essays Aesthetical and Philosophical*. London, 1916.

Schlegel, A. W. *A Course of Lectures on Dramatic Art and Literature* translated by I. Black and A. Morrison. London, 1846.

Schlegel, F. *Lectures on the History of Literature, Ancient and Modern*, translated by J. Lockhart. Edinburgh, 1818.

Schopenhauer, A. *The World as Will and Idea*, translated by R. B. Haldane and J. Kemp. New York, 1961.

Tillyard, E. M. W. *Shakespeare's Problem Plays*. London, 1957.

Wellek, René. *A History of Modern Criticism*, Vols. I and II. London, 1955. An dispensable analysis and survey of all the important theories of tragedy from Dryden to Schopenhauer.

Chapter Two

HAMLET: PHILOSOPHY THE INTRUDER

T. S. Eliot, in his essay "Hamlet," remarks, ". . . Hamlet the character has had an especial temptation for that most dangerous type of critic: the critic with a mind which is naturally of the creative order, but which through some weakness in creative power exercises itself in criticism instead."[1] However true Eliot's insight may be, there exists an even greater temptation for an even more dangerous type of critic and that is the temptation to concentrate upon the philosophical meaning of the play or hero for that kind of critic with a mind which is naturally of the philosophical order, but which through some weakness in philosophical power and, it must be added, aesthetic power, exercises itself in philosophical criticism instead. For the great scandal of *Hamlet* criticism has not been in the reduction of the play to the character of Hamlet, as Eliot suggests, but in the reduction of the play to some one philosophical theme that is abstracted from either the character of Hamlet, the soliloquies, the dialogue, the plot, the imagery, or the general atmosphere of the play and is then proclaimed the meaning of the play.

The soliloquies and dialogue, especially, from Polonius' precepts of worldly wisdom to Hamlet's meditations on life and death, seem to cry out for philosophical generalization. Hamlet abounds in ostensibly key passages, for example:

Hamlet: So, oft it chances in particular men,
That for some vicious mole of nature in them,
As in their birth, wherein they are not guilty

(Since nature cannot choose his origin),
By the o'ergrowth of some complexion,
Oft breaking down the pales and forts of reason,
Or by some habit, that too much o'er—leavens
The form of plausive manners—that these men,
Carrying I say the stamp of one defect,
Being nature's livery, or fortune's star,
His virtues else be they as pure as grace,
As infinite as man may undergo,
Shall in the general censure take corruption
From that particular fault: the dram of evil
Doth all the noble substance of a doubt,
To his own scandal.

(I,iv,23-38)[2]

This passage and the statement that we are about to see the tragedy of a man who could not make up his mind become the opening lines of the Prologue to Sir Laurence Olivier's film version of *Hamlet*. But this passage, both before and after the appearance of the film, has been accepted widely by many critics of *Hamlet* as the meaning of the entire drama because it reflects an instance of the Aristotelian concept of *hamartia* or tragic flaw.

A second example of philosophical dialogue is:

Hamlet: Denmark's a prison.
Rosencrantz: Then is the world one.
Hamlet: A goodly one, in which there are many con-
fines, wards and dungeons; Denmark being one o' the
worst
Rosencrantz: We think not so, my lord.
Hamlet: Why, then 'tis none to you; for there is nothing either good or bad, but thinking makes it so: to me
it is a prison.

(II,ii,246-254)

How nicely this exchange, especially Hamlet's expression of moral subjectivism, invites generalization. Yet, no critic has interpreted it as the philosophy of Hamlet. Perhaps the reason for this neglect is that it is already obvious to us when Hamlet makes his claim for subjectivity that he, more than anyone else in the play, disbelieves and rebels against such a doctrine. The trap laid here in Hamlet's affirmation of moral subjectivism, into which no one has yet fallen, should serve as a warning against similar traps into which critics have fallen when they have pulled certain philosophical remarks out of their dramatic contexts.

Two more examples of dialogue that suggest philosophical generalization are:

> Hamlet: . . . What a piece of work is a man, how
> noble in reason, how infinite in faculties, in form and
> moving, how express and admirable in action, how like
> an angel in apprehension, how like a god: the beauty
> of the world, the paragon of animals; and yet to me,
> what is this quintessence of dust?
>
> (II,ii,307-312)

> Rosencrantz: The cess of majesty
> Dies not alone; but like a gulf doth draw
> What's near it with it. O 'tis a massy wheel
> Fixed on the summit of the highest mount,
> To whose huge spokes ten thousand lesser things
> Are mortised and adjoined, which when it falls,
> Each small annexment, petty consequence,
> Attends the boist'rous ruin. Never alone
> Did the king sigh, but with a general groan.
>
> (III,iii,15-23)

Both Hamlet's speech on man and Rosencrantz's statement on kingship express doctrines that are integral to the general philosophical view of reality as a Chain of Being. For many critics, Theodore Spencer among them, these two passages culminate in a philosophy of optimism that was articulated by the Elizabethan version of the universe as a Chain of Being. *Hamlet* as a whole is interpreted as the dramatization of the conflict between Elizabethan optimism and pessimism, although the conflict is no longer in the background of the action but is instead inside the hero's consciousness.

Two further related examples of philosophy in the dialogue are:

> Hamlet: . . . We defy augury. There is special provi-
> dence in the fall of a sparrow. If it be now, 'tis not to
> come—if it be not to come, it will be now—if it be
> not now, yet it will come—the readiness is all . . . .
>
> (V,ii,217-220)

> Hamlet: Let us know
> Our indiscretion sometime serves us well,
> When our deep plots do pall, and that should learn us
> There's a divinity that shapes our ends,

Rough—hew them how we will—

$$(V,ii,7-11)$$

Both these bits of dialogue addressed to Horatio beg for religious interpretation, and there have been many critics who have gleaned philosophical readings of the whole of *Hamlet* from these and other passages about the providential nature of the *Hamlet* universe.

Two final examples of dialogue that invite philosophical generalization are:

Player King: What to ourselves in passion we propose,
The passion ending, doth the purpose lose.
The violence of either grief or joy
Their own enactures with themselves destroy
Where joy most revels, grief doth most lament,
Grief joys, joy grieves, on slender accident.

$$(III,ii,193-198)$$

Hamlet: And blest are those
Whose blood and judgement are so well co-meddled,
That they are not a pipe for Fortune's finger
To sound what stop she please: give me that man
That is not passion's slave, and I will wear him
In my heart's core, ay in my heart of heart,
As I do thee.
$$(III,ii,66-72)$$

The interpretation given these last two philosophical passages is the interpretation I first wish to consider. In Lily Campbell's book *Shakespeare's Tragic Heroes: Slaves of Passion*, the drama *Hamlet*, like the other major Shakespearean tragedies, is considered fundamentally a study in passion. Indeed, Lily Campbell claims in each of the tragedies the hero is dominated by one passion, which Shakespeare analyzed in accordance with the medical and moral doctrines of his day. The passions are love and hatred, desire and aversion, pleasure and grief, hope and despair, courage and fear, and anger. They are located in the appetitive part of the human soul where they relate intimately to the four humors: blood, choler, phlegm, and melancholy, because the passions influence and are influenced by the humors.

For example, each of the three sons in *Hamlet* is called upon to mourn his father and to avenge a wrong suffered by his father. Each son's response to grief is determined by his individual temperament: Fortinbras, a northerner, is phlegmatic or sanguine; Laertes, a southerner in his love of France, is choleric and hot-complexioned; and Hamlet, also a northerner, is sanguine or phlegmatic, at least before the play opens. Hamlet's development from the sanguine to the sanguine adust or, as it was called, the "melancholy adust," is brought about by excessive grief. It is this tendency toward excess that creates the constant conflict between the passions and the rational part of the soul; it is this conflict that gives rise to the moral problem of how men are to control their passion by reason.

The whole of Elizabethan tragedy is an attempt to present and explain this moral problem by showing a just and computative God who punishes those whose sin and folly are self-induced through the exercise of passion. Dramatic tragedy, because it is imitation that pleases as it teaches, serves as an effective exemplar of "how to avoid ruin and misery by avoiding the loose and ungoverned passions that lead thereto."[3] Consequently, *Hamlet*, because it is a study in the passion of grief, is an example of moral philosophy that delightfully and spiritedly teaches us how to avoid sin and ruin. Indeed, the play is ". . . constructed to show the profound truth of its dominant idea":[4]

> What to ourselves in passion we propose,
> The passion ending, doth the purpose lose,
> The violence of either grief or joy
> Their own enactures with themselves destroy,
> Where joy most revels, grief doth most lament;
> Grief joys, joy grieves, on slender accident.

(III,ii,193-198)

These words of the Player King Campbell glosses as the central idea of a play about a man ". . . impelled by passion to revenge and yet through excess of passion having the cause of his passion blurred in his memory."[5]

But grief is more than diversified in *Hamlet*; it is also tied to the moral philosophy of the age. The main problem is consolation in grief: how men accept sorrow when it comes to them. In *Hamlet* Shakespeare contrasts a grief that seeks consolation with a grief that remains inconsolable and results either in dullness and loss of memory, the sin of sloth, or in hasty anger and rashness, the sin of ire. Fortinbras exemplifies grief consoled by reason; Laertes demonstrates inconsolable grief that results in anger, the sin of ire; and Hamlet embraces an inconsolable grief that culminates in his dullness, the sin of sloth. Hamlet's grief results in a "melancholy adust" and, in effect, provides a case study of a man who will not yield to the consolation of reason, as urged by Claudius and Gertrude, in the moderation of his passion of grief. For this he is justly punished. Ophelia reflects another facet of this problem, for grief in her is exemplified in its most intemperate form, one that leads to madness and destruction. She, Hamlet, and Laertes represent venial sin, that is, passion undirected by reason; for this they are destroyed but not damned. Claudius and Gertrude, on the other hand, represent moral sin, that is, passion in control of and perverting reason; they are destroyed and damned. Fortinbras and

Horatio exemplify reason victorious over passion. Hamlet himself sums up Horatio as one in whom "blood and judgement are so well commingled" that he is no slave of passion, no pipe of fortune to play upon. "And this is but to say," Campbell concludes, "that those who balance passion by reason are not Fortune's puppets. And such is the lesson of tragedy."[6]

Campbell's critical method and interpretation are a paradigm of philosophical intrusion in *Hamlet*. She picks out one passage, her nugget of "profound truth," abstracts it from its dramatic context, paraphrases it by reducing its meaning to the one idea that passion in excess gives rise to sin, and then reduces the whole play to a series of variations on this idea. The rest of the dialogue, the entirety of the action, and the philosophical significance of the play must revolve around this one general idea of the need to balance passion with reason. Indeed, *Hamlet* for her is a case study in philosophy, teaching us how to caution ourselves against divine punishment.

Reduction generally leads to distortion, and Lily Campbell's attempt is no exception. Her reading necessitates a basic perversion of *Hamlet* and Hamlet's grief which is the *donnée* she starts with.

Campbell associates Hamlet with Fortinbras and Laertes—all grief-stricken over a father lost and wronged. But surely Hamlet is grieving for more than this. Remember his first soliloquy:

> O most wicked speed . . . to post
> With such dexterity to incestuous sheets!
> It is not, nor it cannot come to good,
> But break my heart, for I must hold my tongue.

> (I,ii,156-159)

These lines certainly express a grief that goes beyond a father's death and includes a mother's incest; hence, Hamlet's grief calls for more than consolation for a father lost and wronged. So we must ask Campbell, once we comprehend the true nature of Hamlet's grief, if the moral philosophers of the Elizabethan age, or of any age for that matter, have a clear case of the sin of sloth in Hamlet's inconsolable grief over a father murdered and a mother whored? Campbell's method of abstraction forecloses on the full and horrible nature of Hamlet's sorrow as he reveals it to us. Given that sorrow, for which Hamlet is not responsible, the play cannot be reduced to an exemplary study in the avoidance of divine retribution, without making a moral mockery of man's deepest filial feelings.

Similar to Campbell's reduction of the play to one or more selections of dialogue or soliloquy is the equally dangerous attempt to ascribe to another aspect of the language the philosophy of the play. Caroline Spurgeon, in her epoch-making book *Shakespeare's Imagery and What It Tells Us*, argues that the center of every Shakespearean drama is its dominant imagery. It is this poetic imagery that ". . . gives quality, creates atmosphere and conveys emotion in a

way no precise description, however clear and accurate, can possibly do."[7]
For example, in *Hamlet* the pervasive atmosphere is created by ". . . the
number of images of sickness, disease or blemish of the body, in the play."[8]
The dominant imagery is that of an ulcer or tumor that expresses the sickness
of Denmark itself. She enumerates these images: "blister," "sick soul,"
"thought-sick," "mildew'd ear," "mote," "vicious mole," "galled chilblain,"
"probed wound," and "purgation." Rottenness, physical, mental, and political,
is the striking quality of these images. Thus, she says:

> To Shakespeare's pictorial imagination, therefore, the problem in
> *Hamlet* is not predominantly that of will and reason, of a mind too
> philosophic or a nature temperamentally unfitted to act quickly; he
> sees it pictorially *not as the problem of an individual at all*, but as
> something greater and even more mysterious, as a *condition* for
> which the individual himself is apparently not responsible, any
> more than the sick man is to blame for the infection which strikes
> and devours him, but which, nevertheless, in its course and
> development, impartially and relentlessly, annihilates him and
> others, innocent and guilty alike. That is the tragedy of *Hamlet*, as
> it is perhaps the chief tragic mystery of life.[9]

For Spurgeon, then, the philosophy of *Hamlet* is its imagistic affirmation
of the destructive natural condition of man, the tragic fact of life. As profound
as this claim is, or as accurate as her classification of the imagery of *Hamlet*
may be, the reduction of the philosophy of *Hamlet* to the imagery that
expresses a fundamental truth about life does not do justice to the whole play,
especially to the quality of moral responsibility shared by the major characters.

Nor does her concentration on the imagery do justice to the role of the
imagery itself. For as Clemen in *The Development of Shakespeare's Imagery*
shows, *Hamlet* cannot be interpreted in terms of its imagery alone, but the
imagery must be related to the whole play: the plot, characters, and theme.
Spurgeon's statistical method of collecting and classifying images and her
consequent isolation of them from their exact dramatic contexts violate the
organic role imagery plays in the drama. The imagery discloses no ultimate
pattern beneath the characters and plot, rather imagery is but one contributing
element among many others. The plot, not the tragic fact of life, Clemen
points out, dictates the imagery: the murder of King Hamlet and the incest of
Gertrude give rise to the imagery of disease, infection, and corruption. However, as the drama unfolds, ". . . imagery and action continually play into each
other's hands and we see how the term 'dramatic imagery' gains a new
significance."[10] Hamlet's images, Clemen says, are the most striking in the
play. They are not so much similes or metaphors as they are imaginative
translations of real things and persons. They are keen, penetrating
observations of reality, referring as they do to its most ordinary
aspects—trades, callings, objects, games. Indeed, Hamlet is unique in the play

for his spontaneous and unpremeditated images, which reveal him to be no mere abstract thinker or dreamer.

Clemen examines the much-discussed image:

HAMLET: And thus the native hue of resolution
Is sicklied o'er with the pale cast of thought,
And enterprises of great pitch and moment
With this regard their currents turn awry,
And lose the name of action.

(III,i,84-88)

and concludes that the traditional interpretation of this passage—that reflection hinders action—is wrong:

> For Hamlet does not say "reflection hinders action," he simply utters this image. The fact that he does not utter that general maxim, but this image, makes all the difference. For this image is the unique and specific form of expression of the thought underlying it, it cannot be separated from it. If we say "reflection hinders action" we make a false generalization; we replace a specific formulation by an apothegm. And thereby we eradicate in this passage that quality which is peculiarly Shakespeare's or, what is more, peculiarly Hamlet's. Here the image does not serve the purpose of merely casting a decorative cloak about the thought; it is much rather an intrinsic part of the thought.[11]

The adage "reflection hinders action" implies that action and reflection are two opposing moral principles. But in Hamlet's image, ". . . 'native hue of resolution' suggests that Shakespeare viewed resolution as an innate human quality, not as a moral virtue to be consciously striven after."[12] Thought and action are related in Shakespeare ". . . not as an opposition between two abstract principles between which a free choice is possible, but as an unavoidable condition of human nature."[13]

Although it has been established that the philosophy of *Hamlet* is not contained in the imagery alone, nor can it be isolated in the dialogue or soliloquies, some critics still contend that it can be secured in the plot. For example, Francis Fergusson's fundamental thesis about *Hamlet* is that the main action—"the basic situation"—of the play is the attempt to find and destroy the "hidden imposthume" of Denmark. Hence, it is the welfare of Denmark, not the hero's plight, that is central. The whole action is based on the time's being out of joint. Everything reflects this uneasiness; consequently, *Hamlet* must be seen as a series of shifting perspectives on this analogue. Moreover, since everyone in the play has a share in the main action—the welfare of

Denmark—there is nothing irrelevant in it.

Fergusson, thus, divides the action of the play into a prologue (Act 1, scenes 1, 2, 3) in which the malady of Denmark is brought out, the agons or conflicts and contrasts (Act I, scenes 4, 5; Act II; Act III, scene I) in which an attempt is made to identify and destroy the malady, the climax, peripety, and recognition (Act III, scenes 2, 3, 4) in which the hidden imposthume is opened, the pathos or sparagmos (Act IV) in which all the suffering is culminated, and the epiphany or collective revelation (Act V) in which the illness of Denmark is perceived by all.

Hamlet, furthermore, as a multiple-plot structure, parallels The *Odyssey* rather than Greek or French classical tragedy, for The *Odyssey* is also a series of analogues on one major theme—the attempt to return home. Like Homer, Shakespeare composes by analogy, not by emotional or conceptual progression. The anagoge, or ultimate meaning, which is Denmark as it mirrors the world, is present in all the analogical relations within the play: the ironic parallels formed by tragic and comic motifs, the father-son relationships, and the male-female relationships.

But to grasp the total meaning of *Hamlet* we must also see the main action as a manifestation of the ancient myth and ritual pattern of human experience. *Hamlet* is a celebration of the mystery of human life, and it is this celebration rather than form that ties the play inextricably to Greek tragedy and the ancient ritual. There are profound parallels in *Hamlet* and *Oedipus Rex*. In fact, for Fergusson, the main difference between the two plays is that one comes at the beginning and the other at the end of the tradition of theater as ritual. In both plays, the royal personage is associated with pollution; there is invocation for well-being; and there is the interweaving of the individual and society. In *Hamlet*, the rituals show forth the main action; they are ". . . lamps lighting the rottenness of Denmark."[14]   From the beginning when the guards change to the end when Hamlet is borne like a soldier by four captains, there are rituals that function to focus attention on the body politic and ceremoniously invoke well-being. Indeed, the play scene is the center of the drama. "It has a ritual aspect, it is Hamlet's most ambitious improvisation, and it is the climax and peripety of the whole complex plot-scheme."[15] "It reveals the malady of the regime in all its ambiguity, mystery, and spreading ramifications . . . .   It catches more than the conscience of the King."[16] It represents the hidden crime, the incestuous theft, the usurpation. Altogether this scene functions as an anagoge of human weakness.

As the traditional scapegoat—hero, Hamlet is the appointed victim to cleanse the scourge of a sick society:

Hamlet is apparently thought of as undergoing a similar [to Oedipus] transformation, from hero to scapegoat, from "the expectancy and rose of the fair state" to the distracted, suffering witness and victim of Act V.[17]

The other characters also are placed in the ritualistic scheme Fergusson finds in the play. His most important observation is on Fortinbras, who is referred to early in the play as a threat to a (corrupt) regime, is seen briefly in Act IV, scene 4, and is recognized at the very end of the play as the future legitimate monarch . . . . "In the scheme of the whole the role of Fortinbras, though it is very economically developed, is of major importance."[18] He is a symbol of spiritual rebirth after the cleansing of the scourge; consequently, he, too, functions as part of the ancient myth and ritual pattern of drama, the celebration of the mystery of human life.

So much by way of an all-too-brief account of Fergusson's reading of *Hamlet*. For him the philosophy of *Hamlet*, as it is embodied and re-enacted in the plot of the play, is the religious affirmation of the cycle of human life, from birth, struggle, and death to renewal: from Claudius, through Hamlet, to Fortinbras.

It seems to me that there is much to be said for Fergusson's interpretation of *Hamlet*. His emphases on the unity of the action, the multiple-plot, the search for the hidden imposthume, the symbolic value of Fortinbras, and even the purgatorial role of Hamlet are convincing. But that the whole play adds up to a Renaissance version of the ancient myth and ritual pattern in which the mystery cycle of life, death, and renewal is celebrated, or that Hamlet is a mere scapegoat-hero, ". . . a witness and a sufferer for the hidden truth of the human condition,"[19] is not satisfying, primarily because such a reading does not do justice to the important secular and skeptical strands of the play and its hero. Fergusson's interpretation, like other univocal readings, forecloses on the undeniable complexities within the drama that make it much more than a transformation of *Oedipus Rex*. Even if Fergusson be correct on the nature of the plot, the attempt to reduce the philosophy and the meaning of the whole play to his analysis of the plot leaves much unaccounted for.

The failures of Campbell, Spurgeon, and Fergusson to pluck out the heart of the philosophy of *Hamlet* from its dialogue, imagery, and plot suggest that perhaps *Hamlet* has no underlying philosophy. E.E. Stoll says as much. And whatever we may think of his reading of the play, we must allow that it has the decided merit of bodily rejecting philosophy, before the intruder crosses the threshold of *Hamlet*. Stoll has written much on *Hamlet*, but his thesis has never changed. The play is a revenge tragedy or heroic romance, pure and simple, which makes no philosophical or psychological claims about the world. It is in the great tradition derived from Seneca and sponsored in the Renaissance, especially by Thomas Kyd. It is drama of intrigue, blood, and fate in which the hero remains free from defect or tragic flaw throughout the play and attains his appointed revenge. Stoll supports this thesis by an appeal to both external and internal evidence. His external evidence is that the play was regarded as a typical revenge tragedy from its first appearance to the late eighteenth century. Readers and spectators during this early period complained of the defects of the play, but no one complained of psychological deficiencies in the hero.

The internal evidence is the dramatic. Every relevant datum of the text, Stoll claims, supports his contention that *Hamlet* is a revenge tragedy, not a psychological study. First is the delay. Stoll does not deny that Hamlet delays but he does deny that the delay has psychological significance. The delay functions, as it had from the Greeks on, in the epical tradition, not to accentuate the defects of the hero, but to make the deed momentous when it comes. Because tradition and the old *Hamlet* story required the delay, Shakespeare simply relied on established devices. Though woefully misconstrued by later critics, the hero's self-reproaches and exhortations function not as character traits, but as dramatic reminders to the audience that Hamlet's main business, though retarded, is not lost to view. Indeed, the self—reproaches, although they contain execrations, interrogations, even lacerations, serve as exhortations and, finally, as exculpation. Even the Ghost's reminder to Hamlet,

> Do not forget! this visitation
> Is but to whet thy almost blunted purpose

> (III,iv,110-111)

is exhortation, not judgement on Hamlet's character. The highly emotional scenes—the cellarage, the nunnery, the play, the graveyard—are not pathological either, for they are natural enough in the dramatic circumstances. These scenes serve to enhance the emotional pitch and form part of the action; they are art as artifice, not as psychology. Finally, that Hamlet is a heroic figure can be inferred from the fact that no character, except himself and the Ghost, reproaches him and, more importantly, because the end of the play, which is "one of your surest indexes of your dramatist's thought,"[20] also contains nothing but praise for Hamlet and not even a hint of dereliction from Horatio, who should know.

Stoll's interpretation and his wholesale dismissal of both philosophy and psychology in the play rest, of course, on the plausibility of his treatment of the delay. And if this is not convincing, perhaps we can turn to the character of Hamlet for the philosophy of the play. It is Dover Wilson who best counters Stoll's assertion that Hamlet's self-reproaches are exculpation.

> . . . That [Stoll's] thesis is moonshine any unprejudiced reader of the soliloquy in 4.4. may see for himself. Not that the evidence of the soliloquies by any means stands alone. Hamlet's sense of frustration, of infirmity of purpose, of character inhibited from meeting the demands of destiny, of the futility of life in general and action in particular, finds utterance in nearly every word he says. His melancholy and his procrastination are all of a piece, and cannot be disentangled. Moreover, his feelings are shared and

expressed by other characters also. The note of 'heart-sickness' is struck by the sentry Francisco nine lines from the beginning of the play . . . . In short that "the native hue of resolution/Is sicklied o'er with the pale cast of thought," is not merely the constant burden of Hamlet's meditation but the key-note of the whole dramatic symphony.[21]

Much of the tradition, at least from Coleridge to Bradley, has thought that the philosophy of *Hamlet* is in the character of the hero.

Hamlet was the play, or rather Hamlet himself was the character, in the intuition and exposition of which I first made my turn for philosophical criticism . . . .[22]

So wrote Coleridge in 1819, some twenty years after his famous "turn" in criticism. Since this pronouncement, the view that Coleridge is concerned only with character portrayal in *Hamlet* and the whole of Shakespeare's dramas has prevailed. Nothing could be further from the truth. Coleridge's critical interests in Shakespearean drama range from characterization to metaphysical insight, thereby covering the topics of language, unity of feeling, thematic development, and plot. Indeed, his penetrating remark that "Shakespeare shewed great judgement in his first scenes; they contained the germ of the ruling passion which was to be developed hereafter"[23] corroborates the diversity of his interests. Even in his critical remarks on *Hamlet*, fragmentary as they are, Coleridge perceives more in the play than most critics perceive: his observations on the language of the opening scene, Hamlet's wit, the contrast between the playlet and the rest of the play, the judicious introductions of Hamlet and Laertes in the second scene, the sure handling of the Ghost, and the way in which Hamlet's mind operates are cases in point. Where else in Shakespearean criticism is there anything that can match the aesthetic power, for example, of Coleridge's reading of the opening scene?

The language is familiar: no poetic description of night, no elaborate information conveyed by one speaker to another. . . . It is the language of *sensation* among men who feared no charge of effeminacy for feeling what they felt no want of resolution to bear. Yet the armour, the dead silence, the watchfulness that first interrupts it, the welcome relief of guard, the cold, the broken expressions as of a man's compelled attention to bodily feelings allowed no man—all excellently accord with and prepare for the after gradual rise into tragedy . . . .
The preparation *informative* of the audience is just as much as was precisely necessary: how gradual first, and with the uncertainty appertaining to a question—

What, has *this thing* appeared *again* to-night. Even the word "again" has its credibilizing effect.[24]

No, Hamlet is primary in *Hamlet*, not because Coleridge reduces the drama to characterization, but because, for him, Hamlet *is* primary in *Hamlet*. Shakespeare, Coleridge says, never wrote anything without design. In the character of Hamlet, "he intended to portray a person in whose view the external world, and all its incidents and objects, were comparatively dim and of no interest in themselves, and which began to interest only when they were reflected in the mirror of his mind."[25]

Hamlet is called upon to act, to avenge his murdered father; he does not act. Instead he reasons and broods, rationalizes and reproaches himself, "while the whole energy of his resolution evaporates in these reproaches." Yet Hamlet refrains from action not because of cowardice, "but merely from that aversion to action which prevails among such as have a world in themselves."[26] Hence, from a philosophical point of view, Hamlet exemplifies ". . . the moral necessity of a due balance between our attention to outward objects and our meditation on inward thoughts—a due balance between the real and the imaginary world. In Hamlet this balance does not exist . . ."[27] From Hamlet's opening line, "A little more than kin, and less than kind," in which Coleridge says Hamlet expresses his contempt for Claudius as well as his ". . . superfluous activity of mind, a sort of playing with a thread or watch chain or snuff box,"[28] through the soliloquies, indeed, up until the very end, Hamlet remains in words all resolution but in action all words.

Coleridge sums up the philosophy of the play as it is embodied in the character of Hamlet:

> Shakespeare wished to impress upon us the truth, that action is the chief end of existence—that no faculties of intellect, however brilliant, can be considered valuable, or indeed otherwise than as misfortunes, if they withdraw us from, or render us repugnant to action, and lead us to think and think of doing, until the time has elapsed when we can do anything effectually. [29]

For Coleridge, then, Hamlet is central in the play; his inaction, pervasive in him, is caused by his excessive reflectiveness; and this undue imbalance between action and thought dramatizes the moral philosophy of the play that too much philosophy, that is, philosophy without action, is immoral.

Now, Coleridge's reading of *Hamlet*, probably the most influential in the entire history of criticism, has itself been challenged on all major points by many later critics, not least of all by A. C. Bradley who, although he agrees with Coleridge that Hamlet is central in the play, that Hamlet's delay—but not total inaction—pervades him, and that the philosophy of the play is to be found in the hero, disagrees with Coleridge on the cause of the delay and especially on the philosophical significance of Hamlet himself. Hamlet delays, but, Bradley argues, not because he is thought—sick, which he is not, but rather because he is in a profound state of melancholy, a state which has been induced by his predisposition toward brooding and obsession with the mood of the moment and the shock of his mother's hasty, indecent remarriage. In his classic, *Shakespearean Tragedy*, Bradley spells out his theory in magnificent detail. Of course, his own hypothesis about Hamlet's delay has been challenged on textual as well as on purely logical grounds, reduced almost necessarily to the Freudian hypothesis of Ernest Jones, for whom the vacillation is due to a rather stiff double dose of the Oedipal complex, and dismissed entirely, along with all other univocal explanations of Hamlet's behavior, by Dover Wilson, who insists that Hamlet was intended by Shakespeare to remain a mystery:

> In fine, we were never intended to reach the heart of the mystery. That it has a heart is an illusion; the mystery itself is an illusion; Hamlet is an illusion. The secret that lies behind it all is not Hamlet's, but Shakespeare's: the technical devices he employed to create this supreme illusion of a great and mysterious character, who is at once mad and the sanest of geniuses, at once a procrastinator and a vigorous man of action, at once a miserable failure and the most adorable of heroes. The character of Hamlet, like the appearance of his successive impersonators on the stage, is a matter of "make-up."[30]

Bradley, however, admits that the philosophy of *Hamlet* is not in Hamlet the philosopher, Hamlet the procrastinator, or Hamlet the melancholic. It is in Hamlet the tragic hero.

Hamlet alone is tragic in *Hamlet*, not because he dies for a valiant cause, or because he is a slave of passion, or because he is a relatively good man who ruins himself through his tragic flaw, but because in his struggle with the forces of evil his spiritual greatness is destroyed irretrievably. For Bradley, the tragic fact in the world is this ultimate, unexplainable, non-justifiable self-waste of spiritual goodness in its struggle against evil:

> We remain confronted with the inexplicable fact, or the no less inexplicable appearance, of a world travailing for perfection, but bringing to birth, together with glorious good, an evil which it is able to overcome only by self-torture and self-waste. And this fact or appearance is tragedy.[31]

However, only Hamlet exemplifies this mystery of good's expelling evil and being destroyed in the very process. Coleridge, therefore, according to Bradley, is wrong in reducing the philosophy of *Hamlet* to a moral maxim about thought and action. For Bradley the philosophy of *Hamlet* is the dramatization of a perennial truth about man: that man lives in a world where good can vanquish evil and yet be wasted. There is no acceptable explanation of this fact. It remains a mystery.

Many critics agree with Bradley that the philosophy of *Hamlet* is in the tragedy of the hero but they reject Bradley's definition of the tragic as the self-waste of spiritual good. This disagreement turns on the supposed essence of the tragic, which each of these disputing critics claims to state truly. But this issue, it seems to me, cannot be settled in any true or false manner, because there is no such thing as the essence of the tragic. If the philosophy of *Hamlet* be identified with the tragic in Hamlet and the tragic in Hamlet be defined in terms of the essence of tragedy, an essence that is non-existent, then the philosophy of *Hamlet* cannot be determined at all. But I believe it can be determined by turning from dialogue, soliloquy, imagery, character, and tragedy to the tone of the play. Our best critical guide here is E. M. W. Tillyard. His essay on "Hamlet" in *Shakespeare's Problem Plays* is one of the few enlightening pieces of criticism of the play since Bradley.

For Tillyard, the tragic is not primary in *Hamlet*. He distinguishes between three kinds of tragedy: suffering, sacrificial purgation, and regeneration. The third, he says, is the "centrally tragic." Both *King Lear* and *Othello* are tragic in this fundamental sense; *Hamlet* is not since Hamlet never regenerates himself. *Hamlet* is tragic only in the first two senses, but even in these the tragic is ". . . not the principal quality."[32] Rather, for Tillyard it is the tone that is central in *Hamlet*:

> . . . the sheer wealth and vigour and brilliance of all the things that happen . . . . Simply as a play of things happening, of one event being bred out of another, and of each event being described with appropriate and unwearied brilliance, *Hamlet* is supreme . . . .
> One is tempted to call *Hamlet* the greatest display of sheer imaginative vitality in literary form that a man has so far achieved.[33]

If, Tillyard continues, we distinguish between content and form, or recognize what for Aristotle was the difference between imitation and harmony, in the sense in which, say, *Othello* emphasizes the form or ordering of experience rather than the content of it, *Hamlet* ". . . is best understood as a play less of ordering than of sheer explication or presentation, as a play presenting the utmost variety of human experience in the largest possible cosmic setting." *Hamlet* himself serves in the play to render evident ". . . the wonder and variety of all human experience."[34] Thus, *Hamlet* ceases to be a tragedy and becomes instead a "problem play," for:

> When sheer explication, or abundance of things presented, takes

first place, then we leave the realm of tragedy for that of the problem play. Here it is the problems themselves, their richness, their interest, and their diversity, and not their solution or significant arrangement that come first.[35]

Now, much of Tillyard's analysis is open to debate; for example, that the regenerative is the centrally tragic, that *Hamlet* is a tragedy of suffering and sacrificial purgation, that the tragic in *Hamlet* is not primary, that *Hamlet* is essentially a problem play, and that the tone is primary in *Hamlet*. But what is not challengeable, indeed, what is quite indubitable, is his presentation of the tone of the play. Tillyard's description is a necessary reminder of what most critics have utterly forgotten since Dr. Johnson's remark that variety is the distinguishing excellence of *Hamlet*. The tone establishes the beginning as well as the end of any attempt to provide a reading of the philosophy in *Hamlet*. I do not wish to say that the tone is primary in *Hamlet*, but only that it is there, a pervasive quality or *donnée* as obviously and undeniably present as the imagery of rottenness or the blood and guts of melodrama.

There is, however, more to be said about the tone of *Hamlet* than that its range of presented or represented experiences is great, vigorous, brilliant, and vital. As these qualities establish, the tone is also life-enhancing, if I may borrow a term from Berenson. That is, the quality of the sheer love of life, of being alive, is shared by all, including the melancholic Hamlet. Hamlet can gossip with the players, remind them of the rudiments of their craft, partake of the artist's ecstasy over a good play well done; and he can jest with Polonius, the King, and the gravediggers. Of course it is true that he complains to Rosencrantz and Guildenstern that he has of late, he knows not why, lost his mirth; yet minutes before he has pulled off one of his delightful bits of bawdiness in his burlesque of Fortune as a strumpet in whose privates Rosencrantz and Guildenstern enjoy her favors. Hamlet has lost his mirth, but clearly not quite all of it. He can still joke obscenely, yet harmlessly, with Ophelia later in the play. His wit, often expressed for the sheer love of it, is present throughout. Certainly he is bitter and depressed, but the natural delight in wit and humor shines through the darkness.

Mystery, too, pervades much of the play. Many have commented on the predominantly interrogative mood of the drama—all its questioning, doubt, and uncertainty. Harry Levin even reads "question" as the key word of the play. To be or not to be? Is the Ghost an honest one? Is Ophelia honest? Is Gertrude bestial? What is the true nature of man? Why do I delay? These are among the questions of the play.

The variety and the wonder, along with the woe, imply a kind of irreducible complexity of human experience, the idea that man lives in a universe which is inexhaustively vast—from the "majestical roof fretted with golden fire" to the "quintessence of dust." And it is a universe whose vastness reflects itself only in man's infinitesimal comprehension of it. We live in a world in which we can formulate the questions, but we can hardly answer them. Hamlet cannot even answer why he delays. He knows not "seems," he says, but neither does he know what is. It is in this aspect of the tone—the irreducible complexity of human experience as it mirrors man's condition—that I find the philosophy of *Hamlet*. Paradoxically, it is philosophy that rejects the very possibility of a philosophy of man and the universe. In the traditional sense in which philosophy is the attempt to reduce the complexity of experience and the world to a formula, to provide answers to the great questions about the meaning of life, to pluck out the heart of the mystery of the universe, *Hamlet* shows, through its over-all quality of irreducible complexity, that the formula cannot be secured; consequently, philosophy itself functions as an intruder on the human situation. *Hamlet*, then, is a celebration of the mystery of human life, not in the myth and ritual pattern, but in the more basic secular pattern of life as a series of questions to which there are no certain answers. Life is and remains a mystery. Hamlet's delay and his tragedy instance that mystery. As artist, Shakespeare dramatizes the mystery; as philosophical artist, he also dramatizes the denial of any convincing solution to the mystery. In effect, in *Hamlet*, Shakespeare shows us that man lives, questions, affirms, doubts, and dies. The rest is silence.

Chapter Three

OTHELLO: A TRAGEDY OF PERFECTION FLAYED AND FLAWED

That Shakespeare worked the classical philosophical doctrine, first enunciated by Plato in his *Timaeus*, of a perfection as cosmic completeness and hierarchical order, needs no refurbishing. Many of his plays dramatize this doctrine, sometimes as theme, at other times, as thesis about the world and man's place in it. Whether this doctrine, equivalent to an ontology of the universe as "A Great Chain of Being," is central as some distinguished Shakespearean critics, such as Tillyard and Theodore Spencer, have contended, or merely one theme among others, as important, I do not wish to debate here.

The "order-disorder" conflict, dialectic or "synthesis," as it is called, is certainly a dramatic feature in many of the dramas, especially the histories, the tragedies, and perhaps in some of the comedies. But that it is pervasive in each of the plays or in the whole of Shakespeare's dramas is suspect, as indeed, I think, is any overview about a single or unified philosophy in Shakespeare's work.

In *Antony and Cleopatra*, for example, at least in my interpretation of it,[1] Shakespeare dramatizes the theme of perfection, but of a kind of perfection that can find no secure place in the platonic universe of perfection as cosmic completeness and order. Instead, the play revolves around, or at least includes, a kind of perfection in love that destroys itself at the very moment of completion.

The world of *Antony and Cleopatra*, vast as it is, encompasses infinite variety but also gaps in nature. The traditional notion of perfection as variety can accommodate the one but not the other, for these gaps are among the inexplicable missing links of any chain of being. Both the variety and the gaps, however, are linked to the rhythms of transformation: of one thing becoming another; of perennial generation and corruption. The images in the play especially, whether those of normal, to be expected, transformations, or of abnormal, surprising, indeed inverted, transformations, such as an Antony "That grew the more by reaping" (V.ii.88) or a Cleopatra who ". . . makes hungry,/ Where most she satisfies" (II.ii.237-8), reinforce the variety. One, but only one, form of this variety of generation and corruption, of the inexhaustible rhythms of nature and experience, is the love of Antony and Cleopatra, confined to them, that generates a ". . . nobleness of life . . . when such a mutual pair,/ And such a twain can do't" (I.i.36-8). In their relationship, but not in love universal, there is a coming into being (the intensity of fire) of a love (the rarefaction of air) that, though it transcends the baser elements of water and earth, self-destructs in its very perfection. The sustaining implicit image of the play, thus, is not that of a Nile that begets fertility, then famine, but of a Nile that in its abundance of fertility destroys itself. One kind of perfection, in a world of many perfections and imperfections, then, is a love which corrupts itself in its fullness of generated being. In *Antony and Cleopatra* Shakespeare dramatizes this *infima* species of the genus of perfections. He does not reduce this variety or even this perfection to the traditional conception of perfection as (ordered, hierarchical, complete) variety. Indeed, he shows, as he does with many philosophical ideas, how the dramatist as artist may have a truer sense of reality than the philosopher and, in particular, in *Antony and Cleopatra*, that there is a variety of perfections and imperfections but that there can be no convincing resolution of this variety into some metaphysical perfection in variety.

Another example, my chosen one, *Othello*, also shows that Shakespeare is as interested in the varieties of perfection as he is in the orthodox perfection in variety. Here, too, I think, Shakespeare dramatizes a kind of perfection that, though rooted in the disorder of the traditional order—disorder synthesis and dichotomy, is nevertheless a perfection that is more real than any nebulous perfection of a cosmic order.

In approaching *Othello*, let me assume, what I think is true, that all of us have read or seen the play at least a few times and that it has left what Helen Gardner calls that "immediate and overwhelming first impression to which it is a prime rule of literary criticism that all further analysis must conform;" 2 and, perhaps what is not true, that many of us have not already written a definitive piece on it which, at least for most of us, blocks our ability to respond to it freshly, if not innocently. These three conditions are not, I think, special, but rather fairly typical of most of us: we return to *Othello* with some overall conception of what is going on dramatically in the play.

Now, in these circumstances, is it not evident that the temptation scene—Act III, Scene iii—is as much the dramatic center as it is its numerical center? But to say that the scene is the center is not yet to say that it is central. The latter is, I think, a step towards an interpretation of the play, that what happens here—the temptation of Othello and the gulling of him by

Iago—best explains the action and the meaning of the play: that it is essentially the tragedy of a man who is unable to cope with jealousy. As such, it is a tragedy in which the tragic hero, Othello, has his *hamartia* that, played upon by Iago, breaks him and, in doing so, produces the requisite pity and fear along with Othello's final regeneration and suicide.

Of course there are many—some marvelous—variants on this interpretation of *Othello* as basically a drama of sexual jealousy, nourished by Othello's *hamartia*, whether it is, specifically his inability to cope with jealousy or with coping itself or with the social conventions of his age or with the demands of reason over passion or even, as I have heard on one occasion, of his pre-cartesian search for certainty in the resolution of intolerable doubt.

Fundamental to this interpretation and its varieties is the notion of *hamartia*, which is a kind of defect or imperfection that, as Othello's flaw, buttresses the centrality of the third scene of the third act and gives a unifying direction to the whole play.

Is such a reading correct or the most plausible? Is the tragedy of *Othello*, like all tragedies according to this view, tragedy of imperfection? Helen Gardner, for one, does not think so, because such an interpretation, which revolves around the "progressive revelation of the inadequacy of the hero's nobility," violates that overwhelming first impression, Othello's nobility, "the play's most distinctive quality."

Her criticism of the limits of Shakespearean interpretation—that it cannot disregard one's first impression—rests on the descriptive rather than interpretive character of first impression. Whether there is so large a *donnée* that critical analysis can start with and return to is at least open to debate since one critic's first, immediate and overwhelming impression becomes another critic's second, unconvincing interpretation. Nevertheless, Gardner's criterion suggests two small criteria of a good interpretation: that it lay out all the dramatic data of the opening scene and that its coherence remain faithful to these data, whether they impress us overwhelmingly or not. I do not mean to suggest that Shakespeare's openings contain the dramatic seeds that organically germinate the evolution of the drama. That Shakespeare adheres to so classic a principle of unity may be true of some of his dramas; but I doubt that it can serve as a universal criterion of interpretation of all his plays. My criterion is the more modest one: to get as clear as we can about what is given in the opening scenes so that we do not lose sight of it or pervert it by what comes later.

What, then, is presented in the opening of *Othello*? That Iago hates Othello and envies Cassio over the choice of the lieutenancy; that Iago, though a racist and a liar, has an admiration for Othello's generalship which, as we see later, is shared by all; that Iago, though malicious, in his remarks on who gets what and how—on the politics of advancement,—is closer to the ordinary run of human beings than he is to the demi-devil he becomes in III, 3. Scene 2 of the first act gives us Othello's own opinion of himself, his royal ancestry, his social equality with his bride; and his realistic assessment of Brabantio's rejection of his marriage to Desdemona. In the third scene, Desdemona proclaims both the violence of her act of marriage to Othello and her consecration of soul to the marriage.

Before Desdemona's opening remarks, however, her father comments bitterly on Othello's successful wooing of his daughter. It is incredible that Desdemona should "fall in love with what she fear'd to look on" (I,iii,98). Othello, therefore, must have conjured her.

> It is a judgment maim'd, and most imperfect,
> That will confess perfection so would err
> Against all rules of nature, and must be driven
> To find out practices of cunning hell,
> Why this should be
>
> (I,iii,99-103).

Here Brabantio refers to Othello's cunning hell in winning his daughter; and he implies that any other explanation is maim'd. This is surely our first impression: of a father's judgment on a totally miscegenated marriage. But suppose we hear these lines again?

What, now, if we understand them not as a causal explanation of Othello's successful wooing but as a critical interpretation of the whole play? Then the judgement that *Othello* is about a "perfection [that] so would err/ Against all rules of nature, and must be driven/ To find out practices of cunning hell,/ Why this should be" is far from "maim'd" and "imperfect" but instead a sound overall reading of *Othello* as a kind of perfection flawed and destroyed by the cunning hell of Iago, with the Why? of it unresolved in Iago's last:

> Demand me nothing; what you know, you know.
> From this time forth I never will speak word
>
> (V,ii,304-5),

as answer to Othello's:

> Will you, I pray, demand that demi-devil
> Why he hath thus ensnar'd my soul and body?
>
> (V,ii,302-4)

I do not know if Shakespeare intended us to take Brabantio's lines in the way they so stunningly suggest. Nor can I endorse the claim that would find in these lines an unconscious or a supersubtle clue to their real meaning. All I insist on is that Brabantio's observation, without his negative assessment, embodies the best interpretation I have yet encountered about the meaning of *Othello*. If it strikes anywhere near the heart of the play, it explodes completely the traditional interpretation. Perfection flawed is hardly compatible with the tragic flaw.

That *Othello* is a tragedy of the flawing of perfection—of a chrysolite as fragile as it is strong and rare, chipped away at until it is smashed—illumines much in the play, not least the requisite dissimilarity between Othello and Roderigo, both gulled by Iago, but the one out of his native stupidity, the other not. But if not stupidity, what then? Is it Othello's ignorance, social ineptness, proneness to trust too easily, or some other vice that aids Iago in his gulling?

On the inverted Brabantian interpretation, Othello succumbs because of his *areté*, not his *hamartia*. Indeed, the reading of the play as perfection flawed or, as Gardner construes it, as Othello's nobility untainted, seems to rule out as a cause of Othello's actions and inactions after the temptation by Iago as well as the temptation itself, any inherent defect in him. In this connection, it seems to me that Gardner's attempt to retain the nobility straight through while at the same time attributing to Othello the tragic error of reneging on his venture of faith in Desdemona verges on the inconsistency of an ignoble nobility.

This impasse between two contrary, perhaps contradictory, interpretations brings us back to the numerical and dramatic center of the play. Whether III, iii is also central or not, it is nevertheless crucial to our understanding of Othello and, though him, of the play. Here, then, are some of the bare facts, if there are such things in drama (or anywhere else), of this scene.

Iago sets it. He has already succeeded in unseating Cassio as Othello's lieutenant. Now he must ensure it. He also wants to get even with Othello, not so much over the lieutenancy as over "wife-for-wife," having already brooded twice on the rumor that Othello had seduced Emilia. Perhaps, he suggests, at the end of the second act, he can enmesh them all: Cassio, Desdemona and Othello. His desire for the lieutenancy, to be realized at the end of the third scene of the third act, is now in the background, as his need for the deaths of Cassio, Desdemona and Othello is yet to come. Central to his plan in this scene is the unhinging of Othello, since this will entail the estrangement of Desdemona and the permanent unseating of Cassio.

During this scene, Iago improvises more than he plots as he drives Othello to his breakdown which occurs in Act IV, not here. He takes advantage of Cassio's embarrassed departure from Desdemona, who is to plead his case; he reminds Othello of Cassio's role of attendant when Othello wooed Desdemona; he introduces a picture of jealousy as unresolved doubt that he knows Othello cannot tolerate; he comments on the furtive ways of Venetian women; and, more convincingly, to Othello, reminds him of Desdemona's deception of her father; he forces the handkerchief from his wife after she picks it up when Desdemona drops it; he introduces Cassio's dream talk and behavior when Othello demands proof of Desdemona's infidelity; and he refers to the handkerchief as he relates how he saw Cassio wipe his beard with it.

Each of these furthers his aim—to unhinge Othello. But Othello does not crack here. Indeed, Othello's reactions to each of Iago's forays are as much those of a general weighing strategies in the attempt to hold on to victory achieved or to accommodate defeat if and when it comes, as they are of a man who is broken or, more to the point, in the grip of a tragic error. Othello's worst moment, his one gross moment, is his retreat from:

> 'tis better to be much abus'd
> Than but to know't a little

(III,iii,342-3)

to: It is better to be totally abused and know nothing than to be in the anguish of doubt. His:

> He that is robb'd, not wanting what is stol'n,
> Let him not know't, and he's not robb'd at all

(III,iii,348-9),

is Othello reduced to "honest" Iago; even so, we must ask, where is the ignobility of that observation, since he does not accept it any more than he does the dishonesty of Desdemona until Iago introduces the description of Cassio wiping his beard with Othello's sacred handkerchief?

Line by line analysis is required here. Unfortunately, there is neither time nor is this the occasion for it. Suffice it to posit that the evidence, such as it is, points as much to perfection being flayed and flawed as it does to an inherent fault being painfully mined.

The evidence, I say, points both ways. But the situation is more complex than that since the data or dramatic facts themselves are most of them interpretive. That Iago is improvising rather than following a plot; that Othello's "Zounds!" and "O misery!" are interjections to Iago's brittle sociologizing rather than expressions of self—fury and self-pity; that Iago's brooding over Othello's seduction of his wife is any less a self-deception than his earlier fantasy of being able to seduce Desdemona; or even that Othello's Iago-like cynicism about infidelity is a real rather than a speculative possibility—each of these, it seems to me, though based on some datum or verbal *donnée*, is already heavy with interpretation.

When we turn to Desdemona, however, the evidence points only one way. That she is a perfection in the Elizabethan and in our sense of "flawless," characterized as such by her father (I,iii,100) and by Cassio (II,iii, 25) is one of the unchallengeable *données* of the play. That hers is a perfection flayed but not flawed, in this case by Othello's cunning practices on her fidelity, is another, I think, indisputable datum of the play. Her consecration of soul (I,iii,254) to Othello remains intact, never wavering, not even at the moment of Othello's strangling of her. As admirable as her unswerving faith in Othello is, what is truly remarkable in her perfection, however, is that it represents to her, as well as to everyone else in the play, and probably in the Elizabethan audience too, a perfection founded on and sustained by the disorder, hence imperfection, of her "downright violence" (I,iii,249), in marrying Othello.

The marriage—the love of Othello and Desdemona—brief as it is, is then another kind of perfection, wholly different from the love and perfection of *Antony and Cleopatra*. The latter generates its own corruption; the former is generated in a violation of traditional perfection as variety—"against all rules of nature"—yet is a perfection that is destroyed not because it is a form of imperfection in any cosmic order of things, but because of Iago's wickedness, festering and fructifying in the very pit of disorder.

That Shakespeare consecrated part of his art—we cannot speak about his soul—to a perfection of a marriage in love which is not inherently flawed, as it must be according to the orthodox order-disorder scheme, hence a kind of imperfection in a universe in which imperfection is at best part of a greater perfection as cosmic order and variety, but is instead a perfection flayed and flawed, destroyed ultimately by the terrible imperfection of Iago, is surely as remarkable as the play itself. That this lad, later good burgher of Stratford, or player-dramatist and man about town in London, or even mythical lover and rake at the Taverne in Oxford who, in whatever role, probably shared with his Elizabethan audiences Brabantio's views about such a marriage as a violation of the natural and conventional order, could have transmuted with his usual alchemy this traditional form of imperfection into a kind of perfection and, by doing so, to enjoin his later critics and biographers to find out their own practices of cunning hell why this should be yields, as the only possible response Iago's final:

> Demand me nothing, what you know, you know,
> From this time forth, I never will speak word.

The creator of *Othello* remains as enigmatic as his creation. The perfection of an imputed imperfection remains as clear as ever.

Chapter Four

THE COINAGE OF MAN:
KING LEAR AND CAMUS'S *L'ÉTRANGER*

No, they cannot touch me for coining; I am the king himself[1]
(*King Lear*, IV.vi.83)

How much is a man worth? In spite of their vast differences, *King Lear* and
L'Étranger, I shall propose, offer the same ultimate answer: Nothing. Yet from
this answer, Camus derives nothing; Shakespeare, everything. How this is done
it is the task of philosophical literary criticism to discern. That it is done is of
the utmost importance to philosophy itself in its perennial quest to determine
the place of human values in the world.

It is generally admitted that *King Lear* is the most baffling of
Shakespeare's tragedies. Not that any of them is not full of difficulties, but
King Lear, unlike the others, even with the brilliant insights of its great critics
from Coleridge to Bradley, has yielded no convincing reading. Elucidation of
its characters, plot, imagery, symbolism, themes, or its Elizabethan dramatic
and ideational context has not explained the play or located what is central in
it. Contemporary interpretations, which range from *King Lear* as a Christian
tragedy of redemption to *King Lear* as an early version of *Endgame*, leave the
drama as baffling as, perhaps, even more baffling than, before.

Where so many critical angels have not feared to tread and where some
fools have dared to walk, perhaps there is room for one more trespasser.
However, I may as well confess that I certainly do not know what *King Lear*
means, what it is about, or even more soundly, what may be hypothesized as
central and unifying in what I am convinced is a unified masterpiece, perhaps
supreme in western dramatic art. This uncertainty is unique among critics;
indeed it may be all that is unique in what I shall have to say about the play.

In *Hamlet*, Hamlet proclaims to Rosencrantz and Guildenstern:

What a piece of work is a man! How noble in reason! how infinite in faculties! in form and moving, how express and admirable! in action, how like an angel! in apprehension, how like a god! the beauty of the world! the paragon of animals! And yet, to me, what is this quintessence of dust?

(II,ii,305)

In *King Lear*, Lear asks Kent and the Fool about Edgar, disguised as a madman:

Is man no more than this? Consider him well. Thou ow'st the worm no silk, the beast no hide, the sheep no wool, the cat no perfume. Ha! here's three on's are sophisticated; thou art the thing itself; unaccommodated man is no more but such a poor, bare, forked animal as thou art. Off, off, you lendings! Come; unbutton here.

(III,iv,105)[2]

With all of his suffering and self-laceration, Hamlet never reaches the depths of despair about the nature of man that Lear does. For Lear's descent is from man as god—like to man as naked animal. As the play develops, especially during the storm, both outside and within the hovel, Lear comes to see that man's accommodated virtues—his humanity—have no secure place in brute nature. In Elizabethan terms, *Hamlet* calls into question the truth of the Chain of Being and man's link in it; Lear, on the other hand, is forced to reject it forever as he explodes on his wheel of fire.

That man lives in a world without ultimate meaning—without God, gods, providence, or moral laws—becomes the central fact of the King Lear universe. Lear's own development—one can hardly call it progression—is from metaphysical kingship with all of its prerogatives supposedly guaranteed by nature to royal man who comes to realize that his humanity is only his proclamation and no longer a true report on his place in nature.

There are many ostensible philosophical themes in *King Lear*: That good and evil are absolute and that though evil destroys good, it too is destroyed. Almost all of the characters and much of the plot seem to support this theme. Indeed it is remarkable how simply and completely good Cordelia, Kent, Gloucester, and perhaps Albany are, and how simply and totally evil Goneril, Regan, Cornwall, Edmund, and Oswald are. And it is remarkable precisely because Shakespeare dissolves this simple, absolute good and evil into the ambivalence of all value in a morally indifferent universe.

Another theme, recently explored and exploited, is that of the contrast between sight and insight. Much of the imagery reinforces this contrast; and both Gloucester and Lear come to see—without their eyes—what they did not see before. But this contrast and its further contrasting theme of appearance and reality remain obscure until we can ascertain exactly what it is they come to see: just what the reality is behind the appearances they penetrate.

A third theme, that the world is ruled by justice—Albany's "justicers" above (IV.ii.79)—like Gloucester's "As flies to wanton boys, are we to th' Gods;/ They kill us for their sport" (IV,i,36), or even Edgar's "Men must endure /Their going hence, even as their coming hither: /Ripeness is all" (V.ii.9), reduced to a platitude by Gloucester's "And that's true too", though articulated in the play, does not in its intimations of moral order, Fate, or Stoicism express the brute indifference of the *King Lear* universe.

Nor, it seems to me, can one read the play in Christian terms. Lear comes to realize he has wronged Cordelia; and they are finally reconciled. But in spite of his "When thou dost ask me blessing, I'll kneel down, /And ask of thee forgiveness" (V,iii,10), or even his final "Look on her, look, her lips,/ Look there, look there!" (V,iii,310), and even if Lear dies happy (as Bradley insists), he is hardly redeemed or saved in any Christian sense. Lear's "Never, never, never, never, never!" (V,iii,308) shatters everything. And the play ends with Edgar's:

> The weight of this sad time we must obey;
> Speak what we feel, not what we ought to say.
> The oldest hath borne most: we that are young
> Shall never see so much, nor live so long.

This, too, is obituary, not rebirth.

Philosophically central in *King Lear*—an important if not central strand of the whole drama—is man's worth in a morally indifferent universe. Shakespeare's answer, I propose, is that man's worth resides in his commitment to his humanity: a commitment without any metaphysical justification; indeed, *sub specie aeternitatis*, it is a complete superfluity. In the imagery of the play, man's worth is an accommodation, a piece of raiment, not needed, but deeply required if man is to rise above the beasts or is not to become 'like monsters of the deep' (Albany, IV,ii,49), preying on themselves. Human values are luxuries without which human life is impossible. Man mints his own values. But his currency is backed by no standard in the natural world, only by his own regal proclamation. For him, his coinage is everything; for nature, it is worthless, nothing.

Lear first states this philosophical theme of the place of human value in an indifferent universe in his rejoinder to Goneril and Regan while they proceed to strip him of his retinue:

> Goneril: Hear me, my Lord.
> What need you five and twenty, ten, or five,
> To follow in a house where twice so many
> Have a command to tend you?

Regan: What need one?
Lear: O! reason not the need; our basest beggars
      Are in the poorest thing superfluous:
      Allow not nature more than nature needs,
      Man's life is cheap as beast's. Thou art a lady;
      If only to go warm were gorgeous,
      Why, nature needs not what thou gorgeous wear'st,
      Which scarcely keeps thee warm. But, for true need,—
      You Heavens, give me that patience, patience I need!

(II,iv,262)

Lear reiterates this theme of human values in an indifferent world throughout the rest of the play after his final encounter with his two pelican daughters in Act II. One example is his refusal to tax the elements with unkindness during the storm on the heath. Kindness and cruelty, like all virtues and vices, he perceives, are human attributes, utterly foreign to nature's provenance. But his most provocative statement of it comes in Act IV when, broken and mad, he enters, ranting "O, they cannot touch me for coining; I am the king himself" (IV,vi,83). Some scholars annotate this as Lear refusing press—money for military service. But the line cries out something more. Lear's utterance here is a clear reminder of his royal prerogative, joined with its immediate overtones of man as sovereign over his own economy of values. As I read the line in its context of Lear's discovery or insight and in its wider context of the theme of man's worth in a bare universe, what Lear proclaims is that, as King, it is his prerogative to coin money; what he coins is therefore genuine. To counterfeit, to melt him down, to touch him for coining, consequently, is at once necessarily to acknowledge his genuineness, his true coin. Thus, in human terms, to reduce him to a bare, forked animal is already to recognize his humanity.

So Lear sees—Shakespeare sees—that the counterfeit is not coequal with the genuine but parasitical on it. Hence to reduce man to mere animal is not to destroy him but to accept man in order to reduce him. Shakespeare also implies here that good and evil are not coequal either; rather, that good is man's commitment to value which evil can only reject and violate but cannot deny and destroy since evil must acknowledge good in order to exist at all. There are, then, good and evil in the *King Lear* universe. But like the coinage of man, they rest on human prerogative, with no standard in nature to back them up. Evil cannot exist without good any more than the counterfeit can without the genuine. Nevertheless, value, like money, is, from nature's standpoint, utterly worthless. In *King Lear*, nothing ultimately comes from nothing. But in between—in man—everything comes from nothing.

To return to the play. In *King Lear*, I want now to argue, Shakespeare dramatizes this paradoxical philosophical theme of the metaphysical superfluity of human value and yet the absolute requirement of value for man and society in the specific theme of filial gratitude. Here is Lear on its negation, filial ingratitude:

(1) To Goneril:
>   Ingratitude, thou marble—hearted fiend,
>   More hideous, when thou show'st thee in a child,
>   Than the sea—monster.

$$(I,iv,268)$$

(2) To the Fool:
>   Monster Ingratitude!

$$(I,v,40)$$

(3)
>   Regan: I am glad to see your Highness.
>   Lear: Regan, I think you are; I know what reason
>   I have to think so: if thou shouldst not be glad,
>   I would divorce me from thy mother's tomb,
>   Sepulchring an adult'ress.

$$(II,iv,129)$$

(4) To Regan, about returning to Goneril:

>   Never, Regan.
>   She hath abated me of half my train;
>   Look'd black upon me; struck me with her tongue,
>   Most serpent—like, upon the very heart.
>   All the stor'd vengeances of Heaven fall
>   On her ingrateful top!

$$(II,iv,159)$$

(5) Again, to Regan:
>   thou better know'st
>   The offices of nature, bond of childhood,
>   Effects of courtesy, dues of gratitude;
>   Thy half o' th' kingdom hast thou not forgot,
>   Wherein I thee endow'd.

$$(II,iv,179)$$

(6) To the storm on the heath:

Blow, winds, and crack your cheeks! rage! blow!
You cataracts and hurricanoes, spout
Till you have drench'd our steeples, drown'd the cocks!
You sulph'rous and thought—executing fires,
Vaunt—couriers of oak—cleaving thunderbolts,
Singe my white head! And thou, all—shaking thunder,
Strike flat the thick rotundity o' th' world!
Crack Nature's moulds, all germens spill at once
That makes ingrateful man!

(III,ii,1)

(7) To Kent, before the hovel:

Thou think'st 'tis much that this contentious storm
Invades us to the skin: so 'tis to thee;
But where the greater malady is fix'd,
The lesser is scarce felt. Thou'ldst shun a bear;
But if thy flight lay toward the roaring sea,
Thou'ldst meet the bear i' th' mouth. When the mind's free
The body's delicate; this tempest in my mind
Doth from my senses take all feeling else
Save what beats there—filial ingratitude!
Is it not as this mouth should tear this hand
For lifting food to 't? But I will punish home:
No, I will weep no more. In such a night
To shut me out? Pour on; I will endure.
In such a night as this? O Regan, Goneril!
Your old kind father, whose frank heart gave all,—
O! that way madness lies; let me shun that;
No more of that.

(III,iv,6)

(8) To the Fool and Kent about Edgar, disguised as a madman:

Didst thou give all to thy daughters?
And art thou come to this?

(III,iv,48)

and

What! has his daughters brought him to this pass?

(III,iv,63)

and

> Death, traitor! nothing could have subdu'd nature
> To such a lowness but his unkind daughters.
> Is it the fashion that discarded fathers
> Should have thus little mercy on their flesh?
> Judicious punishment! 'twas this flesh begot
> Those pelican daughters.

(III,iv,70)

(9) Albany to Goneril:

> What have you done ?
> Tigers, not daughters, what have you perform'd?
> A father, and a gracious aged man.

(IV,ii,39)

(10) Kent to a Gentleman about Lear's shame in meeting Cordelia:

> A sovereign shame so elbows him: his own unkindness,
> That stripp'd her from his benediction, turn'd her
> To foreign casualties, gave her dear rights
> To his dog—hearted daughters, these things sting
> His mind so venomously that burning shame
> Detains him from Cordelia.

(IV,iii,43)

That Lear is obsessed by filial ingratitude throughout the drama is indisputable. Quantitatively, it is the most articulated theme of the play. But, more importantly, it is as generative of the plot as any other element. It drives Lear from his two older daughters out into the storm and to his ensuing madness. It moves France and Cordelia to invade Britain which, in turn, precipitates the blinding of Gloucester and then the deaths of Cordelia and Lear. Also, or anyhow so it seems to me, it makes dramatic sense of the first scene, especially the love contest. Read as a final, formal request—in reality, a royal command—for an expression of filial gratitude from his three daughters, a request—command which Lear accepts as an integral constituent of kingship and fatherhood in his universe of absolute values, Lear's contest becomes his last official royal proclamation, scarcely the wilful, stupid act of a selfish, vain, puerile old man, as many critics and actors have conceived it. Interpreted as an act of absolute royal command, sanctioned by a universe that justifies it, his banishment of Cordelia, though extreme, is understandable. Her "nothing, my lord", followed by her

> Happily, when I shall wed,
> That lord whose hand must take my plight shall carry
> Half my love with him, half my care and duty:
> Sure I shall never marry like my sisters,
> To love my father all.

(I,i,100)

is a sardonic rebuke. Lear's punishment is of course extreme and foolish as events show it to be—but it is consistent with his absolute commitment to royal kingship and human fatherhood in a value—structured universe.

King Lear, then, as I see it, begins with Lear's conception of filial gratitude—one among absolute values—as a need that can be reasoned, that is, that can be justified as a requirement built into the nature of things. His whole development—and here we can call it progression—is from this need as reasoned requirement through this need as an illusion (especially in the hovel when he sees man as unaccommodated animal) to his final insight that filial gratitude, indeed, all human values, cannot be reasoned or justified. Humanity itself, he sees, is man's royal proclamation and commitment, with no metaphysical justification. The difference between man and animal, brutal and brute, kin and kind rests on tenuous and ephemeral projection, no longer on universal nature which sanctions nothing. Lear says at the beginning "Nothing will come of nothing: speak again" (I,i,90). But as the play ends, he intimates and we see: "Except everything."

In *King Lear*, then, Shakespeare dramatizes, through the specific theme of filial gratitude the proclamatory rather than metaphysical role of human values in a neutral world. As a philosophical theme it explains much of the play. But, we must now ask, does it tie up with all of the constituent elements of the play? Is it an integral, perhaps even the central, controlling element of the play? As I have tried to show, it explains Lear's action, much of the plot, some of the imagery, almost all of Lear's (critically neglected) powerful staccato, non—metaphorical imperatives, such as "Then, kill, kill, kill, kill, kill, kill!" (IV,vi,189) as well as the traditionally attributed themes of sight and insight, good versus evil, and appearance versus reality.

How does the theme of unreasoned, unjustifiable value in an indifferent universe relate to the subplot; to the pristine goodness of Cordelia, Kent, and Edgar, and to the absolute evil of Goneril, Regan, Cornwall, and Edmund; to the suffering and moral regeneration of Lear; and to the tragic in the play?

Much of the Gloucester-Edgar-Edmund subplot parallels the main Lear plot. In both, filial gratitude carries the major burden; in both, there is deception, self—deception, and final insight. The great difference is that although both Gloucester and Lear die undeceived and reconciled with their true kin, Gloucester never learns what Lear does, yet it applies to Gloucester, too: that filial gratitude, required for human life, is an utter metaphysical superfluity. Edgar's words on his father's passing:

> I ask'd his blessing, and from first to last
> Told him my pilgrimage: but his flaw'd heart,
> Alack, too weak the conflict to support!
> 'Twixt two extremes of passion, joy and grief,
> Burst smilingly

(V,iii,195)

as even Lear's last imperative—dare I call it proclamation?—"Do you see this? Look on her, look, her lips, /Look there, look there!" (V,iii,310), must be read in the finality of "Never, never, never, never, never!" That both Gloucester and Lear burst smilingly contradicts nothing about the fundamental philosophical fact of the *King Lear* universe, that nothing comes from nothing, except all that is human, including their last moment of ecstasy.

Good and evil are not coequal in *King Lear*. Instead, good is primary and evil dependent on it. Nor is good as primary a natural fact in a value—infused universe. Of course, Cordelia, Kent, and Edgar are good, and Regan, Goneril, Cornwall, and Edmund are evil; but their evil is a violation and, through violation as counterfeit, an acknowledgement of the genuine, primary character of good. However, since good is proclamatory, hence metaphysically superfluous, in *King Lear*, the goodness of Cordelia, Kent, and Edgar is like filial gratitude to Lear: an unjustifiable requirement for human as against animal life, but having no place in a universe that indifferently destroys both good and evil. There is thus no good or evil in the *King Lear* universe except that human beings project them so—in their ephemeral commitments to their values or to their counterfeits, which vanish forever as nature swallows them one by one.

Lear's suffering and moral regeneration directly relate to filial gratitude, and to its emotional and intellectual consequences. Goneril and Regan drive him to madness through ingratitude. And Cordelia forgives him his own parental ingratitude, the other side of filial ingratitude. This brings him peace, as he expresses it in his poignant transcendence of suffering:

> Come, let's away to prison;
> We two alone will sing like birds i' th' cage:
> When thou dost ask me blessing, I'll kneel down,
> And ask of thee forgiveness: so we'll live,
> And pray, and sing, and tell old tales, and laugh
> At gilded butterflies, and hear poor rogues
> Talk of court news; and we'll talk with them too,
> Who loses and who wins; who's in, who's out;
> And take upon 's the mystery of things,
> As if we were God's spies: and we'll wear out,

> In a wall'd prison, packs and sects of great ones
> That ebb and flow by th' moon.

(V,iii,8)

Lear's royal command is finally obeyed. But moral and religious order are not restored. Only his human commitment has been met. Lear has been touched, but not for coining. Like Job, Lear has solved the problem of evil, through Cordelia and without God.

Finally, what is tragic in *King Lear*? That Lear, Cordelia, and Gloucester die? That good is destroyed by evil? That Lear regenerates himself? That the play purges us through pity and fear? Why not? Any of these will do, as will any of the other traditional theories of the tragic. However, just as securely tragic is the vision of the play that man coins his own values in a world in which he and his currency are as ultimately worthless as the metal and paper it is printed on. And echoing throughout, even more distinctly than in *The Tempest*, is the idea of the poet as the coiner of words, proclaiming the worth of his own currency, that can be neither melted down nor reasoned, yet which gives human life its tenuous significance even though its value comes to naught in a universe ultimately without discourse.

Camus's *L'Étranger*, like *King Lear*, at least in one of its major strands, dramatizes the philosophical problem of human worth in an indifferent universe. Through Monsieur Meursault, who has no given first (Christian?) name, hence is Everyman, Camus presents the ideal existentialist hero, that is, the man who defines his own existence only when confronted by death. A protagonist of nothing, no idealist, not even a thinker, only a seemingly ordinary man, forced by economic circumstances to place his mother in an old people's home and to earn a living as a clerk, Meursault's total involvement is with his present and immediate future: in ordinary food and friends, in ordinary sex and swimming, in everyday sun and shade, but with no greed or even conscious commitment to these as his philosophy of life. Although he is without ordinary responses to death and marriage and ambition, he is normal enough to his friends and to those, like Raymond Sintès or Salamano, who make minimal demands upon him. It is one of these demands, to help Raymond get even in a sordid affair, that prepares the way for his undoing when, during a beach party, for no reason at all except that "And just then it crossed my mind that one might fire, or not fire—and it would come to absolutely the same thing"[2] he kills a man. Meursault is duly arrested, interrogated, tried, and condemned. As the trial proceeds we are made to realize that he is being prosecuted and finally punished not only for killing a man but also for being "an inhuman monster wholly without a moral sense" (p. 120).

In prison, awaiting his execution, Meursault poses the problem of inevitability. He is guilty and must die. The machine in which he is a cog works, and the only consolation he finds is that it should work efficiently. The prison chaplain enters to offer him a different kind of certainty in God and immortality, which he rejects in an "ecstasy of joy and rage" (p. 151). Completely purged after this incident, he summarizes and justifies his whole life:

> Nothing, nothing had the least importance, and I knew quite well why . . . What difference could they make to me, the deaths of others, of a mother's love, or his [the chaplain's] God; or the way a man decides to live, the fate he thinks he chooses. . . . (p. 152).

Meursault's epiphany ends on a Spinozistic rapture: "for the first time, the first, I laid my heart open to the benign indifference of the universe" (p. 154). Everything, he finally sees, comes to nothing.

Meursault is an existentialist hero, but *L'Étranger* is not an existentialist novel, unless existentialism includes in its mixed bag the nihilism which is central in that novel. For relentlessly nihilistic it is. With the rigor of a deductive system Camus in *L'Étranger* demonstrates that nothing ultimately, hence derivatively, matters. The basic premise of his argument is this: That we live in a world without ultimate meaning. This premise is true and its acceptance the mark of authenticity. As a consequence nothing makes any difference, not even our present or immediately future gratifications. The second premise is that most of us refuse to accept this truth. Instead we live as if there were something significant in love, religion, institutions. Because of this self—deception, this demand for inauthenticity, we ruthlessly punish those who attack our game of self—deception or who, like Meursault, will not play the game. Outsiders will not be tolerated. Even so, the conclusion stares us in the face: we are all of us condemned to a meaningless universe, hence as "guilty" as Meursault, and our only hope is his—that the machinery of execution will work without a hitch. Thus, Meursault becomes each one of us, stripped of illusion, thereby authenticated as a bare, forked animal, awaiting annihilation in a benignly indifferent world. We are all outsiders, in a world that accommodates none of our illusions, whether we play the game or not.

Further theorems follow. It does not matter if one fires or not. There is no difference between killing a man and swatting a fly. Nor is there any real distinction between remorse and vexation, as Meursault suggests to his interrogator. Thus, man's worth in an indifferent universe, even as a tenuous, ephemeral proclamation, is all illusion, adding up to zero.

As appalling as Camus's philosophy is in *L'Étranger*, as magnificently as it is worked into the novel, as hard—headed and courageously honest as it seems, and as rigorous as the argument for nihilism appears, there is, it seems to me, one further theorem that Camus does not bring into the novel but which is implicit in it, especially in Meursault's integrity, and which, once deduced, breaks its back entirely. Nihilism, let us assume, is the true view about man in his universe. Nevertheless, we may ask, why should we accept it as our philosophy? What difference does it make whether we accept it or not? Why play the nihilistic game rather than the conventional one? Without some commitment to truth as a value, however superfluous in the universe, and without some commitment to the rejection of falsehood, nihilism simply cannot be urged. Once urged, however, it is seen for what it is—a counterfeit of Shakespeare's true coin in *King Lear*.

Chapter Five

LITERATURE WITHOUT PHILOSOPHY:
ANTONY AND CLEOPATRA

Major claims have been made both for and against Shakespeare as a man of ideas—of his own time and for all time. These point to larger doctrines about the relation between literature and philosophy. In this paper I shall consider Shakespeare as a dramatist of ideas and his contributions to philosophy in literature.

Philosophy and Literature, Philosophy of Literature, and Philosophy in Literature have only one thing in common: each has been designated a non-subject. Of course this is a slight exaggeration, since it is true of the first two but not of the third. Philosophy and Literature is a piece of academic entrepreneurism, motivated by the mutual desire to make philosophy concrete and literature profound. It succeeds in doing neither. At best, it functions as a part of the history of ideas, using both literature and philosophy as reflecting mirrors of each other; at its worst, it is a series of distorting imitations of imitations, to borrow a phrase from the master.

Philosophy of Literature is a piece of philosophical imperialism, sponsored by the obsession that all disciplines have a philosophical dimension that awaits articulation and scrutiny. All that deserve examination, however, are those aspects of literature as an art that distinguish it from the other arts. Traditionally, aesthetics has regarded this problem of the differentia of literature as its proper domain. I see no need to recast or to reject this traditional role and discipline: there is nothing in philosophy of literature that is not already in aesthetics.

What about Philosophy in Literature? Is it a proper subject? According to a major tradition, from Plato to I. A. Richards, it is not. Philosophy and literature are radically distinct: the first aims at truth, the second, at falsehood or affective experience. Even Aristotle's compromise that poetry, though not pure philosophy, is at least better than history, is not much more than a left-handed compliment to the cognitive content of literature.

Having dealt with this issue of the legitimacy of philosophy in literature elsewhere, I do not wish to debate it here. Instead, let me dogmatically assert or reaffirm that they can be combined without the denigration of either. Indeed, it seems to me, that literature, in some cases, is able to convey a philosophy or truth that philosophy itself does not. Ancient Greek tragedy, for example, dramatizes what by implication is an ultimate, irreducible fact of human experience: that it is tragic. Plato recognizes the tragic but argues that it can be overcome by reason; Aristotle restricts the tragic to the stage, construing it only as a representation of the passage from happiness to misery, a passage that also reason can overcome. If we agree that the tragic, however variously conceived, is something irretrievable—a brute fact in the world—then surely Greek tragedy proclaims a philosophical truth that Greek philosophy does not. Greek tragedy, thus, is not only a clear case of philosophy in literature, it is also a striking victory of literature over philosophy in the pursuit of truth.

The rejection of Philosophy in Literature includes one aesthetically valid point that should be applauded, that literature must never be reduced to philosophy or to any nuggets of embroidered truth. This anti-reductionist insistence on the integrity of the individual literary work, however unfortunately conflated with the rejection of philosophy in literature, remains a solid contribution to literary criticism.

I understand by Philosophy in Literature two related doctrines: (1) that some works of literature contain philosophical ideas which are as integral to these works as any of their other constituents; and (2) that there is a place in literary criticism for the aesthetic articulation of these ideas. More particularly, I find it fruitful to ask of any work of literature: does it have any philosophical ideas? If it does, how do they get into the work? and what aesthetic contribution do they make to the work?

In asking the first question, one must distinguish between a philosophical theme and a philosophical thesis. For example, a novel, say *Anna Karenina*, may have many philosophical themes; among them, that we are not to blame, hence not to be judged, for what we do—a theme that is voiced by all the major characters; or that *laissez-faire* is the best philosophy of life, which is exemplified by Oblonsky. But it is not always clear that a philosophical theme, however much it is expressed, serves as the philosophical thesis; neither of these two themes, for example, can be read as Tolstoy's truth-claim about human life in *Anna Karenina*. In fact, the philosophical thesis, at least on my reading of the novels, is not even expressed on the printed pages of the novel but must be elicited from the plot in relation to the other elements. I am also aware of powerful arguments by aestheticians against the distinction between theme and thesis in literature. All of these arguments rest on a confusion of the factual question: Are there philosophical theses in literature? with the normative question: Ought we, when the plot, characters, dialogue, authorial interpolation, tone, and themes are described and explained in a certain way, to construe one or other of the themes as *a* or *the* philosophical thesis in the whole work? In regard to this normative question, it seems to me that there is no compelling reason for a negative reply and good reasons for an affirmative answer, provided we are able to accommodate false, as well as true, philosophical theses in those works that have or imply them.

My model for philosophical literary criticism is a form of the imagistic criticism of Shakespeare's plays. Traditionally—though the tradition is quite recent—the imagistic approach to Shakespeare displays the same conflict over reductionism as philosophy in literature, best seen in the work of Spurgeon and Clemen. Both of these critics explore the imagery of each of the plays. Spurgeon, however, reduces the whole meaning of the play to its dominant image; Clemen, on the other hand, regards the imagery as but one aspect of each of the dramas, sometimes central, sometimes not; but, in any case, as a contributing element to the whole drama, which, cannot be reduced to any central element, including the imagery. For him, the play's the thing, not the imagery. So, too, for me; the literary work is central, not its philosophical theme or thesis, which may or may not be dominant in any particular work.

In a number of essays, I have tried—by way of examples, the only way philosophy in literature can vindicate itself—to practice philosophical literary criticism as a branch of literary criticism. I have tried to show that Voltaire's *Candide*, Shakespeare's *Hamlet* and *King Lear*, Tolstoy's *Anna Karenina*, Proust's *A la recherche du temps perdu*, and Eliot's *Four Quartets* contain philosophical themes and theses; how these are brought into these works; and what aesthetic difference the theses make to the works. This enterprise, I hope, justifies philosophy in literature, both in literature and in philosophy. In turning now to our present subject, *Antony and Cleopatra*, allow me to reiterate in the strongest terms that there is philosophy in (some) literature, consequently that philosophical criticism is as legitimate and enlightening as any other special branch of literary criticism. However—it cannot be overemphasized—this discipline is a part of literary criticism, not of philosophy.

Is there a philosophy or philosophical thesis in Shakespeare? Wholesale affirmative as well as negative answers have been equally disastrous. That Shakespeare presents a unified system of ideas about life and the world simply will not stand up to the diversity of the ideas in his plays. That Shakespeare has no philosophy, offers no profound claims about man—a view put forth by no less a poet and critic than Eliot, in his contrast of Dante as a poet-thinker with Shakespeare as a dramatist-poet—is also suspect when we turn to some of the individual plays. *Hamlet*, and especially *King Lear*, dramatize themes and proffer theses that in their profundity are not only philosophical but challenge, as the writers of Greek tragedy challenged their contemporaries, the naive and pragmatic optimism of his age.

Without agreeing at all with Eliot about Shakespeare, I want to ask, in regard to literature in general and Shakespeare in particular: Can there be great literature without philosophy, that is, without a thesis about man or his world? It has long seemed to me that there can be. In this paper, I want to discuss this question—again by example—and, if I can, to persuade you that in the case of *Antony and Cleopatra* we have a great tragedy which contains a number of philosophical themes but no implied or elicitable philosophical thesis or universal claim. Thus, in the sense that *King Lear* may be convincingly interpreted as a philosophical drama with its dominant thesis about man's worth in an indifferent world; or that *Hamlet* may be seen as a drama with its thesis about man's ability to raise all the important questions without being able to find any of the answers, *Antony and Cleopatra* is not a philosophical drama: it neither makes nor includes any general claim about man and his world. Rather it is a tragedy of two particulars who instance no universal applicable to all.

Among the distinguishable elements of *Antony and Cleopatra*, there are a number of ostensible philosophical themes, each beautifully explored by critics of the play. (Whether these themes are really philosophical or what is a philosophical as opposed to a non-philosophical theme seem to me fruitless questions, resting as they do on the unwarranted assumption that philosophy is fixed and precise, a discipline that can be brought into a real definition, which it cannot). There is, however, one philosophical theme in the play that, so far as I know, has not been given the scrutiny it deserves: the theme of generation and corruption, of coming into being and passing away, a theme as old as ancient Greek philosophy. This theme is richly unfolded in *Antony and Cleopatra*, so intensively that I would venture to call the play Shakespeare's 'pre-Socratic' tragedy.

Antony and Cleopatra is primarily a magnificent love story, full of exciting episodes, fascinating characters, marvelous, luscious poetry, and a traditional tragic theme of the rise and fall of great ones. Let us even grant that it is the Elizabethan-Roman version of the beautiful people, but without the not-yet Jet set.

What does such a *précis* leave out? For one thing, the multiple contrasts between earth and water, Rome and Egypt, Tiber and Nile, land and sea, Antony's victories on land, defeats at sea. Then, there are the epithets of melting Rome in Tiber, Egypt in Nile. Clemen especially has explored the sea-imagery of the play; Spurgeon, the vast expanse of the world. 'World', she shows, is as important in *Antony and Cleopatra* as 'nature' is in *King Lear*.

There is also the imagery of transformation that our summary account of the play leaves out. Here is Antony, preparing for his battle with Caesar, who will fight by sea, not land:

> I would they'd fight i' the fire, or i' the air.
> (IV,x,3)

This reference to the four elements is picked up toward the end of the play by

Cleopatra:

> Husband, I come:
> Now to that name, my courage prove my title!
> I am fire, and air; my other elements
> I give to baser life.
>
> (V,ii,286-9)

It is this theme of the transformation of the four elements, as it embodies the rhythm of nature, that I wish to concentrate on. In *Antony and Cleopatra*, there is much variation on one thing becoming another: the higher becoming the lower; and nature and her gaps of generation and corruption, as in Enobarbus' description of Antony's first sight of Cleopatra:

> and Antony
> Enthron'd i' the market-place, did sit alone,
> Whistling to the air; which, but for vacancy,
> Had gone to gaze on Cleopatra too,
> And made a gap in nature
>
> (II,ii,214-18)

in contrast to Cleopatra's description of a world without Antony—the gap of former greatness:

> The crown o' the earth doth melt.
>   My lord?
> O, wither'd is the garland of the war,
> The soldier's pole is fall'n: young boys and girls
> Are level now with men: the odds is gone,
> And there is nothing left remarkable
> Beneath the visiting moon.
>
> (IV,xv,63-8)

There is also in the play one thing becoming another, either in a normal, expected way or in an abnormal, unexpected way. Antony's description of the Nile expresses ordinary generation and corruption:

> The higher Nilus swells,
> The more it promises: as it ebbs, the seedsman
> Upon the slime and ooze scatters his grain,
> And shortly comes to harvest.
>
> (II,vii,20-3)

The Nile, in its rises and falls, bringing feast and famine, is a perfect exemplar of one kind of normal, to be expected, passage in nature and life: out of the slime arises fertility; from fertility comes sterility, and the cycle is perennial. No surprises here.

There are many of these examples of normal, generation and corruption in *Antony and Cleopatra*. In each, one thing brings forth its opposite. Antony, to the first messenger from Rome:

> O then we bring forth weeds,
> When our quick minds lie still.
> (I,ii,106-7)

Philo, opening the play by reflecting on Antony's change from warrior to lover:

> Nay, but this dotage of our general's
> O'erflows the measure.
> (I,i,106-107)

Antony, on Fulvia's death:

> The present pleasure,
> By revolution lowering, does become
> The opposite of itself.
> (I,ii,121-3)

Charmian, on Cleopatra's strategy for keeping Antony:

> Tempt him not so too far. I wish, forbear;
> in time we hate that which we often fear.
> (I,iii,11-12)

Enobarbus, on Antony's bravura:

> and I see still,
> A diminution in our captain's brain
> Restores his heart.
> (III,xiii,197-9)

Antony, on Enobarbus' desertion:

> O, my fortunes have
> Corrupted honest men.
> (IV,v,16-17)

Cleopatra, in the Monument, after Antony's final defeat:

> our size of sorrow,
> Proportion'd to our cause, must be as great
> As that which makes it
>
> (IV,xv,4-6)

and Cleopatra's reflection on the clown with the asp:

> What poor an instrument
> May do a noble deed!
>
> (V,ii,35-6)

Besides these normal, expected, causally connected passages from one thing to its opposite, there are normal ones whose expectations do not occur. Two striking examples are the anticipated betrayals of Antony by Cleopatra that do not happen; and Antony's and Cleopatra's moves toward death that do not come off.

However, the really challenging examples of generation and corruption are these:

Enobarbus, on Cleopatra's powers:

> I do think there is mettle in death, which commits some
> loving act upon her, she hath such a celerity in dying.
>
> (I,ii,139-42)

Here we expect dying and death to bring inaction; in Cleopatra, they create heightened action. Death does not become its opposite, it is its opposite.

Cleopatra to Antony on his projected return to Rome:

> Riotous madness,
> To be entangled with those mouth-made vows,
> Which break themselves in swearing!
>
> (I,iii,29-31)

A promise normally—some philosophers would say necessarily—embodies the intent to carry it out; here it is broken in its very utterance. The image is that of a vow that not only is not kept but becomes its opposite when it is made.

Lepidus to Caesar and Antony, in attempting to reconcile them:

> When we debate
> Our trivial difference loud, we do commit
> Murther in healing wounds.

(II,ii,20-2)

The comparison of loud debate with murder is apt, the image of murdering in healing wounds is not, yet it is marvelously right as it yields the totally unexpected effect from a related cause. Healing does not cure, it destroys; one thing generates its opposite by being its opposite.

Enobarbus to Agrippa, on Cleopatra in her barge:

> On each side her,
> Stood pretty dimpled boys, like smiling Cupids,
> With divers-colour'd fans, whose wind did seem
> To glow the delicate cheeks which they did cool,
> And what they undid did.
> (II,ii,201-4)

Enobarbus, again on Cleopatra:

> I saw her once
> Hop forty paces through the public street,
> And having lost her breath, she spoke, and panted,
> That she did make defect perfection,
> And, breathless, power breathe forth.
> (II,ii,228-32)

Again Enobarbus on Cleopatra and the possibility of Antony leaving her:

> Never; he will not:
> Age cannot wither her, nor custom stale
> Her infinite variety: other women cloy
> The appetites they feed, but she makes hungry,
> Where most she satisfies.
> (II,ii,234-8)

Hunger normally leads to food and eating; too much food, to satiety. But the image here is that of a food that creates more hunger. One thing generates its opposite in a very unusual, unexpected, yet totally convincing manner.

Enobarbus, this time to Menas, on Antony's marriage to Octavia:

> But you shall find the band that seems to tie their friendship
> together will be the very strangler of their amity.
> (II,vi,117-19)

Ventidius to Silius, on Ventidius's victorious exploits:

> I could do more to do Antonius good,

> But 'twould offend him. And in his offence
> Should my performance perish.
>> (III,i,25-7)

Caesar to Antony, on Antony's marriage to Octavia:

> Most noble Antony,
> Let not the piece of virtue which is set
> Betwixt us, as the cement of our love
> To keep it builded, be the ram to batter
> The fortress of it.
>> (III,ii,27-31)

Octavia, on the strife between her brother, Caesar, and her husband, Antony:

> The good gods will mock me presently,
> When I shall pray, "O, bless my lord, and husband!"
> Undo that prayer, by crying out as loud,
> "O, bless my brother!" Husband win, win brother,
> Prays, and destroys the prayer, no midway
> 'Twixt these extremes at all.
>> (III,iv,15-20)

Octavia, after receiving Antony's approval to go to Caesar:

> Wars 'twixt you twain would be
> As if the world should cleave, and that slain men
> Should solder up the rift.
>> (III,iv,30-2)

Enobarbus on Antony's bravado in defeat:

> Now he'll outstare the lightning; to be furious
> Is to be frighted out of fear.
>> (III,xiii,195-6)

Antony, after his first defeat and before his final battle with Rome:

> To-morrow, soldier,
> By sea and land I'll fight: or I will live,
> Or bathe my dying honour in the blood
> Shall make it live again.
>> (IV,ii,4-6)

Enobarbus, commenting on Antony's generosity after he deserts:

> I am alone the villain of the earth,
> And feel I am so most. O Antony,
> Thou mine of bounty, how wouldst thou have paid
> My better service, when my turpitude
> Thou dost so crown with gold! This blows my
> heart.
>
> (IV,vi,30-4)

Antony, to Eros, after his final defeat:

> Now all labour
> Mars what it does: yea, very force entangles
> Itself with strength.
>
> (IV,xiv,47-9)

Antony to Eros, begging Eros to kill him:

> Come then: for with a wound I must be cured.
> (IV,xiv,78)

Cleopatra, as Antony is being lifted up to the Monument:

> Here's sport indeed! How heavy weighs my lord!
> Our strength is all gone into heaviness,
> That makes the weight.
>
> (IV,xv,32-4)

Agrippa to Caesar, on the death of Antony:

> And strange it is,
> That nature must compel us to lament
> Our most persisted deeds.
>
> (V,i,28-30)

Caesar adds:

> O Antony,
> I have follow'd thee to this, but we do launce
> Diseases in our bodies
>
> (V,i,35-7)

and Cleopatra to Dolabella on her Antony:

> His legs bestrid the ocean, his rear'd arm
> Crested the world: his voice was propertied

As all the tuned spheres, and that to friends:
But when he meant to quail, and shake the orb,
He was as rattling thunder. For his bounty,
There was no winter in't: an autumn 'twas
That grew the more by reaping.
                                        (V,ii,82-8)

There are probably more of these fascinating inverted images that I have missed. The list is long but since it is Shakespeare, it can hardly be tedious. Well now, to borrow from Spurgeon's famous title, What do these unusual forms of generation and corruption tell us about the play? Can it be that there is at least one form of nature and life that grows from itself and becomes fully itself at the very moment it becomes its opposite? In that case, it is not the image of a Nile that begets fertility, and then famine but an image of a Nile that in its abundance of fertility destroys itself, which is suggested by many of these examples of abnormal generation and corruption. One thing becomes itself, generates more and more of itself and, in so doing, generates its own destruction, not successively but simultaneously. In human beings, this kind of generation and corruption is the ascent to the rarified—fire and air—from the baser elements—earth and water—an ascent which transcends and destroys. Listen to Cleopatra again:

Husband, I come:
Now to that name, my courage prove my title!
I am fire, and air; my other elements
I give to baser life.

                                        (V,ii,286-9)

Earlier she says of Antony:

Be'st thou sad, or merry,
The violence of either thee becomes,
So does it no man else.
                                        (I,v,59-61)

For all, except Antony and herself, moderation is in order. But excess—the ascent that is both life—fulfilling and death-fulfilling—is for them. Antony sets this theme at the very beginning of the play:

the nobleness of life
Is to do thus: when such a mutual pair,
And such a twain can do't.
                                        (I,i,36-8)

Contrast this with Ventidius's comment:

> and ambition,
> The soldier's virtue, rather makes choice of loss,
> Than gain which darkens him.
>   (III,i,22-4)

Is, therefore, one theme in the play that there is in Antony's love for Cleopatra a coming into being (the intensity of fire) of a love (the rarefaction of air) that destroys in its very perfection? It seems to me that it is, yielding one implicative claim in the play. But the claim is not universal; it holds only for "such a mutual pair/And such a twain can do't". It does not apply to Ventidius or to you or me: no undeniable feature of human experience is affirmed. All this theme provides philosophically in the play is a pre-Socratic setting, with the Empedoclean principles of love and strife as the sole forces of generation and corruption.

This theme of a form of generation and corruption that destroys itself in its perfection may not be central in the play but it does relate to a number of its elements: the contrast and unity of external and internal vastness; the infinite variety and ultimate enigma of Cleopatra; Antony's role as a middle-aged hero who has experienced the gap of boredom; and the human as well as demi-god in Antony and Cleopatra, both of whom create gaps in nature by their presence and absence. They are made, as all of us are, of earth and water—the baser elements. However they, not we, can become fire and air, can transcend the normal rhythms of nature and life.

If there is anything to this theme that I have sketched, *Antony and Cleopatra* is not Dryden's "All for Love or the World Well Lost" or Enobarbus' "Don't lose your head when you lose your heart". Rather, there is something unique: that there is in the world (to use an image whose banality Shakespeare would not have tolerated) a kind of perfume which in its loveliness suffocates. Without the suffocation, no loveliness: that is the full choice. The alternative is the gap of boredom. Antony in effect chooses a form of generation that destroys itself in its perfection; but it is his escape from what has become to him the gap of Rome.

Two final observations: however one responds to the theme I have set forth, the imagery on which I have based it does not confirm the traditional dichotomizing of the language of the play into the Roman and the Egyptian. The imagery of abnormal forms of becoming is shared equally by the stolid Romans and the sensual Egyptians, as well as by the Egyptianized Romans, Enobarbus and Antony. The imagery of the causally abnormal may not yield the major philosophical theme or thesis of the play: but neither can any reading of the play survive without including it. Nor—to close the critical gap between the explored imagery and the putative absence of any philosophical thesis in the play—can any *philosophical* reading of the play survive with it. For the imagery of the causally abnormal, in its context of the vast varieties of generation and corruption, forecloses on any philosophical formula which, in effect, must needs reduce the variety to a uniformity required by a universal generalization. Unlike, perhaps, *Hamlet*, where the varieties of experience do suggest a philosophical thesis —that we can put forth all the great questions but can secure none of their answers—*Antony and Cleopatra* does not yield even this minimum resolution of coming into being and passing away.

That Shakespeare does not universalize this theme of a perfection that destroys, can perhaps be seen in a final bit of irresistible philosopher's nonsense. If we project the plays of Shakespeare to mirror in some way the relation between the poet and the world he has created, as can be done with *The Tempest* and *Hamlet* and even *King Lear*, perhaps we can see in *Antony and Cleopatra* the same nobleness that, in its intensity and rarefaction —its fire and air—transcends the baser elements of language to create a mode of ecstatic perfection that fulfills without destruction. The vicissitudes and the grandeur of poetry, thus, make it, too, one among the infinite varieties of generation, a form unlike love that does not destroy itself in its perfection. The nobleness of the play transcends even the exclusive nobleness of its two main characters.

Chapter Six

REASONS IN CRITICISM

Critics do many things when they talk about the arts. They describe, compare, analyze, interpret, explain, and evaluate. Individual critics, of course, emphasize one rather than another of these activities. Some critics supplement these with excursions into poetic theory or with protracted disputes with their fellow critics. Others indulge in metaphorical or rhapsodical utterance, sometimes as their fundamental critical activity.

Much, but not all, critical activity involves argument in which reasons are given as support in this argument. Philosophers have investigated the role of reasons in each of these activities and have proffered different and competing theories of it, but especially of reasons in evaluation. Recently, however, mostly because of the persuasive work of C. L. Stevenson, I think, attention has shifted from reasons in evaluation to reasons in interpretation.

In this paper I return to the problem of reasons in evaluation, mainly because neither Stevenson's nor other similar accounts of reasons in evaluation seem to me adequate.

How do reasons function in evaluative criticisms? This I shall take as my main problem.

First, let me choose as an area of inquiry one aspect of the whole of Shakespearean criticism, its various attempts to provide assessments of Shakespeare's dramas, and, further, to choose, as representative examples of this criticism and, perhaps, of evaluative criticism altogether, the evaluations of Dryden, Pope, Johnson, and Coleridge. I should suppose that anything of philosophical interest which could be said about their evaluative criticism and the role of reasons in it would be of vital interest to any general view about reasons in evaluative criticism.

My first example, then, is from Dryden, more particularly, his *Essay of Dramatick Poesie* (1668), one of the most important assessments ever given of Shakespeare. Dryden writes:

> He was the man who of all modern, and perhaps ancient poets, had the largest and most comprehensive soul. All the images of Nature were still present to him, and he drew them, not laboriously, but luckily; when he describes any thing, you more than see it, you feel it too. Those who accuse him to have wanted learning, give him the greater commendation: he was naturally learn'd; he needed not the spectacles of books to read Nature; he looked inwards, and found her there. I cannot say he is everywhere alike; were he so, I should do him injury to compare him with the greatest of mankind. He is many times flat, insipid; his comic wit degenerating into clenches, his serious swelling into bombast. But he is always great, when some great occasion is presented to him . . . .

Johnson proclaimed Dryden "the father of English criticism, . . . the man who first taught us to determine upon principles the merit of composition"; and his account of Shakespeare ". . . a perpetual model of encomiastic criticism." As magnificent as this praise is of Dryden, it as well as Dryden's assessment deserves our scrutiny. Read even in the full context of his *Essay*, Dryden's evaluation remains extremely general: Shakespeare's is a large and comprehensive soul; he is at times flat and insipid; and so on. Dryden gives no examples to support these claims. At best, these claims serve as summaries of traits in Shakespeare's dramas that are not spelled out.

Pope is our second example. In his Preface to his edition of *The Works of Shakespear* (1725), Pope states that Shakespeare is a good subject for criticism since there are many instances of beauties and faults in his work, but that his main business as an Editor is ". . . to give an account of the fate of his Works, and the disadvantages under which they have been transmitted to us." For such an account will ". . . extenuate many faults which are his, and clear him from the imputation of many which are not." Yet Pope cannot forego an evaluation and begins his Preface with an enumeration of the excellencies in Shakespeare's dramas.

Shakespeare is "an *Original* . . . . The Poetry of Shakespear was Inspiration indeed: he is not so much an Imitator as an Instrument, of Nature; and 'tis not so just to say that he speaks from her, as that she speaks thro' him."

This is all Pope says about this first excellence. He gives no definition or clarification of "original;" instead, he relates it metaphorically to a process in nature. He says nothing about the difference between an imitator and an instrument of nature. He is equally silent on the relation between originality and artistic excellence or, more generally, between any quality and artistic excellence. As a critic engaged in a piece of evaluation, Pope simply does not enter upon these problems.

Shakespeare's second excellence is his delineation of character; he creates characters well—as individuals, in their variety, and with a consistency that extends to their language.

His third excellence, which Pope calls Shakespeare's "*Power* over the *Passions*," is his subtle depiction of passion. His dramas move us as they should—through a just and proper handling of passion.

Shakespeare's fourth excellence, his "coolness of Reflection and Reasoning," is the convincingness of the arguments and motives in the dramas.

Pope turns next to Shakespeare's faults which, he says, are as great as his virtues. They are of two sorts, real ones and imputed ones. He tries to extenuate the first and to refute the second.

It is said that Shakespeare is often vulgar in his themes, extravagant in his incidents, bombastic in his language, and pompous in his verse. These are real defects. But, Pope pleads, it is Shakespeare's audience and his part-time profession as a player that are to blame, not Shakespeare: "To be obliged to please the lowest of people, and to keep the worst of company—will appear sufficient to mislead and depress the greatest Genius on earth."

In his attempt at an extenuation of faults, Pope, as evaluative critic, is very much like a counsel for the defense in a court of law who accepts the charge of "guilty" for his client and then goes on to mitigate it. Pope neither questions that vulgarity, bombast, extravagance, and pomposity are aesthetic crimes, nor does he deny that Shakespeare committed them. Rather, what he tries to do is get Shakespeare's sentence in the court of critical opinion lightened.

Shakespeare's imputed faults are that he never rewrote and that he lacked learning. Pope dismisses both by appeals to historical facts about Shakespeare's revisions and his reading.

Pope, thus, does at least three different jobs as an evaluative critic. He praises Shakespeare, he defends him against charges of which he is guilty, and he refutes certain charges of which he is not guilty. What is most interesting from our point of view of reasons in evaluative criticism is what his praising comes to. In praising Shakespeare, Pope formulates or defends no principles, standards or criteria of beauty in art or drama. He offers no definitions or analyses of his key terms. He argues against no principle of greatness in drama, on the ground that it is an erroneous one. And he indulges in no poetics of the drama. One is not even sure that he would subscribe to a universalization of his four criteria as a definition of great drama. What he does is to accept certain principles (standards, criteria) of excellence in art or drama, and apply these in a summary way to the whole of Shakespeare's dramas. In this application he gives no detailed confirmation of any of the principles, i.e., no instances of Shakespeare's originality, characterization, power over our passions, or coolness of reflection and reasoning. Like Dryden in his Essay before him, and many critics after him, Pope rests content with an evaluation of Shakespeare's dramas that is a general attribution of certain established and accepted principles of merit to him.

Johnson is our next example. His major evaluations of Shakespeare's dramas are in his Preface and Notes to his edition of the dramas of Shakespeare (1765).

Shakespeare is great, Johnson contends, because his dramas realize the basic requirement of great drama, which is to present "just representations of general nature." Only these can satisfy: "Nothing can please many, and please long, but just representations of general nature."

Nowhere in his Preface does Johnson discuss the status of this principle that nothing can please many, and please long, except these representations. He seems to accept it as an empirical truth about human beings that ultimately, as he puts it in another context, ". . . the mind can only repose on the stability of truth." As an empirical statement, this is certainly disputable.

Johnson's main concern in his appraisal of Shakespeare's dramas is to clarify the meaning of "just representations of general nature," which he does by showing how his dramas embody them. Johnson contrasts representations of "particular manners" or of "irregular combinations of fanciful invention" with "a faithful mirrour of manners and of life," the latter of which is equivalent to "just representations of general nature." Unlike all other dramatists, Johnson claims, Shakespeare presents this faithful mirror—through his characters, dialogues, plots, and themes. His spelling out of this principle in Shakespeare's characterization must suffice here as an example of Johnson's clarification of it:

> His characters are not modified by the customs of particular places, unpractised by the rest of the world; by the peculiarities of studies or professions, which can operate but upon small numbers; or by the accidents of transient fashions or temporary opinions: they are the genuine progeny of common humanity, such as the world will always supply, and observation will always find.

Johnson also discusses Shakespeare's faults. Like Pope, he finds them ". . . sufficient to obscure and overwhelm any other merit." Among these faults are: "He sacrifices virtue to convenience, and is so much more careful to please than to instruct, that he seems to write without any moral purpose." He lacks in "just distribution of good or evil." His ". . . plots are often so loosely formed. . . and so carelessly pursued. . . ." He is gross and licentious in many comic scenes, and often tedious in tragic ones. And he has too many quibbles: "A quibble was to him the fatal Cleopatra for which he lost the world, and was content to lose it."

Johnson also considers the imputed fault of Shakespeare's neglect of the three unities. As evaluative critic here, Johnson rejects the charge as a fault by refuting the principle from which the imputed fault is derived. First, he pins down the charge to the unities of time and place as neglected in the comedies and tragedies. Then he states the assumption underlying the supposed necessity of these two unities, namely, that they make the drama credible; which he denies, since the truth is that the spectators are always in their senses, and know, from the first act to the last, that the stage is only a stage, and that the players are only players. Delusion is the touchstone of dramatic response; hence any credibility secured by the presentation of the unities of time and place is unnecessary.

D. N. Smith, an authority on Johnson's criticism of Shakespeare, sums up the Preface: "Johnson set himself to review the common topics of Shakespearean criticism, and to give his judgement on the points at issue. There is little new matter in his Preface . . . . Its importance lies mainly in its being a conclusive summing up, by a strong, wise, and impartial mind, of a prolonged discussion."

This assessment seems to me correct. The evaluative critic may do many things. Among them, he may formulate new principles or reformulate traditional ones, and apply them in great or lesser detail to an author. Johnson, I think, chooses to reformulate and apply traditional principles as his major activity in his evaluation of Shakespeare's dramas. If we can say of Pope that he sometimes engages in evaluative criticism as a kind of counsel for the defence, we can perhaps as properly say of Johnson that on the whole he stresses the judicial side of evaluative criticism, not in the traditional sense of the making of official decisions that derive from absolute principles, but in the legal sense of the weighing of all the evidence—all the principles, precedents, and facts of the case, followed by the handing down of a balanced, seasoned verdict. Johnson's verdict? Shakespeare has his virtues and his faults.

Coleridge is my final example. Dryden, as we have noted, had suggested that Shakespeare's judgement is not always consonant with his genius. Voltaire, Pope, and Johnson, among many, concurred, and the charge that Shakespeare, although great, is "irregular," flourished. Coleridge—not the first, to be sure—rejects this charge, and rejects it totally. "The judgement of Shakespeare is commensurate with his genius." This, it seems to me, is the fundamental theme and thesis in the whole of his evaluation of Shakespeare. This theme is tantamount to Coleridge's persistent claim that Shakespeare is great not in spite of his faulty judgements, but because these are also, on analysis, excellencies along with the undisputed ones. Shakespeare's greatness as a dramatic poet inheres precisely in his exquisite congruence of judgement and genius.

Like Johnson, Coleridge attempts a true assessment of Shakespeare's art. This assessment consists in a clarification, justification, and confirmation in the whole of Shakespeare's dramas and in some of the individual plays, of the harmony of Shakespeare's judgement and genius; hence, of his uncompromised greatness. It also includes a refutation of the traditional censure that Shakespeare often lacks judgement. If we may revert to our legal analogy, Coleridge, it may be said, serves as counsel for the defence. But instead of accepting imputed charges and pleading extenuation, he calls into question the principles and precedents of these charges, demands a new hearing for a new set of principles which he affirms as true ones, and then, on the basis of the new set, converts every ascribed fault into a major excellence in Shakespeare. In effect, Coleridge takes his case to the Supreme Court.

Shakespeare's judgement is at fault in his violation of the traditional unities: this is one version of the irregularity thesis. Like Johnson, Coleridge restricts the censure to the unities of time and place, since Shakespeare's dramas do satisfy the essential unity of action, and rejects both the traditional argument from credibility as well as Johnson's reply to this argument that delusion, not belief, governs our response to drama. The drama is an imitation of reality, Coleridge asserts; an imitation is not a copy of reality, but implies a difference. The mind recognizes this crucial difference and is never deceived. Instead it fosters a kind of poetic illusion—"that willing suspension of disbelief for the moment which constitutes poetic faith"—towards the objects, actions, and passions of the drama. Thus, both belief and delusion do not obtain; the unities of time and place, consequently, are unnecessary.

Coleridge also rejects another version of the irregularity charge: that Shakespeare was a kind of wild genius, i.e., one with no basic sense of order or form. To accuse Shakespeare of extravagances, he says, is like arraigning the eagle because it lacks the dimensions of the swan. Shakespeare does have a form or order which is organic in that ". . . it shapes itself from within, and the fullness of its development is one and the same with the perfection of its outward form." Shakespeare's dramas are like the organic forms of nature. Since his plays possess the same unity as nature's, he cannot truly be called wild and irregular.

Coleridge's refutation of the traditional censure raises many questions. But I must confine myself to one, which brings out still another facet of the problem of reasons in evaluation, namely, their consistency in evaluative argument. Coleridge affirms that Shakespeare's unity is like nature's: it is true to what is basic in nature, and it is itself one manifestation of nature's unity. But, now, can Shakespeare's being true to nature and truly natural be said to sponsor poetic illusion? Coleridge in his metaphysical argument for Shakespeare's organic unity does not think so. His emphasis is on the contrary: Shakespeare is great because of his truth, and we respond to him, as we respond properly to truth, not by a kind of illusion but by a straightforward conviction and belief in it.

Coleridge, thus, vacillates between poetic illusion and belief in truth as the ultimate standard of all his criteria of greatness in Shakespeare's dramas. His vacillation can be seen also in his further clarification and confirmation of his thesis that judgment and genius are in harmony in Shakespeare's dramas. His evaluations of the plays as a whole or of the individual plays employ many criteria or principles of dramatic greatness. He develops at length those of characterization, language, psychological insight, and movement of the action. His application of these is as rich in detail as anything in Shakespearean criticism. Yet every specific argument for the greatness of Shakespeare, of the commensurability of judgment and genius, converges on and revolves around one or other of these two basic criteria—that illusion is basic or that belief is basic.

His evaluation of *Hamlet* must suffice here as an illustration of my thesis that Coleridge employs two basic criteria in order to substantiate Shakespeare's total greatness which, employed together, are inconsistent with each other.

Hamlet, Coleridge, says, is a great play, among other reasons, because its main character, Hamlet, is an "ideal reality," a *genus* intensely individualized; its language is "the language of nature"; its theme, the moral necessity of a due balance between meditation and action, is profound; and its plot is dramatically credible. Coleridge clarifies these reasons and, however we doubt the intelligibility of some of them, we must admit he spells them out. Consider, as one example, his remarks on the language of the opening scene:

> It is the language of *sensation* among men who feared no charge of effeminacy for feeling what they felt no want of resolution to bear. Yet the armour, the dead silence, the watchfulness that first interrupts it, the welcome relief of guard, the cold, the broken expressions as of a man's compelled attention to bodily feelings allowed no man,—all excellently accord with and prepare for the after gradual rise into tragedy. . . .

The language of that first scene is a great use of language, then, because it is the language of nature—it is an imitation of, or true to, the language of real life in similar situations. Coleridge uses this criterion to justify not only most of the language, but the delineation of the characters and the dramatization of the theme as well: they are great ultimately because they are true to nature and we respond to them as we do to truth generally, by belief.

But he also defends some of the language and much of the action by a standard that is remote from an imitation of real life. He praises Shakespeare's use of puns, especially Hamlet's, which has been a perennial source of much censure of Shakespeare. To be sure, he praises the puns because they, too, are imitations of real—life situations where punning is a natural expression of feeling. *But* he also praises them because they move the action of the drama, by intensifying the passion that are depicted. This is no appeal to truth. Nor is Coleridge's praise of some of the other dramatic qualities he mentions an appeal to truth: his praise of the deftness with which Shakespeare prepares his audience, the judicious introductions of Hamlet and Laertes in the second scene, the epical contrasts between the Player's speech or "The Murder of Gonzago" and the rest of *Hamlet* and, finally, the sure handling of the Ghost. All this praise is based on aesthetic criteria that do not obviously relate to real life at all. The greatness of the Ghost, for example, depends on his credibility. Is this credibility a matter of truth to reality or of what Coleridge calls poetic illusion? I do not think Coleridge ever made up his mind about it.

So much for our examples. By way of summary now, what do these critics do when they evaluate the dramas of Shakepeare? As our examples show, they do many things: they praise, condemn, defend, extenuate, exhibit, judge, and revaluate.

Do these evaluative activities reduce to one? It seems to me they do not. Johnson, for example, as judge weighing evidence and deciding on principles, makes a verdict; but not all evaluation begins or ends with a verdict. Pope exhibits Shakespeare's excellencies; he does not—as exhibitor—make a verdict. Coleridge challenges traditional verdicts and attempts a revaluation. Is revaluation the making of a judgement, or is it closer perhaps to doing a bit of jurisprudence? What about extenuating Shakespeare's faults? This is neither praising, judging, etc., but closer to ascribing, and in Pope's case, of changing the attribution of blame from Shakespeare to his audience. Of course, there are similarities among these activities, but I find no truth and little point in certain contemporary philosophical accounts that assimilate all these evaluative procedures to one, which is then construed as the paradigm case. It is simply a false description of the logical behavior of critical evaluations to say that *all* of them recommend, or guide our choices, or persuade, or judge, or counsel, and so on.

Our examples also show that at least some critical evaluation is argument. At times, especially when they praise, our representative critics exclaim or compose inspired metaphors. But mostly they argue; and their arguments are based on principles and are attempts to determine what Johnson aptly calls "the merit of composition" of Shakespeare's dramas. As argument, this evaluation involves formulation of new, reformulation or employment of traditional principles or criteria of merit, their clarification, justification, or application of them to the plays. Among these principles or criteria are: the three unities, regularity, comprehensibility, originality, metaphysical or moral truth, true-to-life characterization, individuality, variety, and consistency of character, power of evocation, subtlety of exhibition of passion, ability to create and sustain illusion, and organic integration of the various characters, language, plot, and theme.

Each critic, then, in arguing his case for Shakespeare's merits or lack of them, does so on the basis of reasons. His evaluation contains what we may call an "evaluative utterance" and reasons that are given in support of that utterance. Examples of evaluative utterances are: "Shakespeare's dramas are good;" "They are mediocre;" "In them, the neglect of the unities of time and place is not a fault;" "His dramas are vulgar and obscene, but these defects were forced upon him by his audience;" "The characterization in Shakespeare is superb;" "His dramas are partly good, partly bad;" "His dramas are flawless, uncompromisingly great, masterpieces."

The critic, in making an evaluation, gives or implies a reason (or reasons) that supports his praise, condemnation, extenuation, defence, exhibition, judgement, or revaluation. His central problem is to validate this relation between his utterance and his reason (or reasons); it is not, as many recent philosophers have wrongly claimed, to verify his evaluative utterances, especially to ascertain or locate the referents of his evaluative predicates.

What, then, is involved in the giving of reasons as support for critical evaluative utterance? How, for example, does the critic validate his praise, defence, judgement, etc., of Shakespeare's dramas?

What is involved here, I think, are certain applications of criteria of dramatic merit, the clarification of these criteria, and the justification of them.

The first—the application of criteria—is the giving of reasons in direct support of the utterance; e.g., "Shakespeare's dramas are great because they have P, where P denotes some criterion like "being true to nature." Every evaluative critic of Shakespeare's dramas applies or employs certain criteria of dramatic merit: these are new ones or reformulated or established traditional ones. The application may be very general, as it is with Dryden and Pope, or it may be spelled out with much particularity, as it is with Johnson and especially Coleridge. But in either case, the critic supports his evaluative utterance by showing that the dramas possess the property (or properties) that makes them great.

The critic, in giving a reason as support for his evaluative utterance, also clarifies his criterion (or criteria). Much evaluative criticism has to do with this clarification. Sometimes, e.g., in Coleridge, the clarification ends in a real definition of the criterion. At other times, e.g., in Johnson, clarification proceeds through examples: Johnson does not define "just representations of general nature"; he gives examples of them in Shakespeare's dramas and counter-examples in the dramas of others.

The most troublesome feature of evaluative criticism, however, is not in the application of criteria, or their clarification, or even their consistency—since inadequacies here can be easily remedied—but in the justification of its criteria. Every evaluative critic of Shakespeare's dramas commits himself to P is a great-making property of drama," when he says, "Shakespeare's dramas are great because they have P. His commitment immediately raises the perennial question, "But what has P to do with dramatic greatness?"

This question is a request for a reason for a reason; as such, it implies that a reason can be given in support of a particular criterion, "P", of dramatic greatness. Yet among our four critics only Johnson and Coleridge, I believe, offer such reasons for reasons, i.e., justifications of their criteria. Johnson claims that Shakespeare's dramas are great because they justly represent general nature (they have P), and that P pleases us since we repose only on the stability of truth. Thus, he praises Shakespeare's dramas ("They are great"), gives a reason in support of his praise ("Because they justly represent general nature"), and implies a further reason in support of the first one ("Just representations of general nature satisfy our desire for truth"). Coleridge, or anyhow half of him, also claims that Shakespeare's dramas are great because they are true to nature, and defends his criterion by the further reason that it produces metaphysical insight.

Johnson and Coleridge exemplify the two traditional ways that critics have tried to justify their reasons for their critical praise: to state that the reason given, e.g., "Because Shakespeare's dramas have P, implies that P is a necessary or a sufficient property or a member of a disjunctive set of sufficient properties of dramatic greatness; or that P causes Q (e.g., pleasure in truth or metaphysical insight) and that Q is a necessary or a sufficient property or a member of a disjunctive set of sufficient properties of dramatic greatness.

Are there necessary or sufficient properties of dramatic greatness? Johnson and Coleridge do not succeed in showing that there are. For neither "just representations of general nature" or "truth to nature" (their Ps) nor "pleasure in truth" or "metaphysical insight" (their Qs) are established by them as such properties. Nor have their Ps and Qs withstood the challenge of other critics who substitute and argue for different criteria as necessary or sufficient properties of dramatic greatness. Nor do these critics fare any better than Johnson and Coleridge since their sets of properties have also been challenged and rejected by still other critics. Indeed, the history of dramatic criticism is in great part a history of unresolved disagreement over the necessary and sufficient properties of dramatic greatness. If there are these properties, then, we must nevertheless admit that no one has ever stated satisfactorily what they are. There is no property that has been shown on any grounds—whether, empirical, conceptual, or metaphysical—to be a necessary or a sufficient property or a member of a disjunctive set of sufficient properties of dramatic greatness; hence, there exists no reason in support of the praise of Shakespeare's dramas that can be said to be a good reason on the ground that it states an established necessary or sufficient property of dramatic greatness.

Can there be these necessary or sufficient properties of dramatic greatness that some critics presuppose in their purported justifications of their reasons for their praise of Shakespeare's dramas?

Suppose there can be. Then dramatic greatness is itself a property, albeit a complex one, composed of an exhaustive set of necessary and sufficient or essential properties; and the term, "dramatic greatness," or its adverbial derivative, "dramatically great," is a name of that complex property.

Now, if "dramatically great" is a name of a complex property, it functions grammatically as a predicate that critics use to describe the property of dramatic greatness; "Shakespeare's dramas are great," then, is a referring *cum* descriptive utterance about the property of dramatic greatness in his dramas. From which it follows that praising Shakespeare's dramas is really describing them; what began in critical evaluation as an attempt at a justification of a reason for a reason in support of praise ends in the denial of the activity of praising altogether.

Praising Shakespeare's dramas is not identical with describing them; "dramatically great," when used by critics to praise, does not function as a descriptive predicate. The assumption that there are necessary or sufficient properties of dramatic greatness, the particular statements of which can serve as major premises of deductive evaluative argument and as justifications of evaluative criteria, entails the doctrine that evaluative criticism does not praise but describes; this doctrine is to be rejected because it constitutes an erroneous description of the logical functioning of praise utterance and activity.

Reasons in support of praise are not and cannot be justified by the further reason that these reasons are about necessary or sufficient properties of dramatic greatness. What, if anything, then, does validate these reasons? Are any of them good reasons, i.e., reasons that support the praise?

To answer these questions, we must reject the idea that a good reason in support of praise is one for which a further reason can be given. We must ask whether for every reason of the form, "Because they have P," offered in support of "Shakespeare's dramas are great," the traditional question, "But what has P to do with dramatic greatness?," is legitimate and forthcoming.

It seems to me, as I read critical evaluation of Shakespeare's dramas, that at least some of the reasons offered in support of the praise of the dramas are good reasons, hence validate the praise, not because further reasons for them can be given, but simply because they employ certain criteria—certain Ps—about which the question, "But what have these to do with dramatic greatness?," cannot be intelligibly asked since no answer to it can be given.

In both Pope and Coleridge, there are praise utterances about Shakespeare's dramas that are supported by reasons which are different from those reasons (e.g., "Because they justly represent general nature," or "Because they are true to nature") about which the question, "But what have these to do with dramatic greatness?," is appropriate and legitimate, and leads to the attempt—unsuccessful, I hope I have showed—to justify them. Pope praises Shakespeare's dramas and offers as a reason for his praise that the characters in them are individuals, various, and consistent, even in their language; he neither proposes nor implies a further reason in justification of his reason for praise. Coleridge, too, praises the dramas: one reason he gives in support of his praise of *Hamlet*, specifically, Hamlet's use of puns, is that they intensify the depicted passions, hence move the action of the drama. To be sure, Coleridge imposes on this reason his attempted justification of it in terms of his principle of poetic illusion. But his reason can stand alone; it requires no justification.

Pope's appeal to character delineation and Coleridge's appeal to the dramatic function of language are prime examples of reasons in evaluative criticism that support praise utterance, and are good reasons, not because they are justifiable by further reasons, but because they state properties of a work of dramatic art which, although neither necessary nor sufficient properties of dramatic greatness or even of drama, are such that one cannot sensibly ask, "What have they to do with dramatic greatness?"

There are other examples of good reasons in Shakespearean evaluative criticism. A superb one is Coleridge's persistent employment of the criterion of unity which, unfortunately and quite unnecessarily, he tries to defend by the further and false metaphysical principle of organic form in nature. "Shakespeare's dramas are great because in them character, theme, plot, and language work together to form an integrated whole" stands alone. Once the reason is clarified and applied with particularity to the dramas it needs no justification: for what could be a further reason for the reason, "Because they are unified," offered in support of the praise of Shakespeare's dramas?

One test of a good reason in evaluative criticism, then, is that it employs a criterion of dramatic greatness which is logically unchallengeable. Other tests are the already-mentioned ones of clarity, concrete application, and consistency. Perhaps there are more, but I have not found them.

Is the criterion of unchallengeability—that for some employments of criteria of dramatic greatness the question, "What have these criteria to do with dramatic greatness?," cannot be asked because it cannot be answered—a necessary or a sufficient criterion or a member of a disjunctive set of sufficient criteria of good reasons in evaluative criticism? I do not know if it is necessary or sufficient. But it is a criterion whether it is necessary or sufficient or neither; like unity, which can be a criterion of dramatic greatness without necessarily being a necessary or sufficient property of dramatic greatness, unchallengeability can also serve as a criterion of good evaluative reasons without necessarily being a necessary or sufficient property of good evaluative reasons.

In this paper I have argued that at least some critical evaluative utterances are supported by good reasons. If my argument is correct, it follows that the traditional view that all critical evaluative utterances can be supported by reasons which can be defended by further reasons about necessary or sufficient properties of dramatic greatness as well as the recent view that no critical evaluative utterances can be supported by reasons are both erroneous descriptions of the logical functioning of reasons in critical evaluation. Indeed, the recent view, initiated by logical positivism and sponsored by Stevenson, Macdonald, and Isenberg, among others, according to which reasons do not function as supports of critical evaluative utterances but serve to guide our evaluative decisions, or as parts of persuasive definitions, or as presentations of critical verdicts, or as linguistic directions for experiencing the work as the critic does, represents more than an inadequate philosophical reading of the whole of critical evaluation. For this view itself functions fundamentally as a recommendation, based on a misconception of the role of reasons in criticism, to salvage much critical evaluation by an arbitrary if attractive transformation of all of this evaluation from argument into art.

Chapter Seven

POETICS

The critics of *Hamlet* describe, explain, or evaluate the play. Their descriptions, explanations, and evaluations vary within themselves, but they differ logically only among each other. As we have seen, they function differently—they do different critical jobs. Hence, they are irreducible. Of course, they interrelate not only in a single critical essay, short or long but also, sometimes, in a single paragraph or even sentence of criticism. Nevertheless, because they play different roles, they must be kept distinct if they are to be correctly elucidated.

The critics of *Hamlet* also engage in poetics. That is, some of them theorize, in their critical essays on *Hamlet*, on the nature of poetic drama, tragedy, and the relation between drama and real life. To be sure, many employ these concepts of drama, tragedy, representation, or related concepts without definition; but some also attempt definitions, especially of "tragedy" and "poetic drama," which are put forth as real definitions or true statements of the essence of tragedy or poetic drama.

In this essay, I shall discuss poetics as one aspect of *Hamlet* criticism. The previous examination of description, explanation, and evaluation—if my basic thesis, that they are logically multiple, is correct—should put us on our guard against the assimilation of poetics by any of the other procedures of criticism. Poetics, because of its variety and range in *Hamlet* criticism, may also possess certain logical characteristics that distinguish it from description, explanation, evaluation. Indeed, my main point will be that poetics in *Hamlet* criticism, and elsewhere, is logically distinct from the other procedures of criticism. The recognition of this difference is basic to an understanding and a solution of at least some of the issues in *Hamlet* criticism.

What is poetics? Traditionally, it is the determination of the fundamental principles of one or other of the arts or species of them. What is the nature of literature, painting, sculpture, music, architecture, drama, dance or, latterly, the cinema? What is poetry, drama, or tragedy? These are among the questions traditionally associated with poetics. To each question, a poetics is a purportedly true answer in the form of a theory of the essential, defining or necessary and sufficient, properties of the art in question.

In *Hamlet* criticism, poetics has traditionally centered on attempts to state the defining properties of poetic drama and of tragedy, although some of this criticism has also essayed real definition of characterization, poetry, imagery, ritual, and symbolism.

Poetics, of course, enters *Hamlet* criticism in ways other than the attempts at real, true definition. Some critics, especially the historical, describe and explain the dramaturgy of the Elizabethan age. This, although part of the criticism of *Hamlet*, is not the same as poetics. Stoll, Campbell, Schücking, Spencer, Fergusson, and others state the Elizabethan or Shakespearean theories of drama and tragedy; their statements, as such, are not statements of their own poetics. They may have such a poetics or their historical approach may imply or presuppose a poetics but these are not equivalent to their historical criticism.

Further, some, perhaps all, critics employ certain categories of explanation or certain criteria of evaluation in the criticism of *Hamlet*. This employment may imply or presuppose theories of drama or tragedy or of great drama or great tragedy. But this employment is not the same as explicit essays in theory or real definition.

Eventually this whole question, whether all criticism implies or presupposes a poetics (as well as an aesthetics, i.e., a general theory of art) must be considered. It will facilitate the understanding of the role of poetics and the philosophical issues involved in poetics, however, if I begin instead with some of the particular discussions of the tragic in *Hamlet*. Can a critic say why *Hamlet* is tragic without stating, implying, or presupposing a theory of tragedy? Is there a theory (a poetics, a true statement) of the nature of tragedy? Can there be such a theory? Need there be such a theory in order to guarantee, to render intelligible, critical talk about *Hamlet* as a tragedy or *Hamlet* as tragic? These shall be the focal questions as we turn to the poetics of tragedy in *Hamlet* criticism.

Once more Bradley is an excellent starting point. We remember from our survey that he asks, Why is Hamlet tragic? and Why is Hamlet the only tragic figure in the play? and that his answers are derived from his answers to the more general questions, What is Shakespearean tragedy? and What is tragedy? Hamlet alone is tragic in the play because only he "rises to the tragic level."

For Bradley, both general questions function as factual questions that can be answered truly (or falsely). Indeed, his answer to What is

Shakespearean tragedy? is determined in part by his answer to What is tragedy? Because his answer to What is tragedy? constitutes a poetics or theory of tragedy, poetics is involved in his statement of the nature of Shakespearean tragedy as well as, of course, in his reasons for Hamlet being the only tragic figure in *Hamlet*.

He begins his analysis of Shakespearean tragedy by limiting it to a class of four members: *Hamlet, Othello, King Lear,* and *Macbeth*. They are the "mature" and "pure" Shakespearean tragedies. The others are either "pure" but "immature," i.e., *Romeo and Juliet*; or tragic histories, for example, *Julius Caesar*; or not really tragic at all, in spite of early classifications of them as tragedies, for example, *Troilus and Cressida*. Bradley's question about Shakespearean tragedy, thus, reduces to the more restricted one: What do the four major tragedies have in common?

His answer, briefly, is this: Each is predominantly the story of one man of a high estate. The story concerns his exceptional and unexpected suffering and calamity that lead to and include his death. His fall and death reverberate upon the welfare of his nation. His suffering and calamity contrast with a previous glory and happiness. This suffering and calamity are also the chief source of our tragic emotions, especially pity.

Further, the hero's fall does not merely happen and is not imposed upon him by non-human forces. Rather, it results from human actions, including his own, that are products of his character and for which he is at least in part responsible.

Other elements are present in the story, among them, abnormal conditions of mind, supernatural intervention, or accidental events. But these are not essential to the tragedy, for they neither originate, compel, nor dominate the causal chain that leads to the catastrophe. They are all subordinate to deeds issuing from character.

The action of these tragedies is a conflict not of an undivided soul against an external force but of a divided soul struggling in part against itself.

The hero is not only responsible for his fall but has, as one cause of his fall, a fatal flaw, his fundamental tragic trait. In each of the heroes, there is a marked one-sidedness, "a fatal tendency to identify the whole being with one interest, object, passion, or habit of mind."[1] But he is also touched by greatness (human excellence), even in his flaw. His fall involves the destruction of that greatness, which moves us not only to pity but to the other tragic emotions of terror, awe, and admiration.

This destruction or self-waste of greatness is the center of the tragedy. The hero, morally good or not, when he falls, epitomizes the tragic fact in the world, which is the irretrievable loss of value, spirit, or greatness. Thus, Shakespeare's dramatic universe of the tragedies is one in which, although there is an ultimate power that is akin to good and alien from evil, good is destroyed and wasted in its struggle with and extirpation of evil. We may experience reconciliation to or even exultation in this self-waste of good, especially when we feel that the hero has never been greater than he is at the moment of death, but we are still left with the sense of the painful mystery of this ultimate, undeniable, and unrationalizable fact that something good has been destroyed.

Tragedy, thus, for Bradley, is the inexplicable self-waste of spirit in the conflict of spiritual forces in the world. This is the essence of all tragedy, not only of Shakespearean. Bradley makes this explicit in his essay, "Hegel's Theory of Tragedy": "Tragedy portrays a self-division and self-waste of spirit, or a division of spirit involving conflict and waste."[2]

Shakespearean tragedy is tragic and Hamlet is a tragic figure, then, because they satisfy this essential criterion of tragedy.

What, now, is the relation between the essence of tragedy—the self-waste of spirit in the conflict of spiritual forces, with which there is tragedy, and without which there is not tragedy—and the other properties or characteristics that Bradley enumerates in Shakespearean tragedy: a story predominantly of a man of high estate, his exceptional and unexpected suffering and fall, the social reverberations at his fall, the contrast between his previous happiness and fall, his fatal flaw, his moral responsibility, the conflict between the evil that begets disaster and the good that destroys the evil, the death of the hero, and our tragic feelings of pity, fear, terror, awe, admiration, or exultation?

Some of these (to Bradley) are necessary to all tragedy, for example, the hero's moral responsibility, flaw, great suffering, and fall, the collision and conflict of spiritual forces, and the tragic effect.

Others (to Bradley) are constituent properties of Shakespeare's tragedies (as well as other tragedies) but not necessary to all tragedy, for example, the death of the hero, evil as the source of tragedy, and the social reverberations at the fall of the hero.

What, then, according to Bradley, is the relation between the essential properties of tragedy and the properties of Shakespearean tragedy? One wishes he were clearer than he is on this important question. In line with his remarks on the difference between the essence and species of tragedy in the essay on Hegel, I suggest that the relation for him is this: Those properties of Shakespearean tragedy that are necessary (but not necessary and sufficient, i.e., essential) to all tragedy are aspects of, or entail the property of, the self-waste of spirit in the conflict between spiritual forces; the other characteristics of Shakespearean tragedy Bradley lists are contributory to, but not necessary or sufficient for, tragedy. Thus, Hamlet's stature, flaw, moral responsibility, exceptional suffering, and fall are aspects of or entail the essential self-waste; whereas Hamlet's death, the evil generated by Claudius' murder of King Hamlet, and the restitution of order by Fortinbras are constituent, contributory characteristics of, but neither necessary nor sufficient to, *Hamlet* as a tragedy.

Is Bradley correct in his views on the nature of tragedy, the nature of Shakespearean tragedy, why Hamlet is tragic, and why he is the only tragic figure in *Hamlet*?

Lily Campbell is certainly one critic of our survey who thinks Bradley is not correct. She rejects his theory of tragedy, his account of Shakespearean tragedy, and his reasons for Hamlet being a tragic figure. All three, she claims, are false; in their place she substitutes her own, purportedly true, views of the nature of tragedy in general and Shakespearean tragedy in particular.

She initiates her attack on Bradley as well as the exposition of her counterviews by challenging his attribution of a subordinate character to the three factors of abnormal conditions of mind, the supernatural, and the accidental in Shakespearean tragedy. Far from being subordinate, they (especially the first) are essential parts of the moral pattern of Shakespearean tragedies. The abnormal conditions of mind, for example Hamlet's melancholy, Lear's madness, Macbeth's hallucinations, and Othello's epilepsy, "are landmarks on the inevitable progress to doom."[3] They are among the effects of unchecked passion in the struggle between passion and reason; as such, they are also manifestations of sin for which their perpetrators are justly punished by a retributive God.

What are subordinate for Bradley, then, are among the primary or defining properties of Shakespearean tragedy for Campbell. Each of the major four that Bradley discusses she reconstrues as a study in passion. In it, the central figure suffers because his particular passion has not been checked by reason and falls deservedly because this vice or sin of unchecked passion, for which he is to blame, is divinely punished.

The central figure is a tragic hero when his sin is a venial one in which passion remains unchecked by reason. But he is a "hero—villain," not a tragic hero, when his sin is a mortal one in which passion perverts the will and reason directs this perverted will. Bradley's identification of Hamlet and Macbeth as tragic heroes, therefore, is erroneous; what they share is not greatness and its self-waste but slavery to passion.

The function of Shakespearean tragedy is to teach morals in a lively, pleasing manner; specifically, how men are to avoid sin and its just, divine punishment by a proper balance of passion and reason. Shakespearean tragedy, thus, is religious, and Bradley is again wrong in proclaiming it secular.

Shakespearean tragedy, like all other tragedy, presents evil. But it also explains it, especially the tragic fact which is the change from happiness to misery, "The permanent and essential material of tragedy."[4] The Elizabethan and Shakespearean explanation (she says nothing about other tragedies) is the religious one of divine justice for human folly. Hence, Bradley, once more, is wrong: there is no mystery, painful or not, about tragedy. It is an explicable fact in an ordered universe.

There are serious issues between Bradley and Campbell on the nature of tragedy, the nature of Shakespearean tragedy, and what makes *Hamlet* tragic. But I shall postpone discussion of them until I have reviewed or surveyed other doctrines about the nature of tragedy and the tragic in *Hamlet* which enlarge upon and sharpen these issues.

First, let me review briefly some of the views in our survey about *Hamlet* as a tragedy. For Stoll, *Hamlet* is a revenge tragedy, characterized by blood, intrigue, and fate, in which the momentous deed of revenge, as part of the

Senecan, epical tradition, comes at the end. Its hero, Hamlet, is the Avenger: noble, ideal, and without a tragic (or other) flaw. He is heroically tragic because he dies young, at the moment of his triumph, with much blood on his hands. Neither his tragedy nor the tragic element in *Hamlet*, in which the central fact is the hero's achievement of the revenge, has anything to do with a self-waste of spirit or a just punishment for the sin of sloth. Both Bradley and Campbell, therefore, are in error in their claims about what makes *Hamlet* and its hero tragic. Since *Hamlet* is a test case of Shakespearean tragedy, as well as of tragedy altogether, they are also wrong in their respective theories; Shakespearean tragedies are neither painful mysteries nor moral *exempla*.

Schücking also stresses the role of the passions in Elizabethan tragedy, including *Hamlet*. But these tragedies, he insists, served neither as moral *exempla*, helping to check the passions, nor as real-life imitations, inviting purgation of them. Rather the aim of Elizabethan tragedy was to arouse the passions. Hence, the climax of each of the tragedies was its exhibition of unrestrained passion. This aim and its realization were aspects of the early Baroque in art, which was characterized by great energy, plenitude of power, exuberance, and heightened contrasts. The arousal of the passions, the aim of Elizabethan tragedy, explains also the Elizabethan tragic hero. For this arousal required a sensational or impressive figure, who outstripped ideal or real-life representation in his intensity, eccentricities, extravagances, and self—exaltation. *Hamlet* and Hamlet are instances of these salient features of the early Baroque in tragedy.

For Fergusson, *Hamlet* is a tragedy in the myth and ritual tradition in which the mystery of the cycle from birth, through maturation and death, to rebirth is celebrated. The progress of the play is its tragic rhythm or action from pollution to health, achieved through suffering and death. Hamlet, the tragic hero, is the appointed witness and scapegoat victim in this purgatorial progress. Yet *Hamlet* is tragic not because of Hamlet, but because of the whole situation, which is the attempt to find and destroy the hidden imposthume that is destroying Denmark. Rituals, invocations, and scourgings are present as part of the celebration. Even the form of the ancient myth and ritual pattern is exemplified in *Hamlet*: prologue, agons, climax, peripety, recognition, pathos, and epiphany.

For Spurgeon, *Hamlet* is tragic because it exemplifies, through its imagery of rottenness, the natural condition of man, his physical corruptibility, which itself is tragic.

Dover Wilson, unlike the others of our survey, does not define "tragedy" in his discussion of the tragic elements in *Hamlet*. Instead he employs certain traditional (more or less) Aristotelian criteria of dramatic tragedy: sympathy for the hero; the moral responsibility of the hero; his greatness; his fall as it is caused by affliction or weakness; and the responses in the spectator of astonishment and awe at human endurance. *Hamlet* is "the tragedy of a genius caught fast in the toils of circumstance and unable to fling free."[5] Hamlet is tragic, not because he is weak, but because of his burden:

So great is Hamlet's moral stature, so tough is his nerve, that the back does *not* break. But he is crippled, and the arm which should perform the Ghost's command is paralysed. Thus he continues to support the burden, but is unable to discharge it. That, in a sentence, is "the tragical history of Hamlet, Prince of Denmark."[6]

Peter Alexander, in *Hamlet: Father and Son*, also answers the question, Why is Hamlet tragic? His answer is based upon a poetics of tragedy that differs radically from traditional theories and, for that reason, is worth detailing here, as I turn from this survey of the views of the critics I have already discussed to some other views on *Hamlet* as a tragedy.

Alexander first formulates, then rejects as false, what he calls the "orthodox" interpretation of the tragic in *Hamlet* and the whole theory upon which that interpretation rests.

According to this orthodox interpretation, *Hamlet* is a tragedy of a man who could not make up his mind. As such, it is a clear case of the traditional conception of tragedy in which *hamartia* (the tragic flaw of the hero) is primary and the main cause of his suffering and fall.

On this view, *hamartia* is a necessary property or condition of tragedy. It not only induces the hero's fall; it also explains and justifies the fall, thus effecting in the spectator a rational acceptance of the hero's just and deserved fate. Catharsis is the rational acceptance of the hero's fate.

This orthodox view of *Hamlet* and tragedy as primarily *hamartia* claims support from many sources, among them, Hamlet's famous speech on the battlements (I,iv,13-38), Aristotle's and Bradley's theories of tragedy, and the Greek tragedies. Alexander denies that these sources support the orthodox theory, contending that they serve instead as evidence for his own anti—orthodox explanation of *Hamlet* and poetics of tragedy.

I have already presented Alexander's argument against the orthodox reading of Hamlet's speech in the discussion of his objections to Lily Campbell's reading of it as the key to Hamlet's tragedy. We recall that Alexander points out that Hamlet on the battlements is simply "commenting on a fault in his countrymen that draws on them the censure of the world, and so soils their reputation that their virtues lose all colour and commendation."[7] To read these lines as an explicit or even implicit statement of *hamartia*, then, is to make Hamlet a prophet about himself since, in their context, they are uttered before he could be aware of any dereliction of duty; it is also to make the tragic flaw absurdly large in that the flaw would be present everywhere from "Nature's livery to Fortune's star."

Next, what about Aristotle? Does he, the acknowledged founder of the doctrine of *hamartia*, proclaim it necessary to tragedy? He does not, Alexander says. It is true, of course, that in the *Poetics* Aristotle states that *hamartia* is necessary because without it the spectator would experience revulsion, not catharsis, at the hero's fall. But elsewhere, in his poem on his friend, Hermeias, Aristotle's lines,

> Virtue toilsome to mortal race,
> Fairest prize in life,

pay tribute to Hermeias' death by torture without in anyway finding a fault in him in order to render the tragedy less odious. In effect, Aristotle here glorifies Hermeias' virtue; he does not chastise him for a flaw or mistake that causes and consummates in a catastrophe.

The great tragedies of Greece also exemplify this heroic ideal of virtue shining through suffering and calamity. It is therefore incorrect to view them, in the traditional way, as manifestations of divine attribution for human transgression. To make *hamartia* central in, say, *Oedipus at Colonus* is to reduce the play to a piece of nonsense. Like Aristotle, Sophocles glorifies the virtues; in *Oedipus at Colonus*, he celebrates and commemorates the hero's greatness achieved through terrible suffering.

Bradley, too, has been mistaken as an exponent of *hamartia*, even by himself. For, in spite of his ostensible emphasis upon the tragic flaw, Bradley also turns the flaw into a virtue by making it the source of the hero's greatness.

Tragedy, then, does not dramatize the faults but the virtues of men. *Areté*, not *hamartia*, is central. Tragedy includes the requisite suffering and calamity, but these need not be created and sustained by human frailty or wickedness. Loyalty, honor, and duty can also effect suffering and catastrophe. *Hamartia*, thus, is not a necessary feature of tragedy and was never meant to be in Aristotle, Bradley, or the Greek tragedies.

Moreover, catharsis, as Aristotle understood it, is not a rational acceptance of the fall of the tragic hero through his flaw. Catharsis is reconciliation or redemption, that is, an active mastery over the painful aspects of life. Only the glorification of human virtues can render intelligible this experience of catharsis. Catharsis as active mastery over the painful is already implicit in Aristotle's *Poetics*, especially in his reply to Plato's attack on tragedy. There Aristotle argues, in effect, that tragedy strengthens rather than weakens man's moral stature. It is also implicit in Bradley's remarks on reconciliation as a part of our response to tragedy. Its best formulation, however, is in Wordsworth and Keats, although they describe the same experience in different words.

Tragedy, for Alexander, thus, is the celebration of the virtues of men—their glory achieved through affliction and calamity—which produces in its spectators an intense mastery over life's pain:

> What consumes or sweeps away the disagreeables is not some
> nice calculation arrived at by weighing the hero's fate against

the faults and mistakes that are inseparable from mortality but the sense of something in mortals that has risen superior to their condition.[8]

In his tragedies Shakespeare glorifies *areté*. To regard *hamartia* as central, which the orthodox view does, is to reduce the tragedies of Shakespeare to mere cautionary tales that would have lost their appeal long ago. *Hamlet*, rather than being a tragedy of a man who could not make up his mind:

> is a kind of consecration of the common elements of man's moral life. Shakespeare introduces the common man in Hamlet not for what we are apt to think of as his "commonness" but for this strange power however you care to name it that he possesses—we have used *areté*, or virtue, or we might have borrowed from Henry James "the individual vision of decency."[9]

More particularly, Hamlet, the tragic hero of the play, consecrates the unity of the virtues represented by the two Hamlets, father ard son: "The instinctive wisdom of antiquity and her heroic passions" and "the meditative wisdom of later ages."[10] In the tribulations and final fall of Hamlet, Shakespeare glorifies Hamlet's specific excellence: how to remain humane without loss of toughness.

G. B. Harrison, in *Shakespeare's Tragedies* (1951), also analyzes the tragedies of Shakespeare, including *Hamlet*, by first proposing his (purportedly true) theory of tragedy: "If we are to arrive ultimately at any conclusion or general idea of the quintessence . . . of Shakespearean tragedy, we must first try to define our terms."[11] He defines "Shakespearean," then "tragedy."

So far as "tragedy" is concerned, Aristotle's definition, he says, is still the best. Like Aristotle, we should begin the analysis of tragedy with the concept of dramatic action. Dramatic action has three aspects: actors, a stage, and spectators. Hence, no conception of tragedy is complete without an adequate place for the role of the spectator. "Indeed, Aristotle in his famous definition of tragedy shows that true tragedy only exists when it produces in the spectators a definite emotional reaction, which he calls *catharsis* or purging."[12]

What now, is *catharsis*? Harrison, claiming that he is following Aristotle's meaning, says it is a release: "a visible surrender of the emotions." In order to be indulged in fully, this release requires the public character of the theater performance. When this condition is satisfied, *catharsis* (as release)

> leaves the feelings so utterly stirred and drained that one's whole emotional state and balance are for an appreciable time completely changed . . . . The experience is exalting and cleansing, exactly expressed by Aristotle's word "catharsis"—"purgation."[13]

Purgation, thus, for Harrison, is a defining property of tragedy. But not all so-called tragedies effect this purgation. Harrison meets this difficulty not by rejecting them as tragedies but by distinguishing among tragedies those that purge from those that merely end happily. The first he calls "deep tragedy," the second, "tragedy."

A deep tragedy is *"a play which when adequately acted before a suitable audience can produce a complete cleansing of the emotions."*[14] One test of a tragedy's being deep is that it evokes the response, "Oh, the pity of it all!" Further defining conditions of a deep tragedy are its means of purgation which include: a profound sense of morality, the expression of the pathos in human suffering, craftsmanship, selection, compression, and inevitability of the action.

In Shakespearean drama, only *King Lear* and *Othello* are deeply tragic. *Macbeth* is not. Nor is *Hamlet* because it:

> lacks two of the qualities necessary to produce deep tragedy: a sense of universal morality and inevitability; for Hamlet's death is not the predictable result of error or of mortal frailty but of the chance of combat.[15]

Hamlet is essentially a drama of revenge, which is tragic only because it ends unhappily. But, Harrison adds

> though not deep tragedy of the kind which utterly purges the emotions, *Hamlet* remains the most fascinating and interesting play in the English language, probably in all drama . . . .[16]

H. B. Charlton, in *Shakespearian Tragedy* (1948), also answers the question, Why is Hamlet tragic? His answer rests not on a theory of tragedy or even of Shakespearean tragedy, which he denies are possible, but on a doctrine of inevitability as basic in tragedy.

Tragedy ends in the death of the hero. But, to be tragic, his death must appear inevitable, deriving, as it were, from some ultimate fate of necessity in the universe. In the Greek tragedies, this ultimate fact is Nemesis. In Shakespeare's, where Fate had already lost its vital hold on Elizabethan imagination, necessity or inevitability is centered in the laws governing human nature. Hence, Shakespeare's tragic drama:

> finds its *ultima ratio*, its spring of inevitability, in the interplay of man and the world, in which the subtle though elusive link of psychological cause and effect gives to events sufficient appearance of a cosmic order.[17]

Mere inevitability, however, Charlton implies, is not enough; it must be joined with a greatness in the hero so that his fall holds our sympathy, and it must be integrated with the total inevitability of the action in the particular drama. The inevitable death of a weak person is not tragic; nor is the inevitable death of a hero tragic if his death is imposed upon him by forces that are not integrated in his own nature. What Charlton does, then, is to modify his criterion of inevitability by restricting the range of application of the criterion to a certain kind of inevitability, namely, an inevitability that involves great deeds which issue from character. Consequently, his criterion functions for him as an evaluative as well as a descriptive criterion of tragedy. This dual use of inevitability is most obviously present in his discussion of Shakespeare's early tragedies: *Richard III, Richard II, Romeo and Juliet,* and *Julius Caesar.* They are not really tragic, he argues, because they lack one or other aspect of his qualified criterion of inevitability: Richard III is defeated by God, not himself; Richard II is too weak to retain our sympathy; Romeo and Juliet are destroyed by Fate; and neither Julius Caesar nor Brutus is inevitably doomed.

Hamlet, therefore, is the first of the dramas in which Shakespeare realizes the "tragic idea"—an inevitable death that matters. Hamlet is presented as an admirable person whose failure and death do matter, hence, who retains our sympathy, and whose doom proceeds inevitably from his own nature. Why is Hamlet tragic? Because, great and fine as he is, he fails and dies necessarily. Hamlet, by nature, is incapable of meeting his task. It is not his moral idealism, sensitivity, or reflectiveness that destroys him, but something more fundamental: the way he thinks about things. His mind

> is fired by a temperamental emotionalism and guided by an easily
> excited imagination. The emotion thrusts one factor of the
> thinker's experience into especial prominence, and the imagination
> freely builds a speculative universe in which this prominence is a
> fundamental pillar.[18]

Hamlet, thus, distorts his world. He mistakes the abstract world, constructed and projected by his emotions and imagination, for the real world in which he must act. Given this propensity toward intellectual distortion, his failure to kill Claudius until it is too late and his death are thus inevitable.

E. M. W. Tillyard relates tragedy to Shakespearean drama in two books, *Shakespeare's Last Plays* (1938) and *Shakespeare's Problem Plays* (1950). He distinguishes between three types of tragedies: suffering, sacrifice, and regeneration. The first involves the suffering of a strong, or of a momentarily strong, character, who is not greatly responsible for his plight and protests against it as he reflects upon it and its place in the universe. *The Duchess of Malfi* is an example. The second, that of sacrificial purgation, is rooted in religion. It has for its characters a god, a victim, a killer, and an audience, and for its aim the riddance of a taint on the social organism. The third

> has to do with renewal consequent on destruction. It occurs when
> there is an enlightenment and through this the assurance of a new

state of being. This kind penetrates deep into our nature because it expresses not merely the tragedy of abnormal suffering but a fundamental tragic fact of all human life: namely that a good state cannot stay such but must be changed, even partially destroyed, if a succeeding good is to be engendered.[19]

For Tillyard, "those tragedies which we feel most centrally tragic contain, with other tragic conceptions, this third one."[20]

In his earlier work, *Shakespeare's Last Plays*, Tillyard characterizes this third type as the tragedy of reconciliation, meaning by it, the tragedy of spiritual renewal or reconstruction after disintegration. It symbolizes the cycle of life from birth to destruction that leads to re—creation. One great example of this third type of tragedy is Aeschylus' *Oresteia*, in which the complete tragic pattern from destruction to renewal is recorded. Shakespeare's *King Lear* and *Othello* are other examples.

Hamlet, however, is not an example of the centrally tragic. It is primarily a tragedy of the first type, with elements of the purgatorial as well. But it contains no reconciliation: no revelation, reversal of direction, renewal, or enlightenment. Unlike Othello or Lear, Hamlet undergoes no spiritual change. His speech defying augury (V,ii,217-22) is crucial here; Tillyard, following Bradley, reads it as an expression of quietism rather than of religious enlightenment. Hamlet remains unregenerated; hence, the play is not tragic in the third and fullest sense.

But not only is *Hamlet* not tragic in the fullest sense; even in the other senses, the tragic is not the central quality of the play. Basic in the play are the themes of the effect of Gertrude's remarriage on Hamlet and the call to revenge; the first, especially Hamlet's awakening to Gertrude's guilt, is the more fundamental one. The coherence and structure of the play inhere in the coexistence of the two themes as Hamlet responds to them. Indeed, the greatness of the play has little to do with the tragic but with the richness and variety of presented experience. "*Hamlet* is best understood as a play . . . presenting the utmost variety of human experience in the largest possible cosmic setting."[21] Thus, it is more accurate to classify *Hamlet* as a problem play than as a tragedy:

> When sheer explication, or abundance of things presented, takes first place,   we leave the realm of tragedy for that of the problem play. Here it is the problems themselves, their richness, their interest, and their diversity, and not their solution or significant arrangement that come first.[22]

Hamlet is not fully tragic. Nor is the tragic central in it. Tillyard has one further relevant claim. He defends the view that Shakespeare's last plays, *Cymbeline*, *The Winter's Tale*, and *The Tempest*, are tragic in the third sense. For one element in each play is the regenerative phase of the tragic pattern;

The Winter's Tale even exhibits the whole cycle. This tragic component of regeneration is joined, more or less successfully, he concludes, with the non-tragic themes of romance in each of these last plays.

There are many more critics who state why *Hamlet* or Hamlet is tragic and formulate theories of tragedy in order to do so.[23] And there are as many critics and philosophers who in their statements of the nature of tragedy imply answers to why *Hamlet* and Hamlet are tragic.[24] But they need not be considered here since our examples adequately represent the major issues of poetics in *Hamlet* criticism.

These representative critics raise the issues: Why is, or what makes, *Hamlet* or Hamlet tragic? What is Shakespearean tragedy? What is the nature of tragedy? Can one say why *Hamlet* or Hamlet is tragic without stating, implying, or presupposing a theory of tragedy? Each of the representative critics asks and answers the first question; each considers his answer a true statement about *a* or *the* tragic property in *Hamlet* and some other answers, false statements about this property. Further, although some of these critics raise doubts about the kind of tragedy *Hamlet* is, for example, Harrison on whether it is "deep" tragedy and Tillyard on whether it is "centrally" tragic, not one of them asks, is *Hamlet* or Hamlet tragic? Tillyard comes closest to asking this question when he challenges the primary of the tragic in the play. In the sense in which one could not ask, "Is *Hamlet* really a drama?" without violating the meaning of "drama," could one ask, without violating the meaning of "tragedy," "Is *Hamlet* really tragic?" Much that concerns the logic of "tragedy" turns on the right answer to this question.

What is immediately striking about our critics' answers to the first question is the diversity of the reasons. And what diversity! Thus: Bradley says that *Hamlet* is tragic because its hero, noble in station and virtue, suffers, falls, and dies; that he is partly responsible for his fate as it proceeds from his character, flaw, and inner conflict; and his death involves the destruction, hence waste, of spiritual value which, as we witness this spectacle, induces in us pity, admiration, exultation, and awe at the inexplicable mystery of this waste of good. Campbell counters that *Hamlet* is tragic because it presents the evil exemplified in the sin or vice of unchecked passion, especially in the hero's sin of sloth, and it rationalizes this evil as the just, divine punishment of the hero's fall. Stoll says that *Hamlet* is tragic because Hamlet dies young, with much blood on his hands, but with his task heroically accomplished. For Schücking, *Hamlet* was tragic because it aroused Elizabethans to a high emotional pitch by means of its greater-than-life, impressive hero. (Whether *Hamlet* is still tragic because of its ability to arouse us, Schücking does not say). Fergusson claims that *Hamlet* is tragic because it celebrates the perennial mystery of human life, with its hero reflecting this mystery as the necessary scapegoat. For Wilson, *Hamlet* is tragic because its hero, great as he is, is unable to discharge his inordinate burden. Alexander considers *Hamlet* tragic because it celebrates, through the hero, human excellence or *areté*, achieved through terrible affliction; by means of this celebration, it effects in us a catharsis—active mastery over pain. Charlton says that *Hamlet* is tragic because its worthy hero dies necessarily. Spurgeon finds that *Hamlet* is tragic because it depicts the tragic natural human condition of physical corruptibility. For Harrison, *Hamlet* is tragic because it ends unhappily. Finally, for Tillyard, *Hamlet* is tragic (although not "centrally") partly because its hero suffers, protests against, reflects upon, stoically accepts, and remains not greatly responsible for, his suffering; and partly because Hamlet is a victim in a sacrificial purgation.

In giving a reason for the tragic in *Hamlet*, that is, in saying why *Hamlet* or Hamlet is tragic, the critic states or implies that a certain property or certain properties of the tragic are exemplified in *Hamlet*. These properties serve as criteria for the particular critic's use of the concept of tragedy.

Consider some of these properties: a hero, dramatic conflict, and emotional response; or, more particularly, a noble hero, his flaw or flawless nature, his greatness, his terrible suffering, his fall, deserved or undeserved, his responsibility or lack of responsibility for his plight, the inevitability or contingency of his fall and death, the waste of good, the struggle between good and evil, *areté*, and catharsis as purgation, mastery over the painful, redemption, or exultation. However difficult it may be to comprehend some of these properties—those that are not empirical—at least one thing is clear about them: that *Hamlet* as a tragedy cannot possess all of them since some are inconsistent with each other. For example, *Hamlet* cannot be tragic because its hero has a tragic flaw as well as an ideal (flawless) nature, nor can Hamlet be both responsible and not responsible for his plight. Consequently, whatever else can be claimed for these properties, it cannot consistently be said that they are all necessary to tragedy.

Our representative critics disagree on the need for a theory in order to give a reason for *Hamlet*'s being a tragedy. Some, Wilson and Charlton, for instance, do not support their reasons by a theory. But most do. For them, to say that or why *Hamlet* is tragic is to presuppose or imply a theory of tragedy. Their assumption that criticism cannot say that or why Hamlet or any drama is a tragedy without an explicit or implicit theory of tragedy is shared by all the great philosophical theories of tragedy from Aristotle through Lessing, Goethe, Schiller, the Schlegels, Hegel, Schopenhauer, Nietzsche, and Bradley, to J. W. Krutch, U. Ellis-Fermor, F. L. Lucas, and S. K. Langer, among others.[25] All these critics and philosophers concur on the doctrines that "tragedy" denotes a class of works of art; that this class is distinguishable from all other classes; that the members of this class—i.e., all tragedies—possess certain properties that are common and peculiar to these member-tragedies, by virtue of which properties they are tragic; hence, that these properties are necessary and sufficient, essential, or defining ones of tragedy; that a true statement or real definition of the essence of tragedy is forthcoming; and that without such a true statement of the nature of tragedy, critical discourse about particular tragedies cannot be shown to be either intelligible or true; consequently, that one task of philosophical criticism is to provide such a true theory.

Is there, then, a true theory, a poetics, of tragedy? Do any of our representative critics or any of the traditional philosophers provide a true statement of the exhaustive set of necessary and sufficient properties of all tragedies, their common, essential nature, by virtue of which all of them, including Hamlet, are tragic? Does any philosophical formula cover all tragedies, Greek, Elizabethan, French, and modern, without leaving out any of them or any of their tragic properties?

The fundamental disagreements on the nature of tragedy even among our representative critics seriously call into question the possibility of arriving at such a true theory. To be sure, they are unanimous on the defining properties of a hero, his suffering and calamity; dramatic conflict involving important values; and the tragic effect. But there is little agreement on the specific requisite attributes of the hero, the cause of his suffering, and the particular response of the ideal spectator. And there is no agreement on what is essential in tragedy. For Bradley, the essence of tragedy is the self-waste of value in the conflict of spiritual forces that ultimately leaves us with a sense of wonder at the inexplicable mystery of unresolved pain in the world. For Campbell, it is the presentation and explanation of evil that leave us rationally satisfied with our ordered universe. For Alexander, it is the glorification of human virtue as it produces in us an active mastery over life's pain. For Fergusson, it is the celebration of the cycle of life from birth, through death, to renewal. For Spurgeon, it is the natural condition of physical corruptibility. For Harrison, when tragedy is "deep," its essence is a suffering that cleanses. Finally, for Tillyard, when tragedy is "centrally" tragic, the essence of it is regeneration.

Do any of these formulas cover all tragedies and all tragic properties of all tragedies? Each critic claims or implies that his theory does and that the other theories do not—which is one reason why he puts forward a new theory. But every critic who proffers a purportedly true theory of the nature of tragedy is immediately countered by other critics who reject his theory as false or inadequate. Bradley, for example, claims that spiritual waste is the essence of all tragedies. But Campbell, Stoll, Schücking, Fergusson, Spurgeon, Harrison, Charlton, and Tillyard disagree with Bradley, some contending that Bradley's theory does not even cover the tragic in Hamlet!

Our representative critics also disagree about the necessary properties of tragedy. Do all tragedies have a hero? Do all tragic heroes possess the tragic flaw? Are all tragic heroes responsible for their fates? Do all of them suffer terribly, fall, and die? Are all touched by greatness? Do all get their just deserts? Do all tragedies commemorate human excellence? Do all end unhappily? Do all stir us deeply or at all? Are all inevitable in their action? Are there conflict and collision in all? Do all induce catharsis in any of its numerous senses: redemption, active mastery over pain, purgation, etc.? Do all produce any other uniform effect in their spectators? For each critic who answers affirmatively any of these questions, there is another critic who offers a negative reply. Basic disagreement is rife over both the essential as well as the purely necessary properties of tragedy.

Can this disagreement be resolved? Is there anything that can establish the truth of any theory of tragedy? Perhaps, as most critics think, the disagreement can be resolved by further probing and research.

Two possibilities suggest themselves: dramatic tragedies and the human condition. But neither of these yields a true theory of tragedy. Further research into the whole extant corpus of dramatic tragedies and the resultant probing of their shared properties reveal no essences. What do *Oedipus Rex, Oedipus at Colonus, Medea, Hamlet, Phèdre, Hedda Gabler, The Weavers,* and *The Three Sisters*[26]—to mention but a few tragedies—have in common by virtue of which they are tragic and distinguishable from other works of art? Perhaps they have some similarities but no set of necessary and sufficient properties. Further examination of the human situation will not furnish us with a theory of tragedy either because there is no tragic fact in the world about which a theory of tragedy could be true or which could corroborate such a theory. There may be spiritual waste, loss of greatness, suffering, struggle, defeat, *areté,* regeneration, explicable or inexplicable evil, and catharsis. But that any of these, or a collection of them, is tragic cannot be determined by any investigation, past, present, or future.

There is no established true theory of tragedy, offered by the critics of *Hamlet,* other critics, or philosophers, that states the requisite set of essential properties of all tragedies. Further research and probing, no matter how exhaustive or deep, cannot resolve the disagreements among the theories of tragedy or remedy their failure to provide a true, real definition of tragedy. However, the reason that there cannot be a true theory is logical, not factual. For underlying every theory of tragedy, every purportedly true statement of the essence of tragedy, is the assumption that tragedy has a set of necessary and sufficient properties; this assumption is equivalent to the doctrine that the concept of tragedy or the term, "tragedy," or their adjectival derivatives, have a set of necessary and sufficient conditions for their correct, intelligible use. This doctrine is false. That it is false is revealed by the logical behavior of the concept of tragedy, whose use shows that it does not and cannot have a set of essential conditions of employment. All theories of tragedy, thus, misconceive their basic concept: they attempt a definition of a concept whose very employment requires that it have no defining conditions.

It is the disagreements over the necessary and sufficient properties of tragedy among the critics of *Hamlet* which furnish the clue to the logical behavior of the concept of tragedy and the consequent impossibility of a theory or poetics of tragedy. Because these disagreements, unlike others in *Hamlet* criticism, are not primarily over the application of accepted criteria, however multiple or fluctuating, for the correct use of certain concepts but over the very criteria themselves. What is central in the disagreements among the theories of tragedy are the debates over which criteria shall determine the correct use of the concept of tragedy. The critics do not dispute, for example, the criteria of "adultery" or "madness" when they argue about whether Gertrude was an adulteress or whether Hamlet was mad; they dispute whether certain criteria apply or do not. But it is precisely the dispute over the criteria of "tragedy" that characterizes their arguments when they attempt a true theory in order to answer, Why is *Hamlet* or Hamlet tragic?

The concept of tragedy, thus, is *perennially debatable*. The employment of the concept, especially by the critics in their disputes over the nature of tragedy, reveals that "tragedy" is a term whose every criterion of use is always open to fundamental question, challenge, rejection, and replacement. That the concept of tragedy or the term "tragedy" or their adjectival derivatives are perennially debatable is their most important logical characteristic as they function in *Hamlet* criticism and in all other attempts to state the nature of tragedy. Now, because the concept of tragedy is subject to perennial debate, it cannot (logically) have a set of necessary and sufficient conditions of its use. Hence, any theory, poetics, or real definition of tragedy, which must involve a statement of the necessary and sufficient conditions of the employment of the concept of tragedy constitutes a violation of the logic of that concept: One cannot state the essential conditions for the correct use of a concept whose very use precludes such a set of conditions.

"Tragedy" is not definable in the requisite theoretical sense of a true statement of the necessary and sufficient properties of all tragedies because all the purportedly requisite properties are challengeable, emendable, and corrigible. But "tragedy" is not definable (in the theory sense of true, real definition) for another reason, namely, that its use must allow for the ever present possibility of new conditions. Think of the history of the concept of tragedy. It is simply a historical fact that the concept, as we know and use it, has continuously accommodated new cases of tragedy and, more important, the new properties of these new cases. Thus, a second logical feature of the concept of tragedy is its *perennial flexibility*; that is, its being applicable to conditions that are unlike those that govern the extant use of the concept. "Tragedy," as its historical employment reveals, has been and still is, employed to talk about past or present tragedies; but it is also part of the task assigned the term to be applicable to future tragedies as well which may differ from the past and present ones as much as the present ones (at any particular time) differ from the past ones. To state the necessary and sufficient conditions for the correct use of the concept of tragedy, then, once again, is to foreclose upon the use of the concept which is, at least in part, to accommodate itself to these new conditions.

Elucidation of the concept of tragedy reveals that a theory of tragedy is not only factually difficult but logically impossible. An important consequence for the philosophy of language follows. Wittgenstein showed that it is a condition of our intelligible, correct employment of language that some of its terms do not, hence need not, have corresponding essences that guarantee their meanings. The elucidation of the concept of tragedy enables us to go beyond his rejection of the assumption that there are or must be essences to affirm that it is a condition of our intelligible, correct use of language that at least one of its terms cannot have a corresponding essence; for "tragedy" is a term whose use entails that there cannot be an exhaustive set of necessary and sufficient conditions for its use. Wittgenstein asks and answers negatively, Does the use of every term, for example, "game," depend upon a set of defining conditions? I am asking and also answering negatively, Can the use of every term, for example, "tragedy," depend upon such a set? It is logically impossible—i.e., a violation of its employment and rules of employment—for "tragedy" to perform the tasks it has been designated to perform and at the same time for "tragedy" to depend upon a set of necessary and sufficient conditions.

"Tragedy" is a perennially debatable and flexible term that critics (and others) use to describe or evaluate certain dramas, other works of art, and certain human situations. There are many criteria that govern its correct use; but none, I have argued, that are or can be necessary or sufficient.

Every theory of tragedy—every statement of its essential properties—is not and cannot be a true, real definition of tragedy. Instead, it expresses an honorific redefinition of "tragedy" that restricts the use of the term to a selection from its multiple criteria. Whether "tragedy" is defined as a descriptive or as an evaluative term (for example, Bradley's "pure, mature tragedies," Harrison's "deep tragedies," or Tillyard's "centrally tragic"), the definition represents a selection of, an emphasis upon, and an argument for, some of the many criteria of "tragedy."

It is this selection, emphasis, and argument, rather than the logically vain attempt at real, true definition of what is unamenable to such definition, that give point and value to all the theories of tragedy; for each serves as a recommendation to concentrate upon certain preferred criteria or properties of tragedy that are neglected, distorted, or omitted by other critics. If we attend to these criteria or properties instead of to the unsuccessful essays in essentialist definitions, we can learn much from the individual theories, especially about what to look for in tragedies and how to look at them.

The answer to What is tragedy? then, is not a statement of what all tragedies have in common, of their necessary and sufficient properties. The answer consists primarily in offering undeniable examples, paradigm cases. "*Oedipus Rex* and dramas like it are tragedies" is an adequate answer. *Oedipus Rex*—let us call it A—has certain properties: a hero, terrible suffering, reversal of fortune, reconciliation, momentous action, etc. Let us call these properties, 1, 2, 3, 4, and 5. Now, "dramas like *Oedipus Rex* refers to dramas B-N that contain properties 1-5; or properties 1-3 but not 4 and 5; or properties 2-5 plus new properties 6-8. Thus, dramas B-N, roughly the history of dramatic tragedies, are tragedies because they have properties, 1-5, 1-3, or 2-5, plus 6 and 7; and so on. They are not tragedies because they have properties 1-5 that are the necessary and sufficient ones of all tragedies. Drama $N + 1$ (e.g., *Death of a Salesman*), is a tragedy, then, not because it contains a set of essential properties, but because it is like the recognized tragedies A-N in some respects, although it differs from them in others. Knowing what tragedy is, finally, is not knowing a true theory of tragedy, but being able to cite indisputable examples and to decide on the basis of similarities and dissimilarities what else is to count as a tragedy.

Does criticism need a theory of tragedy in order to give intelligible reasons for *Hamlet*'s being tragic? Must it know the essence of tragedy or assume that tragedy has an essence in order to say cogently that or why *Hamlet* or Hamlet is tragic? If criticism requires such a theory then, because there is not and cannot be this theory, discourse about the tragic in *Hamlet* (or in any other work of art) is not intelligible. But this discourse is intelligible, hence, its intelligibility must depend upon something other than a theory. On what, then, do the reasons depend? The critic says, for example, "*Hamlet* is tragic," and gives a reason, "Because it has *P*, where *P* denotes a property of tragedy. (None of our representative critics ask, "Is *Hamlet* tragic?" Past critics, such as Voltaire, asked this question and denied that *Hamlet* is tragic because it violates decorum, the three unities, and the form of ancient as well as modern [French] tragedy. But Dryden's attack on the French theorists and Johnson's arguments against Voltaire, which were based upon traditional as well as new criteria of "tragedy," established *Hamlet* as one of the paradigms of tragedy. Their arguments against and victory over the French and Voltaire point up once again the perennial debatability and flexibility of the concept of tragedy.) The critic's reason, "Because *Hamlet* has *P*, is intelligible, has a use, not because *P* is necessary or sufficient for tragedy, but because *P* is a member of an open set of acknowledged (yet debatable) traditional properties or argued-for new properties of the tragic. "*Hamlet* is tragic because its hero, noble in virtue and station, suffers, falls, and dies; is partly responsible for his fate as it proceeds from his character, flaw, and inner conflict; and whose death involves the destruction, hence waste, of spiritual value which, as we witness the spectacle, induces in us pity, admiration, exultation, and awe at the inexplicable mystery of this waste of good" (Bradley) is an intelligible utterance because it employs certain criteria of "tragedy," that derive from the Greek tragedies which, after all, constitute the home base of the concept, and from Bradley's own recommendations and arguments for other, new criteria that were suggested to him by Hegel. "*Hamlet* is tragic because it celebrates the virtues of men" (Alexander) employs an entirely new (i.e., newly-formulated) criterion, that is fully argued-for and that achieves intelligibility because of the open character of the concept of tragedy.

I began this essay by asking whether, as many critics claim, criticism of *Hamlet* requires a poetics of tragedy in order to give meaning or intelligibility to its reasons for *Hamlet*'s being a tragedy. I have argued that there is no true poetics of tragedy, that there cannot be such a poetics, and that there need not be in order to guarantee the cogency of the reasons. I have also argued that poetics, unlike description, explanation, and evaluation, is an illegitimate procedure of criticism in that it tries to define what is udefinable, to state the necessary and sufficient conditions of the functioning of a concept whose very functioning shows that it has and can have no such conditions. "What is tragedy?" consequently does not function like "Does Hamlet delay?" "Why does Hamlet delay?" "or Is *Hamlet* a great drama?" In *Hamlet* criticism. "Why is *Hamlet* or Hamlet tragic?" also differs from the descriptive, explanatory, and evaluative questions of *Hamlet* criticism in that it involves not only debates over the clarification and application of established criteria, whether clear, ambiguous, or vague, but often debates over the very criteria themselves. Further, "Is Hamlet the only tragic figure in *Hamlet*"? that is, "Is Claudius also tragic?" cannot be answered as Bradley answers it. For "Is Claudius tragic?" is not equivalent to "Does Claudius satisfy all the requisite essential criteria of the tragic hero?" Rather it is equivalent to "Does Claudius satisfy any of the traditional (yet debatable) or newly argued-for criteria of the tragic hero?" It is certainly within the compass of the concept of tragedy to allow for cogent argument for the tragic stature not only of Claudius and Hamlet but, if one wishes to follow Schopenhauer, for example, of all the characters as they exemplify the sheer suffering of mere existence. There is nothing true or false about "Claudius is tragic." It, too, represents a decision, based on argument for new criteria of the tragic, to extend the concept of the tragic to cover the properties, thence the character, of Claudius.

What about the nature of Shakespearean tragedy as our critics discuss it? Although critics divide sharply on whether they require a theory of tragedy in order to state the defining features of Shakespearean tragedy, it should be clear by now—if my argument against a theory of tragedy is correct—that critical discourse about these features of Shakespearean tragedy is intelligible without such a theory. Instead of beginning with the questions, What makes these tragedies tragic? or Are they tragic? one simply starts with the correct assumption that Shakespearean tragedies are among the indisputable members of the open class of tragedies and form a subclass which have their own set of properties that unite them as well as distinguish them from other tragedies. In effect, one draws a boundary around the concept of tragedy, namely, "Shakespearean" and asks, What characterizes this particular subclass? Each of the theories of Shakespearean tragedies then serves as a statement of the defining features of this subclass of tragedies. In our survey, Bradley's is one such statement; Campbell's, another. Their basic disagreement is not over the presence of the abnormal conditions of mind, the supernatural, and the accidental in Shakespearean tragedy, but over the importance of these in relation to the other features. Even so, theirs is not a factual quarrel that can be settled by a common datum or set of data in the four major tragedies; it involves a disagreement over an explanation of some of the data in the four tragedies, consequently it can be adjudicated only in terms of which hypothesis, Bradley's or Campbell's, is more rather than less adequate in explaining the data of the plays. Perhaps, as Kenneth Muir acutely argues, both are in error in their assumption that even the major four are alike in any important way. In *Shakespeare and the Tragic Pattern* (1958), Muir writes: "There is no such thing as Shakespearian Tragedy: there are only Shakespearian tragedies."[27] All generalizations about Shakespearean tragedies and all attempts to distinguish among them the "pure" as against the "impure," the "major" as opposed to "minor," fail because they exaggerate their resemblances and obscure their differences. The English and Roman historical tragedies, *Titus Andronicus*, *Romeo and Juliet*; and the major four, that is, *Hamlet*, *Othello*, *King Lear*, and *Macbeth*; *Coriolanus*, *Antony and Cleopatra*, and *Julius Caesar* are all tragedies. The assumption, prevalent among critics, that some are not, rests on the false thesis that they deviate from the essence of the major four. But the major four, Muir argues, differ as much from each other as the others do among themselves or in relation to the major four. Thus there are many conceptions of the tragic in the tragedies of Shakespeare:

> The medieval idea of the man in high estate brought to his ruin by the workings of fate; the Senecan idea that calamity was inescapable and that man must endure; the idea that the essential function of tragedy was to warn people against pride, ambition, and other vices; the Marlovian idea of man brought to his ruin by excess; and underlying all the Christian idea that misery is often God's punishment for sin, the punishment falling on the innocent as well as the guilty.[28]

The twelve Shakespearean tragedies, consequently, according to Muir, have no properties in common. If they share any one quality, it is the aesthetic quality of all great art, the intensity noted by Keats in his maxim:

> The excellence of every art is its intensity, capable of making all disagreeables evaporate, from their being in close relationship with Beauty and Truth.

So much for the issue: Why is *Hamlet* tragic? What is tragedy? and What is Shakespearean tragedy? My claim about poetics, that it comprises debates over and recommendations of criteria and not true, real definitions of essences, is relevant to the clarification of other issues as well.

Is *Hamlet* a representation of life? Is it true? Is it to be comprehended as a representation of life? Jones answers these questions affirmatively; Stoll, negatively; Wilson, somewhere in between. But none of their replies is correct because the questions, although they look (grammatically) like factual ones, function normatively—indeed, elliptically for: Should *Hamlet* be comprehended as a representation of life, hence as true (or false)? The answer to *this* question is neither true nor false; it is a decision and recommendation, which one can accept or reject in accordance with the role one assigns to drama (and art) in one's economy of values.

What defines *Hamlet* as a poetic drama? What is the essence of poetic drama? Is *Hamlet*, as a poetic drama, basically character and plot, symbolism, imagery, myth and ritual, or poetry? It should be clear by now that these questions are bogus, in spite of the heated argument they inspire among contemporary critics. *Hamlet* is essentially none of these: not essentially character and plot, or imagery, or poetry, etc.—nor is any other poetic drama—for the simple but conclusive reason that, like tragedy, poetic drama has no essence, no exhaustive set of necessary and sufficient properties. Of course, it has properties: characters, plot, dialogue, imagery, myth and ritual, symbolism, and poetry. Some, for example, characters, plot, and poetry, are necessary; some, for example, myth and ritual or symbolism, are contingent; none is sufficient; and no collection of them is necessary and sufficient. All the theories of the essence of *Hamlet* as poetic drama—in our survey, Bradley's, Knight's, Fergusson's, and Spurgeon's theories—are at best stipulated, honorific redefinitions of "poetic drama," i.e., recommendations of certain properties rather than others, not true, real definitions of poetic drama at all. Like theories of tragedy, theories of poetic drama serve as much needed reminders of what we should look for in poetic drama and how we should look at it. The contemporary doctrine that Shakespearean drama is essentially poetry, not character and plot, a doctrine stated not only by Knight, but by L. C. Knights, especially in his well-known essay, "How Many Children Had Lady Macbeth?"[29] and by D. A. Traversi,[30] among others, is no refutation of Bradley's view of Shakespearean drama; indeed, it plays a more important role than an attempt at refutation, because, in effect, it says: In an age in which character analysis has run riot in the criticism of Shakespearean drama, let us return to the poetry of the dramas. The most effective instrument for initiating and promoting this desiderated shift is the employment of the definitional form: to provide a "persuasive definition" of "poetic drama," which the critics of Bradley have done.

How can we best understand *Hamlet* as a work of dramatic art? Once again, there is no true (or false) answer to this question. To be sure, there are more and less adequate explanations of *Hamlet*; but even a relatively adequate explanation, vague as this is, is not equivalent to the best way to comprehend *Hamlet*. Evaluative, poetic, and aesthetic, as well as explanatory, issues are involved in this question. Every answer ultimately turns on a particular theory of art, an aesthetic. And every theory of art, like every poetics, is neither true nor false, but an honorific redefinition of "art." Consequently, every purportedly true answer to this last question functions instead as a recommendation as to how we, the readers of *Hamlet*, should respond to and comprehend *Hamlet*. Our concern, consequently, should be with the reasons for and the implications of the recommendation, not with its nonexistent truth (or falsity).

Chapter Eight

LITERATURE AND PHILOSOPHY:
SENSE AND NONSENSE

Is there really anything new to be said about the relation between literature and philosophy? Of course, one can always invent a new piece of nonsense. Certain contemporary styles of literary criticism and theory prove the point; the ever-present possibility of nonsense provides a virtual guarantee of novelty. Indeed, this seemingly inexhaustible potentiality of novelty in nonsense ought in all consistency to enjoin certain enterprising contemporary linguistic theorists to postulate, along with their innate mental structures that puportedly explain the generation of new sense, another, more powerful, structure that alone could account for our unlearned capacity for limitless nonsense.

In exploring the relation between literature and philosophy, I shall aim at something new, without nonsense—or more realistically perhaps—at a nonsense that transgresses the limits of sense by trying to say what can only be shown, if it can be shown at all, rather than at that kind of prevalent nonsense that violates both the syntax and the semantics of intelligible critical discourse.

Literature and philosophy, then, to begin, is traditionally at any rate but one species of the genus art and truth, of which another important species, especially from Wordsworth to I. A. Richards, is poetry and science. Much has been written on both the genus and its species, though not as much on literature and philosophy as one might have expected. Plato and Aristotle, among the ancients, raise the problem directly and fully, as does Sir Philip Sidney some 2,000 years later. But in between there is very little: art and truth, not literature and philosophy, becomes a central issue, along with other problems concerning the arts. More surprising, there is equal neglect of the problem of how literature relates to philosophy from Sidney to Croce and I. A. Richards. The great figures of neoclassicism and of romanticism, both

English and continental, have much to say about poetry, literature, criticism and truth in literature; and some, especially the nineteenth-century German philosophers, explore voluminously the nature of art and the nature of philosophy and reality, but they are especially illuminating when they turn from abstract discussions of literature and philosophy to their concrete analyses of tragedies as examples of philosophy in literature. Even Matthew Arnold, in spite of his abiding concerns for both criticism and literature as the best that has been thought and expressed, is not directly worried about the problem of literature and philosophy. It is therefore only in the modern period, beginning with Croce and encompassing I. A. Richards, some of the New Critics, and early Santayana in his *Three Philosophical Poets*[1], that Plato's ancient quarrel is revitalized and new answers offered as to the proper relation between literature and philosophy. Thus, in spite of the antiquity of the problem, the disciplinary rubrics Philosophy and Literature, Philosophy of Literature, and Philosophy in Literature, each of which derives from Plato's quarrel, are mainly contemporary approaches, without the solid historical grounding of other, philosophical, including aesthetic, problems.

What, now, does the tradition say about the relation between literature and philosophy? Plato begins the debate. He revives what he refers to as the ancient quarrel between poetry and philosophy; so presumably, the problem of the relation between literature and philosophy is older than Plato. Plato distinguishes poetry from philosophy. Poetry—neither he nor Aristotle has or coins a word for literature, though Aristotle fumbles for such a word at the opening of the *Poetics*—is the making of certain kinds of objects that include painting, sculpture, music, and of course drama. Philosophy, though a dialectical activity, makes nothing; instead it seeks to grasp the forms: the ultimate entities of reality. What we call literature, what he calls (a species of) poetry, aims at and produces illusions or perspectives of imitations of the real. Philosophy, alone, aims at and grasps the real. Whatever the nuances, subtleties, or deviations may be in Plato's writings (some commentators even regard him as the supreme poet or maker), Plato never wavers on his fundamental and irreducible dichotomy between literature (epic, tragedy, comedy) and philosophy. In effect, he resolves the ancient quarrel not by joining literature and philosophy, but by rendering them asunder once and for all as the irresolvable difference between literature as falsehood and philosophy as truth. They cannot be friends: the putative truth-claims of literature remain just that—pretenses to truth about reality that give us instead (harmful) falsehoods.

Plato does more than divorce literature from philosophy, he also introduces the powerful idea that literature is purely emotive (as well as impurely cognitive). Unlike his successors, he does not identify poetry or literature with the noncognitive, that is, as neither true nor false, only with expressive language; but he does state for the first time the important doctrine that literature, though a tissue of lies and falsehoods, is emotive. And because he regards the emotive as harmful since it is false, his rejection of literature and of any legitimate relation between literature and philosophy is complete and definitive. Whatever modifications he offers in his whole *corpus*, one of the footnotes Plato bequeathes to western thought and literary criticism is that literature can no more be married to philosophy than falsehood can to truth. It is this footnote that serves perennially as the major text in the ensuing discussions about the relation, if any, between literature and philosophy. Moreover, it is not entirely clear, even after 2,500 years, that Plato's separation and his accompanying characterization and castigation of literature, together with his antecedent description and exaltation of philosophy, have been decisively refuted.

Aristotle, not Plato in some of his dialogues according to some of his commentators, is the first to answer Plato. He agrees with Plato that philosophy seeks truth and, when it finds it, is true: and that philosophy (the contemplative life) is best. But he disagrees with Plato on what the real is that truth captures, since for him, the forms or universals that Plato dissociates from their instantiation, at least in the ordinary world of things in space and time are, he claims, precisely in this ordinary world as its generic characteristics. Philosophy, thus, seeks, among other things, the universals in things, not the dubious universals beyond things that Plato postulates. He also agrees with Plato that literature is imitative but, in a master stroke of deduction from his conception of the real, he restricts the imitative to artifacts rather than, as Plato does, construing the imitative as coextensive with all objects, artifactual and natural.

Poetry, then, Aristotle says (and literature, he implies), because it comprises imitative artifacts, contains truth. Poetry (literature) seeks and, when successful, finds a variety of basic universals in things. He says in a famous passage that poetry (literature), which unlike history deals with what might happen, is "more scientific and serious than history": poetry can give general truths, history, only particular facts.

Poetry is more like philosophy than is history. But does this compliment extend to poetry (literature) as philosophy, so that both literature and philosophy aim at and achieve the same things, namely, truth about reality? Aristotle's hierarchy of the intellectual virtues in Book VI of the *Nicomachean Ethics* suggests otherwise: that philosophy, which involves wisdom, differs from literature, which is merely art, requires general truths for its proper practice but that is not, as wisdom is, directly concerned with them. Literature may be better than history, but it is not quite as good as philosophy.

Nevertheless left-handed compliment or not, Aristotle's tribute to poetry (literature) as a repository of truths about the general or shared features of human actions and experiences is the first of many attempts to join literature with philosophy to the enhancement of the first without a necessary denigration of the second. He asks and answers affirmatively: Does literature contain philosophy, that is, general truths about general things? His answer rests upon his denial of the reality of transcendent forms. Hence, if Plato is correct that these forms constitute a necessary condition for the existence of anything else and that there is no philosophy and no truth without these forms, Aristotle's specific reply to Plato's challenge collapses. Literature cannot be joined with philosophy if the objects and truths of the latter differ radically from the imitations and opinions of the former.

Nevertheless, Aristotle's doctrine that literature can and does contain certain truths of the highest ontological order and is therefore philosophical in that sense remains a possibility and a possible defense of the joining of literature and philosophy. Transcendent forms or not, the world as we all live in it exemplifies certain generic features. Why cannot literature include these and by doing so incorporate philosophy?

After Plato and Aristotle, there is further probing into fundamental problems regarding the arts. Plotinus, Horace, Longinus, Augustine, and Thomas Aquinas, among others, introduce or debate many questions that we today recognize as aesthetic, that is, as philosophical problems about the arts. However, to repeat, there is little—I believe, perhaps in ignorance—that is of major importance on our topic of the relation beween literature and philosophy until Sir Philip Sidney's *An Apology for Poetry* (1595).

This essay, in my judgment as profound in its implications as it is scintillating in its presentation, is typically Renaissance as it returns to the ancients for the union of literature and philosophy and just as atypically a *naissance* as it anticipates certain later, mostly modern, doctrines that divorce literature from philosophy. It obviously borrows from Aristotle and Horace; but it also implicitly points to a conception of literature that does not state truths but *shows* them instead, and thereby employs language that is neither true or false nor purely emotive. Literature, on this conception, contrasts sharply with philosophy, which *affirms* truths and is thereby a use of language that in its capacity to state truths (or falsehoods) differs completely from the language of literature. The ostensible emphasis on the feigned fictions and the moral efficacy of literature, stressed by both Sidney and his commentators, becomes incidental in his essay to the implicit main arguments for the two contrary possibilities of literature in relation to philosophy.

Sidney, following Aristotle and Horace, defines poetry as an art of imitation: "that is to say, a representing, counterfeiting, or figuring forth—to speak metaphorically, a speaking Picture; with this end, to teach and delight." To which he adds later: "...it is not rhyming and versing that maketh a poet . . . But it is that feigning notable images of virtues, vices, or what else, with that delightful teaching, which must be the right describing note to know a poet by . . . ."[2]

Whether Sidney offers two definitions of poetry, one that emphasizes teaching and delight, the other, morality, or what is more likely, one definition that specifies the moral or "what else" as what poetry teaches, he does define poetry in a manner that allows it to compete with philosophy.

To be sure, Sidney does not define philosophy. However, it is clear from what he does say about it that he construes philosophy in the traditional terms of (true or false) doctrines about what is, may be, or should be, comprising as it does metaphysics, natural philosophy, and morals. Moreover, philosophy is, like poetry, an art—a practice—whose function is to proclaim truths, including but not identified with truths about how we are to live: it too claims to teach.

Sidney next locates the difference between literature and philosophy not in *what* they teach but in *how* they teach. Philosophy teaches by abstractions, morality in particular, by abstract precepts. Literature teaches by examples, by richly fabricated, feigned notable images. Philosophy proceeds by way of definition, division, and distinction, each dry as dust, that can be understood only by those few who already understand or who are too old for it to make a difference in their actions; in regard to morals, philosophy provides only knowledge of virtue, with no guide as to its practice. Poetry (literature), on the other hand, furnishes richly concrete examples that can move us to be virtuous, not merely to know the virtues. Shifting from considerations of what should be to what is, even here, Sidney claims, literature beats philosophy in their common game of getting at the essences. Consider, for example, anger. The philosopher, Sidney says, analyzes and defines it, the Stoics in particular, as "a short madness." The dramatist (Sophocles), on the other hand, brings an Ajax on the stage, portrays him as whipping and slaughtering sheep, thinking them to be Greek soldiers, beaten and destroyed. Tell me, Sidney asks: "if you have not a more familiar insight into anger than finding in the Schoolmen [or the Stoics, or any other philosophers] his genus and difference." Poetry, thus *is* philosophy, but philosophy rendered richly concrete. Sidney concludes: "the Poet is indeed the right popular philosopher.[3]

Poetry, then, according to Sidney, not only makes virtue attractive, but also makes truth accessible. It differs from philosophy not in its concern with truth, since it conveys all the truths that philosophy does, but it conveys the truth more effectively. What Sidney strongly suggests, then, is that both philosophy and literature contain truths: about what should be and about what is. So they can be, are, and should be joined. Where they differ is that philosophy states whereas literature shows truths. And because showing is more revealing and more moving than saying, literature is superior. Examples, richly invented one might add, are more vivid, convincing, and appealing than abstractions, however persuasively argued. Poetry, Sidney sums up in his defense of poetry against its detractors, is not ". . . an art of lies, but of true doctrine."

How, now, we may ask, can poetry (literature) be an art of true *doctrine* if poetry shows but does not state truths? Are feigned notable images, indeed any image or representation, true doctrine?

Sidney offers an answer: ". . . I think truly, that of all writers under the sun the poet is the least liar, and though he would, as a poet can scarcely be a liar . . . for the poet, he nothing affirms, and therefore never lieth."

If poetry affirms nothing—contains no statements, true or false, about the world as it is or should be—how can it be an art of true doctrine? It cannot. Poetry (literature) can show what is or what should be, but it says, states nothing true (or false).

On this view, literature and philosophy are radically distinct. The first is an art of representation, the second, an art of statement. Truth (and falsity) belong to philosophy, not to literature. The dramatist can still show us anger as a short madness, but he cannot, without affirmation, state what it is or present an insight into or a true doctrine of anger as a short madness. Should he do so, on Sidney's second account of poetry, the dramatist abandons poetry, unconcerned with truth, for philosophy, concerned only with truth. Literature differs from philosophy no longer as competing modes of truth but as radically distinct modes, the one as neither true nor false but feigned representation, the other as either true or false statement. Sidney cannot have it both ways: either literature and philosophy can, are, and should be joined in their mutual quest for affirmed true doctrine or they cannot, are not, and should not be united in their separate quests for feigned fictions and true doctrine. If, as Ben Jonson puts it:

> For he knows poet never credit gained
> By writing truths, but things like truths, Well feigned,[4]

or as Francis Bacon says, "poetry is feigned history," then what Sidney implies in his essay, with Jonson and Bacon, is close to Archibald MacLeish's admonition, centuries after Sidney:

> A poem should be equal to:
> Not true . . .
> A poems should not mean
> But be.[5]

Plato claims that Poetry (literature) pretends to be true and always fails. Aristotle counters that literature pretends to be true and often succeeds. Sidney agrees with Aristotle in one mood but rejects both Plato and Aristotle in his other mood. What, now, are some of the other positions on the relation between literature and philosophy that are formulated or suggested by the tradition?

Wordsworth's Preface to the Second Edition of the *Lyrical Ballads* (1800) is, I think, the first new document, after Sidney, on the relation between philosophy and literature, as indeed it is the first major statement on the opposition of science and poetry.

To praise the originality of the Preface, however, is in no way to discredit the importance of Boileau, Dryden, Pope, Johnson, and other neoclassicists; rather, it is to suggest that their contributions lie elsewhere. On the generic issue of art and truth, they remain Aristotelians and because of their acceptance of the delight as well as the instruction of literature, they are good Horatians too. Boileau's "Rien n'est beau que le vrai: le vrai seul est aimable";[6] Corneille's commitment to *le vraisemblable* and to *le nécessaire*; Dryden's insistence on drama as "a just and lively image of human nature, representing its passions and humours, and the changes of fortune to which it is subject, for the delight and instruction of mankind;" Pope's

> First follow nature, and your judgment frame
> By her just standard, which is still the same.
> Unerring NATURE, still divinely bright,
> One clear, unchang'd, and universal light;[7]

Lessing's adherence to art as *Nachahmung* and to the mimetic principle even as he challenges the doctrine of *ut pictura poesis*; and Johnson's "Nothing can please many, and please long, but just representations of general nature"[8]—whether they epitomize their individual author's views on the relation of art and truth or do not—are but variations on the Aristotelian *cum* Horatian theme of art as delightful instruction in general truths about nature. These authors may differ about art and truth and they disagree about nature. But they never demur from the requirement, hence legitimacy, of literature joined with philosophy in the common pursuit of truth about the world. Thus, the whole neoclassic aesthetic, diverse as it is, concurs on the main thesis that literature and philosophy, though distinct in their aims and effects, can be joined without the detriment at least of literature but without any obvious enhancement to philosophy.

Wordsworth's Preface is "a systematic defence of the theory upon which the Poems (*Lyrical Ballads*) are written."[9] Both the theory and its defense are universally recognized as the first of the great credos of English Romanticism, the second being Coleridge's *Biographia Literaria* (1817). The Preface contains much of importance to historians on the proper subjects of diction in Wordsworth's experimentations with poetry. Of central concern to us, however, is what he says or implies about poetry and its relation to philosophy. In regard to this topic, of major significance is his shift from the putative opposition of poetry and philosophy to his stated quarrel between poetry and science, the latter of which he identifies with "matters of fact"; although even here, he projects a future of reconciliation once science divests itself of its purely quantitative approach to recognize the intrinsically subjective, qualitative content of true scientific knowledge.

It is this theme of reconciliation and unification of human faculties and of nature that pervades Wordsworth's critical theory and poetry. Human feelings, passions, and emotions, directly experienced and subsequently enlarged by an imagination that modifies and synthesizes our sensations, images, feelings and thought, make up poetry and its unified vision of a unified and ordered world.

There is thus for Wordsworth a true picture of poetry that corresponds to the truth about the world: its richly concrete qualitative unity. Wordsworth introduces a number of complications and qualifications but the gist of his theory, and that which has most relevance to us, is that poetry in its verbal, imaginative unity expresses and reflects the nonverbal concrete order of the world. Poetry is a philosophically true rendition of the philosophically true character of the world. His *Lyrical Ballads*, unlike much traditional poetry that he even questions as poetry, are natural expressions of the true unities of feeling and thought—not artificial, ornamental, contrived metric or nonmetric composition—of certain concrete orders of feelings and thought in the world. Poetry—his poetry—is expression that delights as well as avers philosophical truth about reality.

Thus, it is not accurate to reduce Wordsworth's theory to the idea that poetic truth is emotional knowledge or a transcendent vision or revelation of the nature of things. For he believes that poetry is straightforward linguistic expression that in its closeness to real speech is natural, therefore true to this speech, and that it is truly about man in nature. Wordsworth employs both "true to" and, more important, "truth about," in his statement about the nature of poetry in relation to the world. Poetry is true in the sense of "natural" or "true to" our expression of contemplated passion and, at the same time, is "true about" these experiences. This, I think, is the correct as well as fairest interpretation of Wordsworth's contribution to the relation between poetry and philosophy as he promotes their union in the same way that he seeks unity and synthesis in all things. At any rate, this is how I read the relevant portions of his Preface and especially its marvelous, frequently quoted, remarks: the poet ". . . has a greater knowledge of human nature, and a more comprehensive soul, than are supposed to be common among mankind." "For all good poetry is the spontaneous overflow of powerful feelings," to which he adds the important qualification: "it takes its origin from emotion recollected in tranquillity: the emotion is contemplated till, by a species of reaction the tranquillity gradually disappears, and an emotion, kindred to that which was before the subject of contemplation, is gradually produced, and does itself actually exist in the mind."[10] ". . . Poetry is the most philosophic of all writing: . . . its object is truth, not individual and local, but general, and operative; not standing upon external testimony, but carried alive into the heart by passion, truth which is its own testimony . . . Poetry is the image of man and nature . . . the poet writes under one restriction only, namely the necessity of giving immediate pleasure to a human Being . . . ." ". . . The Man of science seeks truth as a remote and unknown benefactor; he cherishes and loves it in his solitude: the Poet, singing a song in which all human beings join with him, rejoices in the presence of truth as our "visible friend and hourly companion. Poetry is the breath and finer spirit of all knowledge; it is the impassioned expression which is in the countenance of all Science.[11]

Like Coleridge (and others), we may reject much of the Preface, especially Wordsworth's naive view that poetic diction is the ordinary language of ordinary men; but what remains hard-headed and unsentimental, perhaps even unromantic in its rejection of any pathetic fallacy, is Wordsworth's very clear theory about how one kind of poetry (that he takes, rightly or wrongly, to be the only kind) is, as poetry, true to one kind of reality (again, that he takes to be the only kind). If the world is a particular kind of concrete unity, then a poetry that expresses, imitates, or represents it is true in precisely the sense that a poetry (or poetic pretense) that rejects or distorts this unity is false. In the end, Wordsworth's argument for the union, not identity, of poetry and philosophy rests upon his specific, not so implausible, theory and philosophy of the world itself. We can ask no more of an adequate theory of the relation between poetry (or literature) and philosophy, even if we cannot share the metaphysics that sponsors and supports it. Wordsworth, like Johnson, believes that poetry provides knowledge of certain general truths about general facts. To call this claim to knowledge irrational intuition or revelation is to do injustice both to the English language and to Wordsworth; to label it "insight" is to commend it as knowledge, not to applaud or castigate it as something higher than or different from knowledge. Finally, to claim, as some commentators do, that Wordsworth identifies truth with sincerity and thereby changes the question "Does poetry (literature) contain truths about the world?" to "Is poetry sincere?" is to conflate the poetic process with its product. The poet is sincere, true to himself, his feelings, and thoughts: but his poetry is true (or false), as he is sincere, when and only when it expresses and communicates to others the requisite unity of feeling and thought that constitutes reality.

Coleridge, like Wordsworth, celebrates the union of poetry and philosophy. He says of Wordsworth's poetry that it is "the union of deep feeling with profound thought",[12] which he generalizes into a principle in his assessment of Shakespeare: "No man was yet a great poet without being at the same time a profound philosopher."[13]

But Coleridge challenges Wordsworth's theory of poetry and his philosophy of nature. Wordsworth, he claims, is wrong in his naive theory of poetic diction and he is inadequate in his metaphysics in that he neglects the fundamental organic character of reality. More important, however, than these two objections is Coleridge's deep feeling and profound thought that Wordsworth does not grasp the full significance of union as an organic fusing of elements rather than as a mechanical juxtaposition of compatible, even if discordant, elements. For the defining principle of union to Coleridge is the secondary imagination that he struggles, perhaps in vain, to formulate and clarify, an imagination that germinates rather than fructifies (that he calls the primary imagination). In this regard, Coleridge relates to Wordsworth as Kant's Second Edition Deduction of the Categories in the *Critique of Pure Reason* does to the First Edition Deduction. Kant, too, sees that without the (Second Edition) transcendental synthetic unity of apperception as the noncategorical, nonconceptual basis, there can be no unifying principle of experience that can overcome the limitations of his First Edition Threefold Synthesis of Knowledge.

The analogy to Kant is meant to be exact. Coleridge realizes that Wordsworth's (and traditional) conceptions of the imagination as a synthesizing faculty cannot account for the originative and organically unifying "permeative, blending and fusing" power of the imagination. Coleridge's theory of the secondary imagination, vague and maddeningly brief as is his account of it, is nevertheless the absolute center of Coleridge's theory of poetry (literature) and of a philosophy that purports to be a true metaphysics of art and nature; and, most important for our topic, at the very root of philosophy in literature.

Although Coleridge comes close to identifying art and nature, both being like growing plants; the concept allows him to hold on to a mimetic view of art as an imitation of processes of nature; and although he comes close to identifying poetry and philosophy, he refuses to do so. Poetry, he contends, gives us pleasure, derived both from its separate parts and as individual wholes: philosophy, like science, on the other hand, seeks only truth about the world, however organic that truth must be about an organic world. Poetry alone, seeks a union—a fusion, not a juxtaposition—of passion, truth and pleasure. It is, says Coleridge in one of his occasional pieces, the "union of passion with thought and pleasure which constitutes the essence of all poetry."[14]

There is little to say in favor of Coleridge's organicism as the fundamental metaphysical principle, derived no doubt from Schelling's aesthetic philosophy of nature. We can safely ignore it, even though Coleridge does not, contending that the organic in art replicates the organic in nature. But this view presupposes that art and nature are themselves organically or internally related, which they are not.

On the other hand, there is everything to say for Coleridge's organicism as a fundamental aesthetic principle. That each item in a work of art is interrelated, as a harmony of concordant and of discordant elements, and that this unifying, processive character can best be explained by an imagination that permeates, blends, and fuses is one of the few great contributions in the history of aesthetics or the philosophy of art.

As attractive as Coleridge's organic theory of art is, it is in its application by him that the theory comes to glorious life, as his criticisms of the dramas of Shakespeare—even as the (for the most part) reports and marginalia they are—so beautifully reveals. For me, as for many others, his Shakespeare criticism is one of the great moments in the history of literary criticism. All of it, whether we quarrel with parts of it, for example his treatment of *Hamlet*, or with the whole of it, is replete with his aesthetics of organicism. He sees each of the plays as germinating from the first scenes and as individual organic wholes, growing like a plant, being born and being nourished by an imagination that fuses everything, even the discordants that Keats is later to refer to as the disagreeables that evaporate in the work "from their being in close relationship to Beauty and Truth." Omnipresent Deity or not, Shakespeare, for Coleridge, is the supreme example of the union of passion, pleasure, and thought.

We cannot here go into the details of his assessment of Shakespeare. In any case, I have done this elsewhere. Suffice it to say that, for Coleridge, philosophy—profound true thoughts about the world—enters into literature exactly as do the other elements of character, plot, dialogue, etc. Of course literature relates to philosophy: it joins them not by juxtaposing them but by fusing them into an organic whole that is the individual work of art. Coleridge sees as clearly as anyone before or after him that the relation between philosophy and literature is one in which the philosophy is in the literature, when it is, in exactly the same sense in which the other distinguishable but not separable elements are germinating and contributing to the whole interrelated work. No wonder that he celebrates the union of poetry (literature) and philosophy! It is also he who invents and legitimizes Philosophy in Literature as a proper discipline with a proper subject. We can applaud the achievement without accepting the dubious union of art and nature that Coleridge insists on. Literature can be organic without the nature it depicts being itself organic and organically related to the literature that depicts it. Moreover, I think that Coleridge agrees with me: for the two principles of his criticism of Shakespeare—that the dramas are illusory and enjoin a willing suspension of disbelief that he calls poetic faith and that the dramas are true to life (which feature enjoins belief, not suspension of belief or disbelief)—are themselves as discordant as they are fundamental. Is Coleridge able to reconcile these disagreeables as he believes Shakespeare and poetry do? I think not. In the end, Coleridge is terribly torn between the organic in art as a replication of the organic in nature and the organic in art as a deviation from the organic in nature. Both art and nature may grow like plants; but in art the growth is accompanied and fused by a pruning secondary imagination, a power that is entirely lacking in the plant of nature. No one, I submit, is more aware of this difference than Coleridge, as his specific exegeses of the various movements in the plays of Shakespeare show again and again.

After Coleridge's "Copernican Revolution" against traditional conceptions of the relation between literature and philosophy, a revolution that locates the planet of philosophy in the universe of literature rather than, as the tradition has it, a planet revolving around and being attracted to or repelled by the independent planet of literature—indeed, a revolution that is less vulnerable than Kant's "Copernican Revolution" or, for that matter, as it has turned out, Copernicus'—the offerings on our topic are slim, at least in comparison with Coleridge's. Lamb, Hazlitt, Shelley, De Quincey, and J. S. Mill provide addenda to the problem of poetry (literature), truth, science, and philosophy. Hazlitt's view of poetry as the language of the imagination that ". . . is not the less true to nature, because it is false in point to fact; but so much the more true and natural, if it conveys the impression which the object under the influence of passion makes on the mind" ("On Poetry in General") is worth noting. So is De Quincey's famous distinction between the literature of knowledge and the literature of power, the latter of which "is a rarer thing than truth—namely *power* or deeper sympathy with truth."[15] Shelley's "A Defense of Poetry" is a great paean to poetry which claims, without much argument but with much eloquent exhortation, that poetry reaches after eternal truth, that Shakespeare, Dante, and Milton, for example, "are philosophers of the very loftiest power," and that poetry "is at once the center and circumference of knowledge," and that "Poets are the unacknowledged legislators of the world."[16] Mill's essay, "Thoughts on Poetry and Its Varieties" (1833), ten years before his *Logic*, is of great fascination because it is written by a philosopher who, as a no—nonsense nominalist, rejects the traditional search for real definitions of the genus differentia or essence variety and yet who, in his writing on poetry, lays down as exact and real a definition of poetry as has ever been given, in which he reduces poetry—"true poetry"—to the soliloquizing lyric, meant to be not heard but overheard, and best exemplified in Shelley, not Wordsworth, where all is the truth of human feeling. In a language that out—romanticises the romantics, Mill characterizes poetry—its inner essence—as the "delineation of the deeper and more secret working of human emotion," as "feeling confessing itself to itself, in moments of solitude," as "the natural fruit of solitude and meditation," as "impassioned truth," in which the truth of poetry "is to paint the human soul truly," not "to give a true picture of life," and, finally, as "Feeling itself, employing Thought only as the medium of its expression." As audacious and legislative as his definition of poetry is, his application of it to the purely poetic as against the oratory of music, especially to the *"Dove sono"* in Mozart's *The Marriage of Figaro*—"Who can imagine *"Dovo sono"* heard? We imagine it overheard—redeems all."[17]

Only Keats, among the romantics after Wordsworth and Coleridge, makes a major contribution. His notion of negative capability is on a par with Coleridge's notion of the secondary imagination as the germinating and integrating force of literature. However, because his notion applies more to the difference between philosophy in literature as against the philosophy in philosophy than it does to the relation of literature and philosophy—our present topic—I shall return to his notion later, as one of the brilliant ways of understanding the difference not between literature and philosophy but the difference between philosophy in literature and the philosophy in traditional philosophy.

Of the continental theorists I have said and will say nothing about the French and Italians, although Leopardi's radical dichotomy between poetry (literature) and philosophy is worth remembering: "the more poetry is philosophical, the less it is poetry . . . . Philosophy wants truth, poetry falsity and illusion. Philosophy harms and destroys poetry . . . . There is an unsurpassable barrier, a sworn and mortal enmity between them, which cannot be abolished, reconciled or disguised"[18]

The Germans are another story. From Lessing and earlier writers, through Goethe, Schiller, Schelling, the Schlegels, to the philosophers Hegel, Schopenhauer, and Nietzsche, there is a running concern for the metaphysics of art, poetry, literature, life, nature, reality, and of philosophy itself. There may even be some profoundly new ideas on the relation of literature to philosophy. But I must leave this possibility to the future historian who has yet to write the first book on this fascinatng, for the most part neglected, subject. For me, as I have already indicated, the great contribution of these Germans to the problem of how literature relates to philosophy is not in their abstract metaphysical speculations, brilliant as they are, but in their concrete discussions of the tragic in the tragedies they discuss. Hegel, for example, shows how the dialectic works best in philosophy and literature when he applies it to some of the ancient Greek tragedies, especially his exemplar, Antigone. Here we are offered full illustrations of how philosophy joins with literature. Nevertheless, because these philosophers are more interested in the metaphysics of tragedy as an abstract philosophical problem than they are in elucidating the tragic in the tragedies they discuss, like most philosophers who deal with literature, they commit the heresy of paraphrase, by abstracting the tragic from the tragedies in order to explore the tragic rather than the actual literary tragedies. As a result, they do philosophy of literature, not philosophy in literature. A. W. Schlegel, perhaps, is the great exception, as his lectures on Shakespeare's tragedies amply testify. But then he is a critic, not a philosopher.

This brings us to Arnold and the moderns. Arnold has many memorable words and phrases, among them "touchstone," "sweetness and light," and "culture and anarchy"; there are also many memorable ideas such as his notion of literature "as the best that has been thought and said," his definition of criticism as "a disinterested endeavour to learn and propagate the best that is known and thought in the world," his statement of the function of criticism and of the critical power in all knowledge as "to see the object as in itself it really is," and his conviction "that poetry (literature) is at bottom a criticism of life."[19] In his essay "Literature and Science," Arnold meets their quarrel with an attempt to reconcile them through the reminder that both are in the same business of acquiring and transmitting knowledge. Presumably this would be his answer too to Plato's ancient quarrel between philosophy and poetry.

Unless we become bewitched by any of these words, phrases, or ideas, and treat them as touchstones of Arnold's achievement as a critic, each of them is, even if memorable, vulnerable, and some of them, such as his ideas of literature, criticism, and poetry, are downright unacceptable. It is not so much that these doctrines are false, which they are; rather, that if they are (taken to be) true, they reduce poetry, literature, and criticism to mockeries of what they so heterogeneously are.

What about Arnold's (implicit) idea of the relation between literature and philosophy, once we skip over his facile reconciliation of literature and science and look elsewhere? I know of no essay in which he tackles the problem head-on. However, there is an answer or at least the suggestion of one in his essay on Wordsworth, in which he introduces his selection, *Poems of Wordsworth* (1879).

Poetry, he begins, ". . . is nothing less than the most perfect speech of man, that in which he comes nearest to being able to utter the truth. It is no small thing, therefore, to succeed eminently in poetry." To this he adds: ". . . the noble and profound application of ideas to life is the most essential part of poetic greatness. . . . A great poet receives his distinctive character of superiority from his application under the conditions immutably fixed by the laws of poetic beauty and poetic truth, from his application, I say, to his subject, whatever it may be, of the ideas 'On man, on nature, and on human life.'"[20]

Many poets meet this criterion, including, Arnold contends, Wordsworth, at least in his best poems. Indeed, Arnold claims, Wordsworth is superior to any of his contemporaries, English and continental, because "he deals with more of life than they do; he deals with life as a whole, more powerfully." However, it is not, as some say, Wordsworth's philosophy of life, but his poetry about man, nature and human life, that makes him great. We read him not for his abstract ideas but for ". . . the extraordinary power with which Wordsworth feels the joy offered to us in nature, the joy offered to us in the simple primary affections and duties: . . . the extraordinary power with which, in case after case, he shows us this joy, and renders it so as to make us share in it . . . ." Arnold concludes: "Wherever we meet with the successful balance in Wordsworth, of profound truth of subject with profound truth of execution, he is unique." It is therefore his poetry that "is the reality, his philosophy . . . is illusion."[21] And what is true of Wordsworth, Arnold suggests, is true of all great poetry, that its reality is in its concrete criticism of life, not in its abstract statement of philosophical ideas.

As consistent as Arnold's criteria of poetic greatness in Wordsworth are with Arnold's overall conception of poetry as a criticism of life, and as dubious as these criteria may be as unchallengeable ones or as sole criteria of poetic greatness, Arnold implies at least the central idea that the great difference between literature and philosophy—both deeply concerned with truth—is that the truth of literature lies in the truth of concrete execution of ideas whereas the truth of philosophy is abstract. And if this is so, Arnold, in the end, simply reiterates one version of the relation between literature and philosophy: both deal with truth, the one with its concrete immediacy of feeling, the other with its abstract remoteness of thought. There is truth in literature, but no philosophy. Philosophy and literature, therefore, remain distinct. Coleridge's implicit contention that there can be philosophy in literature, just as there can be character, plot, or dialogue in drama, is forsaken for the more traditional view that though poetry may be more philosophical than history in its general truths, it is not less philosophical than philosophy. Instead, poetry is not like philosophy or philosophical at all. Philosophy in literature must be an illusion.

That there is or can be philosophy in literature is an illusion is also the cardinal tenet of at least two of the moderns who deal with the relation of literature to philosophy: Benedetto Croce and I. A. Richards. And, if my reading of Arnold is correct, Arnold anticipates the modern radical divorce between philosophy and literature as much as he sums up one version of the Aristotelian tradition. For both Croce and Richards present powerful indictments against the joining of literature and philosophy in any harmonious way. Whether their arguments for their indictments are as powerful as their indictments is another story. Croce makes his case by demanding a radical distinction between art and philosophy in his hierarchy of knowledge; Richard makes his case by insisting upon a radical distinction between the two fundamental uses of language: the emotive versus the symbolic or descriptive or referential. Croce's not implausible conclusion,[22] that art (literature) is not philosophy—that the expressive, intuitive is not the conceptual—rests upon the entirely implausible premise that the aesthetic, the intuitive, the expressive—that is, art—is nonconceptual, a kind of unmediated immediate experience, a knowledge by acquaintance, which because it is intuition without conceptualization, is incoherent. Richards' equally plausible conclusion[23] that science or philosophy and poetry are two distinct kinds of utterance, the one, true-false, the other, affective, rests upon the unacceptable premise that there are these two radically distinct and different kinds of utterance. Richards' emotive-symbolic distinction, a direct influence on both Logical Positivism and C. L. Stevenson's metaethics, reduces the many different kinds of use of utterances—what today we call Speech Acts—to an arbitrary two and an equally arbitrary radical division between them. For there are many different kinds of uses of language whose variety cannot be reduced to any dichotomy of expressing or emoting and describing or referring.

But deeper than this objection is that Richards, like the Positivists, Stevenson, and others, simply assumes that the convention for construing sentences as statements and therefore as true-false scientific or philosophical claims is fixed in such a manner that one can easily distinguish the sentences of literature from the sentence-statements of science and philosophy. It may very well be that there is such a convention for converting the sentences of science and philosophy into statements. But although there is a similar convention for reading the sentences of literature as sentences, not statements, the convention Richards subscribes to, it is precisely this convention that is debatable and exchangeable; indeed, it goes right to the heart of the whole problem of philosophy and literature. With the sentences of science or of philosophy, we do not ask, "Are they statements?" That they are is built into our notions of science and philosophy. But with the sentences of literature—of poems, dramas, novels—there is this question, "Are they, or at any rate some of them, statements?" To say that literature is not philosophy or science, on Richards' or any linguistic account, is in effect to deny that the sentences of literature are in any sense statements. This denial purports to be based upon the description of the function of the sentences of literature. It is nothing of the kind; the denial is not the factual disclaimer that the sentences we read in literature are statements, it is the normative recommendation not to take them as statements, which we may accept or reject, an option not open to us with the sentences in science or philosophy.

Richards' program, then, and the whole dichotomy between literature and science or philosophy conflates the injunction against the reading of a certain class of sentences as statements with a mythical factual description of that class, that it contains no statements. Whether the sentences in literary works are or are not statements revolves around two equally powerful conventions, unlike the one convention that governs the sentences of science and philosophy. There may be no philosophy in literature. But the argument that there is none cannot rest on the incoherent premise of Croce's nonconceptual immediate knowledge or the confused and arbitrary premise of Richards' emotive as against symbolic use of language.

So much for our brief and ever so cursory survey of some of the major traditional positions taken on the relation between literature and philosophy. These range from the view, best stated by Plato, reiterated by Sidney in one of his moods, and most recently revitalized by Croce and Richards and their numerous, if diverse, followers, that literature and philosophy are radically distinct enterprises which cannot lie joined without the detriment of both and without the enhancement of either, to the view, first stated by Aristotle, repeated by Sidney in his major mood and by many others in different ways, that they can be joined without compromising either and perhaps with the enhancement of both.   In between are views that literature, as insight, revelation, or intuition, is the higher philosophy; that literature is concrete philosophy; that literature includes or may include philosophy; and so on. And throughout there hovers the whole problem of art and truth. Rather than entering once again into this interminable debate, I wish now to argue for the aesthetic legitimacy of philosophy in the works that contain it. I want to defend the presence of philosophy in literature and the happy joining of them. This is my topic, the academic subject of which is Philosophy in Literature. I shall say no more about the topics of philosophy and literature or philosophy of literature, except that, at least to me, as academic subjects, Philosophy and Literature and Philosophy of Literature are closer to academic entrepreneurism and philosophical imperialism than they are to genuine subjects of inquiry. As academic subjects, the first strikes me as a part of the history of ideas, and the second as the exploitation of literature for the promotion of concrete examples for philosophy. Neither, I think, serves the purpose of enriching our understanding of literature as works of art.

I understand by Philosophy in Literature two related theses: (1) that some works of literature, certainly not necessarily all, contain philosophical ideas that are as integral to these works as any of their other constituents; and (2) that there is a place in literary criticism for the aesthetic articulation of these ideas. More specifically, I find it fruitful to ask of any work of literature: "Does it have any philosophical ideas?" If it does, "How do they get into the work?" and "What aesthetic contribution do they make to the work?"

In asking the first question, we must distinguish between a philosophical theme and a philosophical thesis. For example, a novel, say, *Anna Karenina* may have many philosophical themes, among them that we are not to blame, hence not to be judged, for what we do—a theme that is voiced by all the major characters; or that *laissez—faire* is the best philosophy of life, which is exemplified by Oblonsky. But it is not always clear that a philosophical theme, however much it is expressed, serves as a philosophical thesis; neither of these two themes, for example, can be convincingly read as Tolstoy's truth-claim about human life in *Anna Karenina*. In fact, the philosophical thesis, at least on my reading of the novel, is not even expressed on the printed pages of the novel but must be elicited from the plot in relation to the other elements. I am also aware of powerful and persuasive arguments by modern aestheticians against the distinction between theme and thesis in literature. All of these arguments, I believe, rest, as do the arguments against the distinction between sentence and statement in literature, on a confusion of the factual question "Are there philosophical theses (statements) in literature?" with the normative question "Ought we, when the plot, characters, dialogue, authorial interpolations, tone, and themes are described and explained in a certain way, to construe one or other of the themes (sentences) as *a* or *the* philosophical thesis (statement) in the whole work?" In regard to this normative question, it seems to me that there is no compelling reason for a negative reply and every good reason for an affirmative answer, provided that we are able to accommodate false as well as true philosophical theses (statements) in those works that have or imply them.

My model for philosophical literary criticism is, of course, Coleridge's organic aesthetics (without the metaphysics). My more immediate model is a form of the imagistic criticism of Shakespeare's plays. Traditionally—though the tradition is quite recent—the imagistic approach to Shakespeare displays the same conflict over reductionism as philosophy in literature in contrast to philosophy abstracted from—philosophy of—literature, best seen in the work of Caroline Spurgeon and Wolfgang Clemen. Both of these fine critics explore the imagery of each of the plays. Spurgeon, however, reduces the whole meaning of the play to its dominant image; Clemen, on the other hand, regards the imagery as but one aspect of each of the dramas, sometimes central, sometimes not, but, in any case, a contributing element to the whole drama, which cannot be reduced to any central element, including the imagery. For him, as for Coleridge (and others), the play's the thing, not the imagery. So, too, for me, the literary work is central, not its philosophical theme or thesis, which may or may not be dominant (or even present) in any particular work.

In a number of essays I have tried—by way of examples, the only way philosophy in literature can vindicate itself—to practice philosophical literary criticism as a branch of literary criticism, not as a part of philosophy. Whether successfully or not, I have tried to show that Voltaire's *Candide*, Shakespeare's *Hamlet* and *King Lear*, Tolstoy's *Anna Karenina*, Proust's *À la recherche du temps perdu* and Eliot's *Four Quartets* contain philosophical themes and theses: how these are brought into these works and what aesthetic difference these make to the works. This enterprise, I hope, justifies philosophy in literature, both in literature and philosophy, without reducing the one to the other and with the one interrelatedly contributing to the other. I have also tried to show, again by example, this time with another of Shakespeare's great tragedies, *Antony and Cleopatra*, that there can be and are great works of literature without philosophical theses. (I am also convinced that there can be and are great literary works, lyrics, for instance, that have no and need have no philosophical themes. Literature without any philosophy is therefore possible and, indeed actual, in spite of certain philosophers' dogma that *all* art, including literature, must be philosophical and true).

Let me now attempt to show how certain literary works not only contain philosophy but a philosophy that in its truth gets at the facts of nature and experience in a way that philosophy proper that deals with the same facts presents falsehoods about them. To reverse Plato's charge, then, I wish to argue that some philosophy can be said to be false in competition with some philosophy in literature that is true.

I begin with that paradigm of both philosophy and literature, tragedy. To say that *X* is a tragedy or that *Y* is tragic is, whatever else it is or comes to include in its reference, an indisputable example of a statement about a literary work and a statement about human life. In any case, there exists a number of dramatic works by Aeschylus, Sophocles and Euripides that are ancient Greek tragedies, and that serve to locate the home base of the concept of tragedy. Now, however these have been analyzed and assessed, from Plato and Aristotle to the present, they are, each of them, indisputable members of the class of tragedy. They are paradigms of the genre of tragedy. But because they are paradigms, they need not be such in virtue of some paradigm set of properties that they all share and must share in order to be legitimate members of the genre. It is this unwarranted assumption, reinforced by Plato's dogma that things called by the same name must have a common defining core, that has, from Aristotle on, given rise to competing theories of tragedy, each of which holds that it and it alone captures the essence of all the paradigms. The assumption implies that if *X* is an indisputable, paradigmatic, home-base example of dramatic tragedy, then *why X* is tragic can also be answered definitively by a paradigmatic property. But the fact is that agreement on paradigm examples of dramatic tragedies has never yielded an agreed-upon set of paradigm properties common to and determining the tragic in these tragedies. Thus, as absurd as, for example, "Is *Oedipus Rex* a tragedy or tragic?" is, "Why is *Oedipus Rex* a tragedy or tragic?" is as alive today as it was to Aristotle. What this suggests is that these ancient Greek tragedies are tragedies even though the tragic in them is variously interpretable and not necessarily some univocal, defining tragic property that guarantees their being tragedies.

Now, however variously interpretable the tragic is in the extant tragedies of Aeschylus, Sophocles, and Euripides one thing is clear and cannot be denied: that these dramas show, say, or imply something about a tragic fact in the world of man's existence. Greek tragedy, whatever else it is, is a metaphysical view about a nondramatic tragic fact in the world which exists independently of its mimetic depiction in the tragedies. Whether this tragic fact is fate, transgression of moral or theological law, human fragility or vulnerability, the celebration of the mystery' of human life, or *areté* shining through *hamartia* and suffering, transcending them; that is, however variously interpretable all of the tragedies are as a group or even severally, they point unmistakenly to an undeniable, irresolvable tragic fact in the world. Aeschylus,

Sophocles, and Euripides make or imply metaphysical statements about the tragic in their dramatic tragedies, even if these statements or the critical commentary about them do not reduce to a univocal claim about what is really tragic. Each of them, all of them, characterize the tragic fact that—whether homogeneous or (as I think) heterogeneous—*is* a fact in the world, undeniable by any putatively true picture or description of the world. The tragic exists as an ultimate, brute, sometimes brutal, ontological fact. Our three dramatists make truth-claims about this tragic fact that, however, disagreement is possible on exactly what it is, cannot be eradicated or rejected.

Now, if we turn from the Greek tragedies to the Greek philosophers, what do we find in regard to this ultimate, irreducible tragic fact? Plato reluctantly recognizes the tragic in the world—suffering, evil, etc., as constituents of the world of appearances or becoming—but argues that it can and must be overcome by reason. Aristotle restricts the tragic to the stage, construing it only as a representation of the passage from happiness to misery, a passage that also reason can overcome. If we agree that the tragic, however variously conceivable it is, is something irredeemable—a brute fact in the world—then surely Greek tragedy proclaims a philosophical truth about the world that Greek philosophy denies. Greek tragedy, thus, is not only a clear case of philosophy in literature, a conception of what is tragic in life as a constituent in the tragedies, but is also, I think, a striking victory of literature over philosophy in the common pursuit of truth about the ways things are.

Aeschylus, Sophocles, and Euripides dramatize the tragic fact that may be understood but cannot be overcome, not even by resignation, acceptance, or reason. Both Plato and Aristotle agree that there is such a tragic fact however they describe it or explain it away, but they deny that it is ultimate and cannot be overcome by the dialectic of human reason. Who is right? It seems to me that, on this issue of the power of reason being strong enough to mitigate, or to overcome, or to transcend the tragic in human life, that Plato and Aristotle speak falsely or naively in a way that our three tragedians speak truly and realistically about the world and man's destiny in it. If there is anything tragic in the world, the Greek literature of tragedy speaks more *philosophical* truth than Greek philosophy. Aristotle, thus, should have said: "Poetry may be more philosophical than history but it is not, at least when it comes to philosophical claims about the universality of the tragic, less true than philosophy, it is more." In this ancient quarrel between philosophy and poetry, the poets win: by honesty, by truth, by knowledge. Greek tragic poetry is philosophically true; Greek philosophy of tragedy is false. Here in Greek tragedy, philosophy in literature integrates and, if only philosophy could learn from it, enhances philosophy as much as it does literature by expanding the range of philosophical truths about the world.

What about Shakespeare, another paradigm of literature and, for many, of philosophy as well? Is there a philosophy or philosophical thesis in Shakespeare's work? Wholesale affirmative as well as negative answers have been equally disastrous. That Shakespeare presents a unified system of ideas about life and the world simply will not stand up to the diversity of ideas in his plays. That Shakespeare has no philosophy, offers no profound claims about man, a view put forth by no less a poet and critic than T. S. Eliot in his contrast of Dante as a poet-thinker with Shakespeare as a dramatist-poet, is also suspect when we turn to some of the individual plays. *Hamlet* and especially *King Lear* dramatize themes and suggest theses that in their profundity are not only philosophical but rival, as the writers of Greek tragedy did their philosophical contemporaries, their naive and pragmatic optimism and pessimism of his age.

We may also ask of Shakespeare, are any of his tragedies without a philosophy, that is, without a thesis about man in his world? *Antony and Cleopatra*, I think, is a great tragedy which contains a number of philosophical themes but no implicit or elicitable philosophical thesis or universal claim. Thus, in the sense that *King Lear* may be convincingly interpreted as a philosophical drama about man's worth in an indifferent universe, or that *Hamlet* may be seen as a drama with its thesis about man's ability to raise all the important questions without his being able to find any of the answers, *Antony and Cleopatra* is not a philosophical drama: it neither makes nor includes any general claim about man and his world. Rather it is a tragedy of two particulars who instance no universal applicable to all.

There are many themes, some philosophical in any traditional sense of philosophical, in the dramas of Shakespeare. None of the plays, not even the tragedies, reduces to these themes; neither do the themes add up to a unified system; nor do the theses, to a unified philosophy. There may be a unifying quality in Shakespeare's work—what Dryden characterizes as the "largest and most comprehensive soul" and Johnson, as "inexhaustible plenty"—but there is no unifying philosophy. Shakespeare is, when he is, a philosophical poet, not a poet with a philosophy. His themes and theses, homogeneous as they may be, are not univocal. In each of the plays, especially the tragedies, there may be themes and theses, most implied by the totality of the elements in the play; but any philosophy in Shakespeare must be distinguished from any philosophy of Shakespeare. In *Hamlet* and *King Lear* the philosophical themes and theses are central or at least are among the controlling elements of these dramas. In *Antony and Cleopatra*, the philosophical theme of generation and corruption, of coming into being and passing away, is as important as anything else in the play. But there is no philosophical thesis, hence, no philosophy in *Antony and Cleopatra*.

The German philosophers are not the only ones to attribute a unified philosophy to Shakespeare. Tillyard and Theodore Spencer, among many others, invest an overall thesis in all the dramas of Shakespeare. Their claim raises the problem of conflicting philosophies in the same literature and just how one is to decide which, if any, is the philosophy in the literature under discussion. Their claim is this: that the doctrine of the universe as a great Chain of Being is the pervasive doctrine in all the plays, such that without knowledge of this doctrine, Shakespeare's philosophy and work are lost to us.

Now, according to this doctrine, first enunciated by Plato in his *Timaeus*, perfection is a kind of cosmic completeness and hierarchical order, which in its completeness includes disorder as a necessary constituent of a larger order.

The "order-disorder synthesis," as it is called, is certainly a dramatic feature in many of Shakespeare's dramas, especially the tragedies, the histories, and maybe in some of the comedies, for example, *The Taming of the Shrew*. But is it and its related doctrine of perfection as completeness pervasive or even present in the whole of Shakespeare? In *Antony and Cleopatra*, Shakespeare dramatizes the theme of perfection but of a kind of perfection that can find no secure place in the platonic universe as cosmic completeness and order. Instead, the play revolves around or at least includes a kind of perfection in love that destroys itself at the very moment of completion.

The world of *Antony and Cleopatra*, vast as it is, encompasses infinite variety but also gaps in nature. The traditional notion of perfection as variety can accommodate the one but not the other, for these gaps are among the inexplicable missing links in any Chain of Being. Both the variety and the gaps, however, are linked to the rhythms of transformation, of one thing becoming another, of perennial generation and corruption. The images of the play especially, whether those of normal, to be expected transformations, or of abnormal, surprising, indeed inverted, transformations, such as an Antony "That grew the more by reaping" (V,ii,88) or a Cleopatra who "makes hungry,/ where most she satisfies" (II,ii,36-38), reinforce the variety. One, but only one, form of this variety of generation and corruption, of the inexhaustible rhythms of nature and experience, is the love of Antony and Cleopatra, confined to them, that generates a ". . . nobleness of life . . . when such a mutual pair/And such a twain can do't" (I,i,36-38). In their relationship, but not in love universal, there is a coming into being (the intensity of fire) of a love (the rarefaction of air) that, though it transcends the baser elements of earth and water, self—destructs in its very perfection. The sustaining implicit image of the play, then, is not that of a Nile that begets fertility then famine, but of a Nile that in its abundance of fertility destroys itself.

One kind of perfection, in a world of many perfections and imperfections, thus, is a love that corrupts itself in its fullness of generated being. In *Antony and Cleopatra* Shakespeare dramatizes this *infima species* of the genus of perfection. He does not reduce this variety or even this perfection to the traditional conception of perfection as (ordered, hierarchical, complete) variety. Indeed, he shows, as he does with many traditional philosophical ideas, how the dramatist as artist may have a truer sense of reality than the philosopher, and in particular, in *Antony and Cleopatra*, that there is a variety of perfections and imperfections but that there can be no resolution of this variety into some fictitious, metaphysical perfection in variety.

Othello shows that Shakespeare is as much interested in the varieties of perfection as he is in the orthodox perfection in variety. Here, too, I think, Shakespeare dramatizes a kind of perfection that, though rooted in the disorder of the traditional order-disorder synthesis and dichotomy, is nevertheless a perfection that is more real than any nebulous perfection of a cosmic order.

The traditional interpretation of *Othello* is that it is essentially the tragedy of a man who is unable to cope with sexual jealousy. On this reading Act III, scene iii is not only the numerical but the dramatic center of the play: the temptation of Othello and the gulling of him by Iago. It is Othello's inability to deal with his jealousy that reveals his *hamartia* which, played upon by Iago, breaks him and, in doing so produces the requisite pity and fear along with Othello's final regeneration and suicide.

Fundamental to this orthodox interpretation and its many variants is the notion of a kind of defect or imperfection in Othello that buttresses the centrality of the third scene of the third act and that gives a unifying direction to the whole play.

But there is another, I think, stronger possibility, suggested by Brabantio's explanation to the Senators of Othello's seduction of Desdemona. It is incredible, Brabantio says, that Desdemona should "fall in love with what she fear'd to look on" (I.iii.98). Othello therefore, must have conjured her.

> It is a judgment maim'd, and most imperfect,
> That will confess perfection so would err
> Against all rules of nature, and must be driven
> To find out practices of cunning hell
> Why this should be.[24]

Here Brabantio refers to Othello's cunning hell in winning his daughter, and he implies that any another explanation is maimed.

What, now, if one understands these lines not as a causal explanation of Othello's successful wooing but as a critical interpretation of the whole play? Then the judgment that Othello is about a "perfection [that] so would err/Against all rules of nature, and must be driven/To find out practices of cunning hell/Why this should be" is far from maimed and imperfect but instead a sound overall reading of Othello as a kind of perfection flawed and destroyed by the cunning hell of Iago, with the Why of it unresolved in Iago's last

> Demand me nothing, what you know, you know,
> From this time forth I never will speak word[25]

as answer to Othello's

> Will you, I pray, demand that demi-devil
> Why he hath thus ensnar'd my soul and body?[26]

I do not know whether Shakespeare intended us to take Brababantio's lines in the way they so stunningly suggest. Nor can I endorse the claim that would find in these lines an unconscious or supersubtle clue to their real meaning. All I insist on is that Brabantio's observation, without his negative assessment, embodies the best interpretation I have yet encountered of the meaning of *Othello*. If it strikes anywhere near the heart of the play, it explodes completely the traditional interpretation. Perfection flawed is hardly compatible with the tragic flaw.

That *Othello* is a tragedy of the flawing of perfection—of a chrysolite as fragile as it is strong and rare, chipped away at until it is smashed—illumines much in the play, the details and of course the vindication of which we must forgo here. Suffice it to say that the data of the play, especially the crucial III, iii, point as much to perfection being flayed and flawed as they do to an inherent fault being painfully mined.

When we turn to Desdemona, however, the evidence points only one way. That she is a perfection in the Elizabethan and in our sense of "flawless" is one of the *données* of the play. Hers is a perfection flayed but not flawed, in this case by Othello's cunning practices on her fidelity. Her consecration of soul (I,iii,254) to Othello remains intact, never wavering, not even at the moment of Othello's strangling of her. As admirable as her unswerving faith in Othello is, what is truly remarkable in her perfection, however, is that it represents to her, as well as to everyone else in the play, and probably to the Elizabethan audience, too, a perfection founded on and sustained by the disorder, hence imperfection, of her downright act of violence in marrying Othello (I,iii,249).

The marriage—the love of Othello and Desdemona—brief as it is, is then another kind of perfection, wholly different from the love and perfection of *Antony and Cleopatra*. The latter generates its own corruption; the former is generated in a violation of traditional perfection as variety—"against all rules of nature"—yet is a perfection that is destroyed not because it is a form of imperfection in any cosmic order of things, but because of Iago's wickedness, festering and fructifying in the very pit of disorder.

In *Othello*, Shakespeare consecrates part of his art—we cannot speak of his soul—to a perfection of a marriage in love that is not inherently flawed, as it must be according to the orthodox order-disorder schema, but is instead a perfection flayed and flawed, destroyed ultimately by the terrible imperfection of Iago. This reversal of a traditionally conceived imperfection of a miscegenated marriage into a kind of perfection that violates all the rules of conventional philosophical conceptions of perfection as ordered, hierarchical being is as remarkable as anything in the play. That Shakespeare, who probably shared with Brabantio and his Elizabethan audience negative views contrary to the positive view he dramatizes of a recognized form of imperfection into the highest kind of perfection, is a supreme instance of the negative capability (that Keats finds so abundantly in him),the irresolution of doubts that extend even to Iago's motives for his demonic malignancy. Great alchemist that he was, he transmutes the dross of orthodox imperfection into the gold of a real perfection of a marriage in love that leaves his critics as baffled as Othello ("Why he hath thus ensnar'd my soul and body?") by Iago's:

Demand me nothing, what you know, you know,
From this time forth I never will speak word.[27]

The creator of *Othello* remains as enigmatic as his creation. But the perfection of an imputed imperfection remains as clear as ever: as one of the great themes in Shakespeare even without any univocal philosophical thesis about the nature of perfection in the world. *Antony and Cleopatra* and *Othello* together and by themselves prove beyond a doubt that there is and can be a philosophy in Shakespeare's dramas that must be elicited from the plays, not imposed upon them by critics who are too knowledgeable about the ideational history of the Elizabethan age and not sufficiently sensitive to the artistry of its leading poet.

Keats says of Shakespeare's plays that, like all great poetry, dramatic or other, they have "negative capability." Keats means by this the capability "of being in uncertainties, mysteries, doubts, without any irritable reaching after fact or reason." The poet, he adds, should not be "incapable of remaining content with half knowledge." Again: "We hate poetry that has a palpable design upon us." We do not want ". . . to be bullied into a certain philosophy."

If to Keats' "negative capability" we add "affirmative or positive capability"—the refusal to remain in uncertainties, mysteries, doubts, the obsession with certainty, being content only with full knowledge then we have a distinction as illuminating as any between philosophy in literature and philosophy in philosophy plain or proper. Literature, in seeking philosophical truth about the world and the range of human experience in it, is the depiction of the ultimately irreducible complexity or multivalence of experience, a complexity which cannot yield any simple formula. Philosophy proper, on the other hand, seeks a truth that reduces these complexities to universal formulas and which thereby attains a knowledge relieved of doubts.

Now, if it is true, as I think it is, that much, perhaps most human experience—the appetitive, the emotional, the intellectual, and especially the moral—does not reduce to simple formulas, then that range of discourse which embodies this claim is true to experience in a way in which that range of discourse which attests after certainty and simple, univocal answers is false. If literature, or at least most of it, exemplifies the first kind of discourse and philosophy the second, then literature is a truer philosophy than philosophy proper. Keats is profoundly right: it is negative, not positive capability that reflects human experience, its inexhaustible, irreducible range. Literature is philosophically true in its implication of negative capability; philosophy proper is philosophically false in its affirmation of positive capability. Once more, literature can be understood as the victor in its perennial competition with philosophy to depict correctly the nature of human experience.

This is not to imply, however, that all literature realizes Keats' negative capability or what he calls in another letter "making all disagreebles evaporate, from their being in close relationship with Beauty and Truth." Much of literature is, when it contains philosophical themes or a philosophical thesis, as direct a statement about the essences of things as is traditional philosophy. Any good novel, such as Camus's masterpiece *L'Etranger* with its devastating Cartesian nihilism as the fundamental theorem of human experience and destiny, would be truly absurd without its affirmative capability. Literature with or without negative capability, then, is still literature: the question is not whether it is, but which has the better claim to knowledge into the way things actually are? Thus, Keats' notion and my generalized contrast cannot state by themselves a definitive criterion for distinguishing literature and philosophy. Negative (or negative as against positive) capability serves (1) to remind us of the kind of true, philosophical knowledge that some literature (but no traditional philosophy) offers; and (2) to suggest that certain general truths—namely, that there may not be these universals in vast areas of human experience—can better be learned from literature. This may be the lesson Proust's narrator learns in his quest for the creation of a philosophical novel in which the search for the essences, stated in the last volume, leads only to the dissolution of essences, narrated and dramatized in all the previous volumes, from *Du côté de chez Swann* to *Le temps retrouvé*. Or it may be the lesson taught, if only we listen, by Michel's story in Gide's *L'Immoraliste*: that, though there may be univocal answers of the typical traditional ethical kind to moral questions regarding the extreme cases (for example, of a life with the body denied or the mind and will suppressed), the univocality of the moral as against the immoral evaporates in the disagreeables of those middle cases of human life in which our moral choices affect others, such as Marceline, Michel's wife. Gide's bitter fruit of a novel that quenches no one's thirst ends as it starts, except that the title grows a question mark which though invisible is there for all who would seek to see. His novel remains a great challenge to traditional philosophical morals and ethics and their fundamental conviction that all questions about right and wrong, of what is moral as against immoral, have and must have definitive answers. Gide dramatizes the dubiety of this traditional conviction. He does not proclaim it false, he shows that it is naive and facile; and he implies that it is itself wrong: life is simply not that simple. His philosophy of morality—a philosophy of negative, not positive, capability and, in any case, a philosophy in the novel, to be related to all the other elements, including the geographical split between the north and the south of Europe, so important to Michel's physical and spiritual travels in looking for but never finding himself, not a philosophy to be abstracted from the novel, Gide's other novels or his journals—may not satisfy moralists and philosophers, ever questing for certainty. But it does satisfy those who are more concerned with truth than they are with unequivocal answers to basic moral problems.

One final example: In his *The Hedgehog and the Fox: An Essay on Tolstoy's View of History*, Sir Isaiah Berlin reminds us of the parable of the fox who knows many things and of the hedgehog who knows one big thing, and goes on to distinguish between the seeker of multiplicity and the seeker of underlying unity, a division that, on the fox side, parallels Keats' negative capability and which Berlin applies to writers and thinkers. Tolstoy, he says, is the supreme fox in his novels, and a supreme hedgehog in his beliefs.

> Tolstoy perceived reality in its multiplicity, as a collection of separate entities round and into which he saw with a clarity and penetration scarcely ever equalled, but he believed only in one vast, unitary whole. No author who has ever lived has shown such powers of insight into the variety of life . . . No one has ever excelled Tolstoy in expressing the specific flavour, the exact quality of a feeling . . . the inner and outer texture and 'feel' of a look, a thought, a pang of sentiment, no less than that of the specific pattern of a situation, of an entire period, of the lives of individuals, families, communities, entire nations. The celebrated life-likeness of every object and every person in his world derives from this astonishing capacity of presenting every ingredient of it in its fullest individual essence, in all its many dimensions, as it were . . . an event fully present to the senses or the imagination in all its facets, with every nuance sharply and firmly articulated.

> Yet what he believed in was the opposite. He advocated a single embracing vision; he preached not variety but simplicity, not many levels of consciousness but reduction to some single level—in *War and Peace*, to the standard of the good man, the single, spontaneous, open soul . . . .[28]

As magnificent as Berlin's assessment of Tolstoy's achievement as a novelist is—the full quotation reveals a texture as rich as Tolstoy's—and as accurate as the overall conflict he finds in Tolstoy the novelist and Tolstoy the thinker or essayist may be, I think he has missed Tolstoy's union of the hedgehog and the fox in at least *Anna Karenina*, Tolstoy's supreme achievement and perhaps the European novel's supreme achievement. For while it is true that the dominant tone of *Anna* is that largess that Berlin so beautifully details, a largess that celebrates the abundance of nature and life, covering a variety of human experiences from eating and dancing to marrying and having children, it is not outside the novel that Tolstoy seeks the unity underlying this largess, but in the novel and, in particular, I think, in the implicit significance of the two most important, if not absolutely central, events in the plot of the novel, the suicide of Anna and the conversion of Levin. What ties these events together—if they are not tied, the novel fails as an organic whole, with everything left dangling after Anna's suicide—must be itself tied to the principle underwriting the largess. I believe it has something to do with the principle of creativity or fertility in nature, that some call God, but that Levin recognizes in the secularly sacred, through Fyodor, the peasant, and that Anna aborts in her refusal to give Vronsky more children and a legitimate family. I am hesitant about how best to state this principle without doing violence to Tolstoy's insight; but I am convinced that in *Anna Karenina* Tolstoy joins the hedgehog with the fox, just as he joins a particular philosophical thesis about the principle of the good with the multiplicities of goods that there are in the world and which he presents and lingers over in his great work. Nature, of course, cannot mate the hedgehog and the fox; perhaps neither can most of us, including most artists and thinkers. But Tolstoy as artist-thinker does mate them in *Anna*. His genius transcends both nature and God, as it partakes of the very principle of creativity that unites the multiplicity of the good in *Anna*. It also enables him to offer the strongest example of a literature and a philosophy in literature in which his richly endowed negative capability both accommodates his richly stringent positive capability and is itself its finest product.

In this essay I have hardly scratched the surface of the various possibilities of philosophy in literature. Much remains to be done on many works of literature that almost cry out for an account of them that includes the philosophical themes and theses which enrich the totality of these individual works without at the same time reducing the work to a philosophical nugget to be extracted from the work and exploited as an exmple of some philosophical problem. As I hope my examples show, a literary criticism that elucidates the philosophy in the literary works that contain it as an integral, aesthetically contributing part of them is as legitimate and self—justifying as any branch of literary criticism, so long as the whole of the literary work is kept in focus. Without engaging in futile discussion about what criticism is, or what philosophy or literature is, so that these crucial concepts are rendered precise and even definable, we begin with the paradigms. We know that there are works of literature, philosophical writings, and essays in literary criticism. No true definition of literature, philosophy, or criticism is needed or even possible. Nor would such definitions serve as criteria for distinguishing the clear, indisputable cases from the marginal ones. That myth, that these concepts—indeed, that all concepts—rest on clear, precise definitions of them, the Plato-Frege myth we may call it, is not, as western thought has assumed, an overall necessary condition for intelligible discourse, and certainly not for the discourse of literature, philosophy and criticism. The late work of Wittgenstein explodes this myth forever.

But Wittgenstein, in both his early work and his late work—in the *Tractatus Logico-Philosophicus* and *Philosophical Investigations*, challenges as radically as anyone has ever done the very possibility of the union of literature and philosophy, especially as I have been promoting it. For one of the assumptions of the legitimacy of philosophy in literature is that both philosophy and literature, whatever else they are, are fundamentally engaged in the making of truth-claims about the world. Both, that is, are capable of embodying and proclaiming ideas or doctrines, whether ontological, anti-ontological moral, psychological or, as Sidney puts it, "what else" about the world. Both, but especially philosophy, purport to be true doctrine or systems about how things actually are. That philosophy is the search for doctrinal truths about the world, however philosophers differ on what these truths are, is a proposition shared by every philosopher in the tradition from Plato to early Wittgenstein.

In the *Tractatus*, Wittgenstein claims, although in avowed violation of his strictures on what can be said or shown, that philosophy, unlike science, is not a series or system or truth-claims about anything. Rather, it is an activity, not a theory or doctrine of anything (*Tractatus* 4.112). Whatever the changes, whether radical, as I believe they are, or continuous, as some commentators contend, Wittgenstein never wavers on this fundamental point, reiterating it, again as central, in the *Investigations* (paragraph 109).

As activity, not as doctrine making, Wittgenstein changes his mind on what this activity is but not on philosophy as an activity, that is, as neither ontological nor anti-ontological, neither common sense, nor science.

That traditional philosophy is nonsense also remains intact from the *Tractatus* to the *Investigations*. In the *Tractatus*, nonsense is either trying to say what can only be shown (*sinnlos*) or trying to say what cannot be said, because it violates the syntax of the one language of science or because it has no syntax at all (*unsinnig*). In the *Investigations*, nonsense is misconstruing grammatical remarks for ontology or anti-ontology or it is the violating of the logical grammar of concepts.

In both works philosophy functions therapeutically, to expose the nonsense that results when we transgress the limits of language. One, but only one of these bits of nonsense would be the attempt to impose on literature a philosophy or to pursue what I have been calling philosophy in literature: to find true or false statements in a use of language that at least so far as its philosophical aspects are concerned is vacuous nonsense. That there is no such thing as philosophy in literature is no true or false doctrine either; rather it serves as a reminder of the inability of philosphy to function in a doctrinal capacity and as a further remindder of the function of sentences in literature. It is therefore, on Wittgenstein's view, philosophy in literature that is nonsense, not literature.

So devastating and radical is Wittgenstein's conception of the nonsense of traditional philosophy, it is no wonder that he has critics as avid in their objections as he has followers who proclaim his the greatest revolution in the history of philosophy. Revolutionary or not, nihilistic or not, Wittgenstein offers the most powerful indictment ever against traditional philosophy and its history. But he also offers philosophy a choice it has not had before: either to recognize and accept what he says about the inadequacy of traditional philosophy as true-false doctrine or to continue producing more nonsense. The choice is this, then: doing philosophy his way or else doing it another way; if he is right, there is no other way!

In discussions of contemporary painting, art historians and critics distinguish between traditional representational art, formalism, and abstractionism. The distinction parallels that of philosophy as traditional ontology, logical atomism of the sort that Russell formulated in his middle period of 1914-1918, in which both language and facts are logically reduced to their ultimate corresponding, isomorphic logical forms, and Wittgenstein's further restriction of philosophy to logical syntax (in the *Tractatus*) and logical grammar (in the *Investigations*), with no regard, in either case, for the correspondence of language to fact or for the nature of the facts themselves, which inquiry properly belongs to the sciences anyway. Philosophy's sole concern is with language: in the *Tractatus*, with the syntactical rules that determine and govern the formation and functioning of the (only) language of science: and in the *Investigations*, with the rules, syntactical and semantical, exact or inexact, that govern but do not determine the formation and the functioning of any language that is operative rather than idling.

Abstractionism also contends that traditional representational painting is, as painting, plastic or pictorial forms that may not include representations, neither the harmful nor the harmless, to be dissolved into their plastic or pictorial equivalents, as the Formalists allowed, but is pure nonrepresentational forms, which constitute the essence of painting in its purest, undefiled state. The essence of painting is the purely plastic or pictorial: lines, colors, textures, shapes, designs, etc. It is this that is proprietary to painting, that gives it its uniqueness among the arts; and it is this that makes abstract painting autonomous, that is, independent of all else, including the heteronomous mimetic connections with the world. The autonomy of painting, like that of music, consists in this rejection of all the heteronomous elements that tie painting to the world. And because it accepts the abstract in good traditional or formal painting, Abstractionism is not a subtraction from painting, rather an art stripped of all its unessentials and irrelevancies.

Now if by the autonomy of painting we mean, as we should, not the doctrine that art exists for its own sake, but rather that it exists independently of the world and is not a replication of it, however realistic or ideal, then perhaps we may say of Wittgenstein's exclusive concern with logical syntax or logical grammar that he, too, is an abstractionist in philosophy, practicing an activity that is also purely autonomous, again not in the sense of doing it for its own sake, but in the sense of doing it independently of the heteronomous promotion of true-false doictrine about the world, or even in the semiheteronomous search for the logical forms of language and fact. Like the Abstractionist, Wittgenstein centers on what is proprietary to philosophy, its logical syntax or logical grammar that parallels the plastic or pictorial forms sought by the Abstractionist.

Where he differs from his Abstractionist counterpart is in his denial that the proprietary is the essence and that this essence, without the encumbrances, is what makes traditional philosophy or formal analysis philosophical. There are no essences or, better, we need not assume that there are essences in order to explain the intelligibility of discourse and thought about the world; and it is certainly not true that traditional philosophy and formal analysis are ultimately logical syntax or logical grammar. What they are are conflations of bad logical syntax or grammar with ontology: clouds " . . . of philosophy condensed into a drop of grammar," (*Investigations*. Part II, xi, p.222e).

Further, although Wittgenstein does not, like Abstractionists, sever the semantic or mimetic connection with the world, since for him language reaches out to the world in the *Tractatus* and is in the world in the *Investigations*, he does sever the connection between philosophy and putative doctrine about the world. So his emphasis, like that of the Abstractionist, is on the syntax rather than the semantics of his discipline, where in each case the painting or the philosophy exists autonomously, independently of their heteronomous uses, whether for bad, as in representational painting, or for good, as in science.

Quite independently of the parallel I have drawn (whether accurate and illuminating, especially for those outside of philosophy, in the arts, and whatever the ultimate convincingness of Abstractionism as a theory of true painting), at least the beauty of Wittgenstein, especially as it applies to our problem of the relation of literature and philosophy, is in his pristine rejection of any such subject as Philosophy in Literature: not, as Richards has it, because of the exclusive use of emotive language in literature, but because of the nondoctrinal character of philosophy. The vulnerability and arbitrarily legislative character of Abstractionism in art vanishes in the striking, shocking truth of Wittgenstein's devastating attack on the traditional conception of philosophy. This, accompanied by his equally striking substitution of logical syntax, then logical grammar, for philosophy, reduces our concern throughout for a proper, fruitful joining of literature and philosophy to but one more piece of traditional nonsense that requires treatment, not further futile effort.

What, now, of literature? Without asking what its essence is—in any case a question as futile as it is fatuous—but instead beginning with some of the paradigms, of which there are plenty, we ask what, if anything, is proprietary to literature? Or is it, too, autonomous, independent of its heteronomous, mimetic connections with the world? That literature is the unique use of sentences to create a world—a heterocosm—not to imitate the one we have, that it consists of sentences alone or of a self-referring use of language, in which the syntax of literature, not its semantics, is all-important, is certainly a possible view and indeed one argued before with much force from neoplatonist aestheticians to A. C. Bradley in the history and theory of literary criticism. But, as we have seen, this view is after all only one option, certainly not the dire implicative conclusion of Wittgenstein that, since philosophy is logical syntax or logical grammar, there cannot be anything like philosophy in literature, unless it is itself logical syntax or logical grammar or nonsense. If Wittgenstein is right that acceptable philosophy is elucidation of those concepts that traditional philosophy has nonsensically misconstrued, we have no other option than his of repudiating Philosophy in Literature. There is nothing so stringent in literature: for with literature, there is the other option, again as we have seen, of construing the sentences of literature, or at least some of them, as statements, as truth—claims about the world and

133

therefore as heteronomous, with nothing proprietary to it. That literature is in the world and about the world is as valid as that though it is in the world, it need not be about the world. Instead, literature is the creation of possible worlds: pieces of fiction, not pieces of truth in fiction.

As attractive as the first option may be—of literature as autonomous, in which the mimetic ingredients are to be rendered nonmimetic, as aspects of presentational structures rather than as representational structures, as the creation of worlds that satisfy the imagination and that may even invite new possibilities for future human actions, the latter fortuitous, not indigenously heteronomous, because this option is just that, and not a conclusion drawn from true premises against statements in literature—this option vies with the more orthodox option that literature, of all the arts, is mimetic. In the end, then, that literature contains certain sentences which sometimes are read as statements—whether as attractive as its rivals—is the option that is the more conventional and natural, and to be rejected only by a recommendation to convert literature, which does not function as an abstract art, to abstract art, as some convert the painting in all painting to abstract art, and both to the abstract art of music. Nevertheless, stringent and truncated as it is, the autonomy option—it cannot be or be regarded as a thesis about literature as literature—is as possible as it is plausible and attractive. And, once accepted or chosen, it gives us the final answer to our question about the proper relation between literature and philosophy; that there is none. How could there be, since both are complete strangers to each other, inhabiting entirely different worlds?

So, how shall we decide between these two options? If literature is taken to be autonomous and if philosophy is autonomous and *cannot* be taken as anything else, provided Wittgenstein is right; and if literature is proprietarily the creation of nonmimetic, fictional worlds, made up out of sentences alone and philosophy is proprietarily the formulation of the logical syntax of the language of science or the elucidation of the logical grammar of the conceptual life, then there is literature and there is philosophy but neither contains truth-claims about the world and us in it. If, on the other hand, philosophy is autonomous and literature is not, or not taken to be, then literature but not philosophy contains statements, including truth-claims about the world. But these truth-claims cannot be philosophical. What, then, are they? Only statements about matters of fact, some particular, some general. Literature, on this heteronomous view, can be said to be close to history and perhaps to science although, when one thinks about science, full of theories, models, hypotheses, laws, but very little on matters of fact except as reports on relevant confirming or disconfirming data, already invested with theory, literature being like science seems very remote indeed. So we are left with literature being close to history and those sciences that emphasize reporting on matters of fact: sciences or, some say, pseudosciences such as sociology or psychology. In any case, this comparison of literature to disciplines that concentrate on matters of fact rather than on matters of science or philosophy is likely to please no one, not even Aristotle, who complimented literature as being more philosophical than history.

My subject, Philosophy in Literature, and my above vindication of it, is viable, then, only within the classical conception of philosophy as true-false doctrine and system about the world, a conception that Wittgenstein shows is nonsensical and which verdict I accept, since I agree with him in his resolution of philosophy into logical grammar, done either badly, as in the tradition, or well, as in the *Investigations*. Nevertheless, if classical philosophy—ontology and the rest—is misguided, disguised logical grammar, poorly practiced, there remains one reminder that may yet salvage our battered subject of Philosophy in Literature, and that is to return to the original sense of philosophy as the love of wisdom. Construed as philosophy, as ontology, formal analysis, logical syntax, or logical grammar, wisdom is also nonsense. But wisdom is none of these. I do not know what it is; again we must fall back on the paradigms, not a buttressing definition that states its essence as true doctrine. I know wisdom is not philosophy as ontology, logical grammar, etc.; I also know it is not science or history or sociology or psychology or matters of fact. I am also convinced that, though not true-false doctrine, wisdom is close to knowledge, without at the same time being a form of or identical with knowledge. It is what it always was, and it will not go away; some philosophers had it: perhaps even some scientists or lesser beings who are more than prudent, sagacius, sensible. But artists, especially writers of literature, have it: it may even be what is proprietary to literature. And it may still be characterized as nonsense (*sinnlos*) in trying to show what cannot even be said, but it is not nonsense (*unsinnig*) as violation of logical syntax or logical grammar. Wisdom and wisdom in literature is the kind of nonsense we can live with, and since nothing else has it, it is the kind of nonsense we need if we are to be more than philosophers, scientists, historians, or surviving masters of matters of fact. Philosophy in literature, then, is the presentation of wisdom, to be provided only by literature. If I have been able to show that and how some literature contains wisdom—which is all that is left of *philo sophia* (even though construed as philosophy, it is nonsense)—I am satisfied. Who can ask for anything more?

Chapter Nine

GENRE AND STYLE

Genre and style are basic concepts in traditional aesthetics. Particular genre concepts, such as tragedy, have been of philosophical concern at least since Aristotle and are as vigorously discussed today by aestheticians and literary critics as ever they were in the past. Particular style concepts, such as Gothic, High Renaissance, or Baroque, are of relatively recent concern—although there are seminal intimations of them as far back as Vitruvius. Unfortunately they have been of primary interest not to philosophers but to art historians.

Much has been written on the history of genre concepts; the history of style concepts has hardly been started. In twentieth—century discussions of the arts, genre is still the central concern of aesthetics and literary criticism. At the same time however, style has become the most important concept of art history.

More striking than this contemporary division is that, historically, style seems to play a minor role in literary criticism, and that genre, except in the special sense of a kind of secular painting, plays an even smaller role in art history. For example, it is a surprising discovery that although there are great critical essays on the characters, plot, philosophy, poetry, symbolism, and imagery of Shakespeare's dramas, there is no comparable work on Shakespeare's style.[1] Obviously, other concepts, which may or may not be equivalent to certain uses of style in literature, have been found to be more efficacious and illuminating than style in the analyses of Shakespeare's dramas. And we can accept, it seems to me, the major corpus of the criticism of those plays, now annotated by ten generations of critics, as a paradigm of literary criticism. If we substitute for Shakespeare's plays the paintings of Leonardo or Raphael, or Rembrandt or Rubens, we can hardly mention a major critical or historical study that does not focus on the style of these artists. In literary criticism, the concept of style seems to be dispensable in a way that it is not in art history. But genre is not dispensable to the literary critic. There is scarcely a book on the tragedies of Shakespeare that does not contain a first or last chapter on the nature of tragedy, a chapter included as an indispensable part of the discussion and judgment. This recurring concern with genre plays no role in art history. There are no first or last chapters on the nature of portraiture, landscape, religious painting, or the nude, when the historian of art tells his particular story. Indeed, when we read Kenneth Clark on *Landscape into Art* or *The Nude*, or Max Friedländer on *Landscape, Portrait, Still-Life*, we realize how ludicrous it would be for these historians to begin, end, or intrude with a definition of these genres, so obvious are they to all.

Whatever the vagaries of the history of genre and style concepts have been, one assumption about these concepts remains invariant: that they are definable in the Aristotelian sense of real definition, i.e., that necessary and sufficient criteria can be stated for their correct use, and that without such definitions, particular genre and style concepts cannot sustain their assigned roles. Many philosophers, literary critics, and art historians concur in this doctrine that there are such definitions and, consequently, they direct much effort to formulating theories of genre in literary criticism, and of style in art history.

In previous writings I have shown that the traditional assumption, shared by aestheticians and literary critics, that all genre concepts are or must be definable in order to render critical discussion and judgment intelligible, is false. For example, the concept of tragedy, examined in its actual role in literary criticism, exhibits itself as an open concept rather than, as it has been traditionally assumed, a closed concept. That the concept of tragedy is open in the precise sense of having no undebatable necessary criteria can be seen in the range of disagreement over the nature of the tragic in general, and over why or whether a particular work is tragic. The tragedy-giving reason—that is, reasons given as answers to, What is tragedy?, Why is X tragic?, or Is X tragic?—provide the clue to the perennial debatability of the concept and its openness in that sense.

In an early paper, "The Role of Theory in Aesthetics,"[2] I argued that a number of genre concepts are open, in contrast to the traditional assumption that they are all closed, i.e., governed by definitive sets of criteria. Thus, I claimed that "novel," "drama," "satire," "tragedy," and "art" itself are open. But considering all these together conflated two very different kinds of concepts, neither of which is governed by sets of necessary and sufficient criteria: those which have no undebatable necessary criteria and those which have some undebatable criteria even though they are neither necessary nor sufficient. "Drama," "novel," and "art"—as their uses reveal—have certain criteria that are neither necessary nor sufficient, yet are undebatable, in a way in which "tragedy" does not. For example, "*X* is a drama because it has plot" cannot be challenged in the way that "*X* is a tragedy because it has *hamartia*" can. "Plot" is neither necessary nor sufficient for something to be a drama, but neither can it be intelligibly challenged, as "*hamartia*" or any other criterion of "tragedy" can.

Thus I prefer to say that some genre concepts in aesthetics are open in the sense that they have no necessary or sufficient criteria but do have some unchallengeable ones; and that some are open in the sense that they have no necessary or sufficient criteria and no unchallengeable ones. Misled by Waismann's notion of open texture, I erred in thinking, as he did, that the perennial flexibility of concept entails its perennial debatability. It does not, as the logic of the concept of drama itself shows.

What, now, about style? Are there definitive sets of criteria for the concept of style or for every particular style concept? This is a question I should like to consider here. Instead of beginning with philosophical theories of style, which I find surprisingly unhelpful, I propose to contrast what art historians say about style with how they use particular style concepts when they write art history. Although some philosophers pay lip service to the need for detailed examination of style concepts, it has not yet been heeded, in spite of the fact that such elucidation is basic in any attempt to determine the nature of style and style concepts.

I shall discuss, in particular, the views of Meyer Schapiro, James Ackerman, Arnold Hauser, and E. H. Gombrich—all art historians—on the nature of style in art history, and then test their claims in relation to the style concept of Mannerism, especially as it has been explored and developed by Walter Friedlaender, Max Dvorak, Craig Smyth, John Shearman, and Sydney Freedberg, all leading art historians of Mannerism and the *maniera*.

I

Meyer Schapiro's "Style" is a deservedly acclaimed classic on the nature of style in art history.[3] Its prime achievement, however, is its compendious and brilliant survey of the major theories of style from Wölfflin to the present day. Schapiro's classification of these theories into cyclical, polar, evolutionary, psychological, and sociological is of singular importance in any philosophical attempt to understand the concept of style in art history. Of special value are his incisive criticisms of the presuppositions and doctrines of Heinrich Wölfflin, Alois Reigl, Paul Frankl, and others. Without making it explicit, he makes us see that theories of style in art history have conflated two distinct problems: What is a particular or period style in art?, and, How does it arise, mature, and change into a different style? As he abundantly reveals, most theorists are concerned with the second—the causal—question, rather than with the first—the substantive—question; much of Schapiro's critique centers on the deficiencies of the causal theories, especially their implicit determinism, which he rightly attributes to the influence of Hegel.

So far as the substantive question is concerned, Schapiro reminds us of the paucity of explicit definitions of style in art history. Instead of laying down definitive sets of criteria, art historians have applied those criteria that they have found to be "the broadest, most stable, and therefore most reliable"[4] for their purposes of dating and authenticating works of art and narrating a coherent history of art. These criteria—which, Schapiro says are insufficient but which he implies are at least necessary in the art historian's use of style concepts—are "form elements or motives, form relationships, and qualities (including an all-over quality which we may call the 'expression').[5]

Other criteria, advanced by certain theorists, such as technique, subject matter, and material, Schapiro concedes to be important, especially when they are interpreted in formal terms, i.e., as form elements and relations; but he denies that they are necessary features of the concept of style in art history.

Unfortunately, Schapiro does not enlarge upon these formal and expressive criteria, but only because of the encyclopaedic intent of his essay. Nevertheless, the terms are clear enough, both in the tradition of aesthetics and in his own use. For unlike, say, Wölfflin's criterion of *malerisch*, Schapiro's criterion of form element, which he clarifies by means of the example of the pointed as against the round arch, or his criterion of expressive quality which, again, he clarifies by means of the example of the cool or warm tertiary qualities of certain colors, are at least semantically unobjectionable as criteria of style in art.

What is most important and provocative in his essay, I think, and what we must later relate to the practice of art history, is Schapiro's own specific view of the concept of style. "By style [he writes], is meant the constant form—and sometimes the constant elements, qualities, and expression—in the art of an individual or a group."[6] Does his claim about the constancy of certain properties as basic to style or a particular style correspond to, for example, the actual use of the concept of Mannerism, as that concept is employed by the art historians of Mannerism? I hope to show that testing this claim brings to light the fundamental weakness of Schapiro's elucidation of the concept of style.

James Ackerman means, by a theory of style, a definition of style and an explanation why style changes.[7] For him both are essential to art history. Style for the art historian is not a discovered concept but one created by abstraction from the ensemble of characteristics of works of art found in a particular span of time and place; this concept he then employs as a tool for dating individual works of art and, more important, as a pattern to provide a structure of stability and flexibility in the history of art.

Works of art have many characteristics; consequently, from among them the art historian must choose those that best satisfy the criteria of stability and flexibility in order to establish an historical order out of the continuum of self-sufficient works of art. On this basis, Ackerman rules out the characteristic of materials (e.g., wood or stone), because it is not sufficiently changeable; he rules out as well the characteristic of unique expressiveness, because it is too ephemeral. These are symptoms, not determinants of style. Rather than these characteristics, or even techniques, which are important to style only when they enhance formal or symbolic elements, Ackerman chooses conventions of form and symbolism because they "yield the richest harvest of traits by which to distinguish style."[8] Conventions include "an accepted vocabulary of elements—a scale of color, an architectural Order, an attribute of a God or a saint and a syntax by which these elements are composed into a still-life, a temple, or a frieze."[9] The assigned meanings of these conventions define the element of symbolism in style.

In explaining why styles change, Ackerman, like Schapiro and others, rejects the traditional determinist theory that style and changes in style follow a preordained pattern of evolution. In place of the notion of stylistic evolution as a succession of steps toward a solution of a given problem, Ackerman argues—and this, I think, is his most original and radical thesis—that we must explain this evolution "as a succession of steps away from one or more original statements of a problem."[10] The history of style is not a series of solutions of problems but "a succession of complex decisions as numerous as the works by which we have defined the style."[11]

This emphasis upon the history of style (and hence, of art) as a series of statements away from an original statement rather than as a sequence of attempted solutions culminating in an ideal statement enables Ackerman to lay down his criteria for the cogency of particular style concepts. Any particular style concept is formed on the assumption that a particular ensemble of conventions and symbolism is sufficiently stable, distinct, and relevant to justify hypothesizing it as a style. Each ensemble represents a class of related solutions to a problem which differs from distinguishable previous or later problems. Because of the limited, restrictive nature of a problem in art, the more modest the extension of a particular style concept, the more rewarding it is for study. There is no such defining problem in the Renaissance or Baroque; hence these are too grand for style analysis. Mannerism, on the other hand, is a limited style, with an ensemble of conventional and symbolic characteristics, embodied in a clearly distinguishable series of statements away from the original statement of a problem.

Ackerman's article raises many issues, all of which merit scrutiny, but I must confine myself to the one issue that relates most immediately to our problem of theory and practice in art history: Is Ackerman's theory of style consonant with the use of the concept of Mannerism by the art historians of that style? Does "Mannerism" serve to mark out, in a challenging, hypothetical way, an ensemble of conventions and symbolism or a series of related solutions to a clearly statable problem? Here, too, as with Schapiro, I shall try to show that Ackerman overstates his case.

Arnold Hauser writes on the nature of style and changes in style in two books, *The Philosophy of Art History* and *Mannerism: The Crisis of the*

Renaissance and the Origin of Modern Art.[12]   Both are vigorous defenses of the sociological conception of art which, in his modified Marxist version, explains art as an expression, rather than crude reflection, of certain specified economic and social conditions.   On his view, Mannerism, for example, is best understood "as an expression of the unrest, anxiety, and bewilderment generated by the process of alienation of the individual from society and the reification of the whole cultural process."[13]

Styles are sociologically conditioned. But to explain them—to do art history—is to understand style itself, without which there can be no history of art. Consequently, much of Hauser's philosophy of art history deals with the substantive question, What is style? In a remarkably eclectic and sometimes penetrating analysis of about 150 pages, in which style is compared to institutions, Gestalts, language, musical themes, and ideal types—and is contrasted with entelechies, organic wholes, predetermined goals, and platonic ideas—Hauser finally settles on his doctrine of style as "a dynamic relational concept with continually varying content, so that it might almost be said to take on a new sense with each new work."[14]

In his book on Mannerism, Hauser so beautifully articulates the meaning and the implications of this doctrine that I cannot forego quoting his full statement:

> It can rightly be complained that there is no such thing as a clear and exhaustive definition of mannerism, but the same complaint can be made of every, other style, for there is and can be no such thing. There is always a centrifugal tendency in the nature of any style, which influences a variety of not strictly adjustable phenomena. Every style manifests itself in varying degrees of clarity in different works, few, if any, of which completely fulfil the stylistic ideal. But the very circumstance that the pattern can be detected only in varying degrees of approximation in individual works makes stylistic concepts essential, because without them there would be no associating of different works with each other, nor should we have any criterion by which to assess their significance in the history of development, which is by no means the same thing as their artistic quality. The historical importance of a work of art lies in its relationship to the stylistic ideal it seems to be stridng to achieve, and that provides the standard by which its original or derivative, progressive or retrograde, nature can be judged. Style has no existence other than in the various degrees of approximation towards its realisation. All that exist in fact are individual works of art, different artistic phenomena differing in purpose. Style is always a figment, an image, an ideal type.[15]

As I understand this statement, Hauser's central thesis is that the concept of style or any particular style concept is and must be governed by a set of definitive criteria which guarantees its use in the historical ordering of artistic facts. With this as his fundamental premise, he then argues that because these criteria—as a complete set—obtain in no one work of art and yet are essential to art history, they must constitute a fictional ideal. His theory of style as a necessary ideal fiction rests upon his presupposition that style concepts, as they are employed in art history, are logically closed. He shares this doctrine with all the traditional theorists whom he rejects; it is the most vulnerable, I think, when it is contrasted with the actual procedures of style-giving reasons in art history. Do the historians of Mannerism, for example, talk about its particularity and unity without assuming or needing to assume any set of definitive criteria, ideal or not? Here, again, the contrast between what the art historian says about style and how he uses it becomes glaring.

Our fourth example, E. H. Gombrich, has been much concerned with the many aspects of what he calls "the riddle of style." Among his writings, the two essays "Norm and Form: the stylistic categories of art history and their origins in Renaissance ideals" and "Mannerism: the historiographic background" are most pertinent here.[16]

In "Norm and Form" Gombrich's central theme is the derivation of all traditional style terms from an acceptance or rejection of the Classic. The origins of the concepts of the Romanesque, Gothic, Manneristic, Baroque, Rococo, and Romantic (all initially terms of abuse) as well as the origins of the concepts of the Classic, Renaissance, and Neo-classic are normative, not descriptive. From Vasari's castigation of the Gothic or German manner of "Confusion and Disorder" which he bases on Vitruvius' similar denunciation of certain wall decorations of his day, Gombrich contends, traditional concepts of style and particular style concepts in art history blend norm and form, evaluation with description. Every attempt to dissociate these norms from their forms fails, and is bound to fail, because these styles cannot be described without normative criteria. Even Wölfflin's five sets of polarities—linear and painterly, plane and depth, closed and open form, multiplicity and unity, and clarity and obscurity—which Wölfflin claims are descriptive, and which Gombrich reduces to certain principles of composition and representation—function in his art history as normative: i.e., as the classical versus the less than classical.

Traditional style terms are inevitably normative. But, Gombrich suggests, their norms, although historically rooted in the great classic reconciliation of ordered composition and faithful representation, need not be divided neatly into classical and anticlassical. The latter, articulated by the exponents of classicism, tend to be vices or sins to be avoided, and hence function according to "the principle of exclusion." But there are movements or styles in the history of art which do not reject the values they oppose, as anticlassical styles do; rather they recognize the multiplicity of artistic values and choose priorities among them. Such styles, Gombrich says, function according to "the principle of sacrifice." Even though it is difficult to draw a line between these styles, which Gombrich calls "unclassical," and the anticlassical, or between these two and the classical, it can be done by determining which of the two principles is operative. Mannerism has been described as an anti-classical style. But, Gombrich asks, Is it so clear that Mannerism aimed at an avoidance of order and harmony rather than at a shift in priorities?

Gombrich poses this question in his essay on "Mannerism." Here, he argues, as he had in his *Story of Art*, that Mannerism is fundamentally a style of experimentation, of virtuosity, of attempts to outdo one's immediate masters in invention and caprice. It has nothing to do with spiritual or personal crises occasioned, as some historians claim, by social or religious dislocation.

That Mannerism is unclassical, not anticlassical, that it exemplifies a shift in priorities, not a revolt against classic balance and representation: this, Gombrich insists, is a hypothesis, as indeed are all style concepts. Articulated and defended by Vasari, in the form of *bella maniera* (or *maniera moderna* or *terza e perfetta maniera*), and reformulated by Bellori and later critics who censured it, "Mannerism" as a style concept was created to meet a historiographic need: to secure an artistic ranking for those who emulated and restored the ideal perfection of classical antiquity as against those who merely imitated the great *Cinquecento* masters. Modern historians, such as Dvorak, who praise Mannerism as the sixteenth century style of spiritualism in its perennial struggle against materialism (or even Gombrich himself, who characterizes Mannerism as a distinct style of virtuosity and experimentation) also hypothesize in their efforts to meet their historiographic needs.

I can hardly do justice here to the subtlety of doctrine and argument of these two essays, let alone to the issues they raise. Gombrich's primary achievement, however, must be noted: namely, his insight that no understanding of the concept of style or of particular style concepts is possible without a delineation of the role of these concepts. His brilliant attempt to establish this role in the historical home base of the concepts—in Vasari and Vitruvius—as essentially normative is of great philosophical importance. But is he correct in his central claims that style concepts are hypotheses and that at least the traditional ones are inevitable blends of norm and form? Do the historians of Mannerism, of which he is a distinguished representative, employ the term as a hypothetical norm? It seems to me that Gombrich's interpretation of the concept is more a stipulation as to how we ought to regard it than a correct elucidation of how it is actually used in art history.

Other historians of art theorize about style and its changes. A full account should include at least the theories of Wölfflin, Reigl, Panofsky, Frankl, and even the metaphysical conception of Malraux that style in art is a transformation of the meaning of the universe. Moreover, certain rejections of style as the crucial concept of art history are relevant to our problem. For example, George Kubler has recently pleaded for the replacement of the concept of style by what he calls the idea of "a linked succession of prime works with replications, all being distributed in time as recognizably early and

late versions of the same kind of action."[17]   Then, too, we must not overlook
the fact that great histories of art have been written without the concept of
style; it is a refreshing shock, for example, to reread Berenson's *Italian Painters
of the Renaissance* and discover, unless I have missed it, that he does not even
mention "style."   To be sure, he refers to "schools," but the categories by
which he analyzes them are the aesthetic ones of form, tactile values, and
illustration; obviously, Berenson thought that these aesthetic concepts were
sufficient for coherence in his history of art.

Important as all these considerations are, I reluctantly pass them by and,
on the assumption that our four examples constitute a fair sample of theory of
style in art history, ask instead whether what they say about style corresponds
to what art historians do with it when they turn from theory to practice? What
can we now learn from the historians of Mannerism about the concept of
style?

II

I begin with Walter Friedlaender's "The Anticlassical Style."[18]   This
essay, a historical gem of iridescent argument and flawless organization, helps
lay the foundation of our modern conception of Mannerism.   Mannerism,
Friedlaender contends, begins in Florence around 1520 as a conscious revolt
against the ideals of the High Renaissance, especially as these ideals are
embodied in the paintings of Andrea del Sarto and Fra Bartolommeo, and is
initiated by two of their pupils, Jacopo da Pontormo and Rosso Fiorentino.

That there is such a break and that it is recognized by their
contemporaries, Friedlaender documents from Vasari's condemnation of
Pontormo's Certosa frescoes (1522-25).   In these frescoes, Vasari narrates,
Pontormo repudiate's his former beauty and grace to take over the German
manner of Dürer lock, stock, and barrel. Vasari, Friedlaender points out,
correctly perceives in these frescoes a rejection of the ideals of the High
Renaissance—the ideals epitomized in the *terza e perfetta maniera* of Leonardo,
Raphael, and Michelangelo.

What are these ideals? According to Friedlaender—and this he feels is
basic to understanding the origin's of the Anticlassical style—they are certain
aesthetic and ethical norms that govern the representation of the human figure
in pictorial space. Central in the classical art of the High Renaissance, which
for Friedlaender lasts only twenty years and does not include Michelangelo but
is best exemplified in the mature work of Raphael, is an objectively idealized
harmony of figure and space.

Decisive in Anticlassical Mannerism is the rejection of this normative
conception of art. "The canon apparently given by nature and hence generally
recognized as law is definitively given up. It is no longer a question of creating
a seen object in an artistically new way . . . 'as one ought to see it.'. . . Rather

. . . it is to be recreated . . . from purely autonomous motives, [as] one would have it seen."[19]   A new conception of the human figure in pictorial space, with its attendant new rhythmic beauty is central in the new style. Figure and space can be distorted. Volume can displace space or create a space that is no longer three-dimensional. Instability rather than harmony becomes the ideal. Friedlaender sums up Anticlassical Mannerism as a spiritually subjective movement, directed primarily against the canonically objective art of the High Renaissance.

Pontormo is the pioneer of the new style. After a classic and even transitional period, Pontormo, retreating from the plague in Florence, composes five scenes from the Passion in the Certosa of the Valdema near Florence. "As if impelled by the tragedy of the theme toward another and more inward style, Pontormo . . . shed all that was graceful and shining in the Renaissance atmosphere. All that had been established by Andrea del Sarto and his circle, the emphasis on the plastic and the bodily, the material and coloristic, the realized space and the all too blooming flesh tones——everything outwards now disappears. In its place are a formal and psychological simplification, a rhythm, a subdued but still beautiful coloring . . . and above all an expression rising from the depth of the soul and hitherto unknown in this age and style."[20]   The figures, Gothically thin or bodiless, swaying or elongated; the space, unnatural or unreal; the discordant motifs; and the intense religiosity—in part derived from Dürer, some anticipated in Pontormo's early work, but now transmuted—all these establish Pontormo as the first great artist of Mannerism. Pontormo's translation of the artistically observed object into subjectively spiritual terms is paralleled by the work of Rosso Fiorentino. After his own period of classicism, followed by one of vacilation, Rosso "takes the decisive step away from the balanced and classical towards the spiritual and subjective"[21] in his *Deposition from the Cross*, in Volterra (1521). Intertwinings of vertical ladders and elongated, swaying figures, unreal space, sharp light and color, even cubistic surfaces and angularity, together with emotional intensity contribute "to a new spirituality, an astonishing soulful expressiveness, which even Rosso himself rarely reaches again. . . . Everything is heightened, and everything that would disturb or diminish this heightening—space, perspective, mass, normal proportion—is left out or transformed."[22]

Rosso's *Moses Defending the Daughters of Jethro* (before 1523) goes further in the quest for pure abstraction. Psychic depth is supplanted by an aesthetics of form, color, ornamental overlapping, and spatial layers, which produce an unstable tension between picture surface and spatial depth. In construction and color, Friedlaender says, "this painting . . . is the strangest, wildest picture created in the whole period, and stands quite apart from every canonical normative feeling."[23]

The third of the founders of Anticlassical Mannerism is the non-Florentine, Francesco Parmigianino. In Parma, under Corregio's tutelage, he inclines toward the bizarre and unnatural. But it is in Rome (1523-27), where he probably encounters Rosso, and after the sack of the city (1527) when he leaves Rome, that his mannerist style emerges. His famous verticalism, so pronounced in his *Vision of St. Jerome* (before 1527) and especially in his *Madonna of the Long Neck* (1535-40), where it becomes elegantly elongated, is probably influenced by Rosso and is certainly anticlassical. The *Madonna of the Long Neck*, not only in its elongations of figure and column but in its astonishing and ambiguous asymmetrical relations and its over-all expressive quality of exquisite grace, becomes another of the paradigms of the early Mannerist style of Italian art.

The new style, thus, rests on Pontormo, Rosso, and Parmigianino. It is fully formed between 1520 and 1523. From Florence it proceeds to Rome where, after the sack and the consequent scattering of artists from Rome, it spreads, mainly through Rosso and his follower Primaticcio to the court at Fontainebleau and then to northern Europe. Through Parmigianino it enters the Venetian art of Bassano and Tintoretto, and through Tintoretto influences the greatest of the Mannerists, El Greco. In Florence Pontormo's pupil, Bronzino, carries on the style that then evolves into the *maniera*—or second generation of Mannerism—which Friedlaender in a later essay, "The Anti-Mannerist Style," characterizes as a degeneration of "the noble, pure, idealistic, and abstract style"[24] of Anticlassical Mannerism.

Friedlaender draws two important conclusions from his account: that Michelangelo is not the founder of Mannerism, and that Mannerism is not a weak imitation of Michelangelo. While it is true that Michelangelo is anticlassical almost from the beginnings of his work, that there are strong mannerist elements in his treatment of space as far back as 1511 in the spandrels of the Sistine Ceiling, and that his *Last Judgment* (1541) is the "overwhhelming paradigm of Mannerism," his characteristic elongations and distortions—so typical of Mannerism—turn up after 1520. Indeed, Friedlaender argues, Michelangelo is a Mannerist only from 1525 to 1530, when he returns to Florence to create the *Medici Madonna* and the *Victor*; and he is manneristic only in some of his works since this is the period of his great non-Mannerist *Times of Day* of the Medici Chapel.

Friedlaender's brilliant revolutionary essay has been much praised and criticized. Few if any question what is undoubtedly his greatest achievement: that of bringing us to look at the work of three neglected great artists in a new, historically grounded, and enhancing light. Many, however, object to his chronology, his specific attributions and explanations of influence, his particular examples or criteria of Mannerism, and his interpretation of the work of Pontormo, Rosso, and Parmigianino in relation to that of the *maniera* proper.

What has not been done and needs doing if we wish to understand the concept of style in art history is to elucidate the role Friedlaender assigns to his basic style term, "Anticlassical Mannerism."

What Friedlaender does is to employ a style term which he borrows from the seventeenth—century detractors of the *maniera*, and which he extends to cover the sources of the *maniera* in Pontormo, Rosso, and Parmigianino, in order to distinguish, characterize, relate, and revaluate a whole group of artists and their work. As he employs the term to cover the first generation of painters he is concerned with in his Inaugural Lecture, "Anticlassical Mannerism" functions under certain criteria, but these criteria add up to no definitive set and correspond to no essential set of properties shared by all anticlassical mannerist works. Friedlaender offers no definition—hence, in one sense of theory, no theory of Mannerism—no statement of its essence. Nor does he state or imply that without such a definition he can give no cogent reasons for particular works being manneristic. All Friedlaender suggests is a "decisive" criterion: a new artistic relation to the observed object that, more particularly, is a spiritual or subjective (in a nonoptical sense) conception of figure and space in their asymmetrical relations. It is this criterion that he falls back on both to characterize Mannerism and to contrast that style with the normative, balanced, unambiguous, and stable ideal governing the relations between figure and space of the High Renaissance.

That Friedlaender has no definitive set of criteria for his style term, and hence no real definition of "Anticlassical Mannerism" can be best seen if we look at the various reasons he gives for particular works being manneristic. They comprise a large group. A particular painting, he says, is manneristic because it has crowding of figures, a narrow layer of space, half-figures seen from the back, bodiless figures, elongated figures, swaying figures, spilling of figures or, pictorial elements over the frame, impetuous or harsh color, preciosity, cubistic surfaces, rejection of perspective, overlapping of spatial layers, compression of space, elegant grace, violence, turmoil, the bizarre, or a particular kind of spirituality. And there are others.

As diverse as these reasons are, they function as "mannerist reasons" for Friedlaender, I submit, only because they derive from or center on the decisive criterion of the subjective relation between figure and space. This criterion, I have already suggested, is not necessary and sufficient—definitive—for Friedlaender. But is it either necessary or sufficient, as he uses it? It seems to me absolutely clear that this criterion is not sufficient since he rejects certain works, such as Michelangelo's late frescoes, *Conversion of St. Paul*, *Crucifixion of St. Peter* and his Rondanini *Pietà*, as manneristic even though they satisfy this criterion. We must acknowledge, however, that the criterion is necessary for him because there is no example in his essay of a work that is in the Mannerist style that does not satisfy this criterion.

And now we must ask, Is this criterion clear? If we spell it out, as Friedlaender so beautifully does, as an asymmetrical, uncanonical relation between figure and space with its consequent artistically subjective, spiritual, expressive quality or, even more fully, in terms of all the "mannerist reasons" he presents throughout his essay, we do have a criterion or rather a related cluster of criteria regarding unnatural space and figure, asymmetry, violence, elongation, elegance, and the like, that are as empirically grounded as they can be. They have their empirical counterparts in the world outside of art. If, for example, "elongation" is vague, its vagueness rests on its ordinary use, not on its use in talking about style. So too, it seems to me, for all the criteria surrounding Friedlaender's one decisive criterion. The possible exception is spirituality. But here again, I think, Friedlaender provides clear, empirically grounded criteria: painting an observed object as you would want it seen as against how it ought to be seen according to an objective canon.

I do not wish to suggest that all of Friedlaender's criteria or reasons, even if they are clear in the sense of being empirically grounded, are descriptive of properties in works of art in the same way. It may well be, as I think it is, that "spiritual," unlike, say, "violent," or "elegant," is more interpretive or explanatory than descriptive. I shall return to this problem later. All that needs saying here is that Friedlaender's criteria are not vague in the way other criteria of style concepts, such as Wölfflin's *"malerisch"* or even Dvorak's own use of "spiritual," are. The vagueness is not in Friedlaender's decisive criterion or cluster of criteria for "Mannerism" but in the concept itself. This vagueness is the clue to the logic of style concepts, which is not to be found in Friedlaender or any other art historian considered in isolation, and which hence has been overlooked by all the art historians writing about style concepts. It can be discovered only in the disagreements among the art historians over the criteria—clear or vague—for their style concepts as they employ these concepts in their separate histories.

"El Greco and Mannerism," by Max Dvorak, is another classic in the modern conception of Mannerism.[25] Starting with the climax rather than the beginnings of sixteenth—century Mannerism, Dvorak finds in the Spanish work of El Greco the culmination of three tendencies: the late antinatural form of Michelangelo, the antinatural color and composition of Tintoretto, and the new spirituality of St. Theresa and the Spanish mystics. All three influence El Greco, all three are embodied in his work, and all three, with minor variations on the new spirituality, characterize the whole of sixteenth century European Mannerism and show it to be an expression of the perennial conflict between spiritualism and materialism in European culture.

There are great methodological differences between Dvorak and Friedlaender regarding the explanation of the origins of Mannerism. Dvorak concentrates on cultural, Friedlaender, on artistic factors in the development of the new style, but there is little disagreement on the distinguishing features of Mannerism itself as a post High Renaissance style. Dvorak emphasizes a particular range of light and color perhaps more than Friedlaender, but both stress antinatural figure and space. And both center on the new spirituality. Their great difference is over the content of spirituality. For Friedlaender, we remember, it is purely formal, having to do with an autonomous, subjective mode of observing artistic objects. For Dvorak, it is not formal but iconographical, having to do with artistic embodiments of the doctrine that our knowledge of God and of the Christian mysteries consists in their immediate emotional certainty: "to know what you do not know." This rejection of rationality for mysticism, already present in the late works of Michelangelo and his disillusionment with the ideals of the Renaissance, and dominant in the visionary style of Tintoretto as well as in the French artists, Dubois and Bellange, culminates in the works of El Greco in Toledo.

"What I see," said St. Teresa, "is a white and red that cannot be found anywhere in nature, which give forth a brighter and more radiant light than anything man can see, and pictures such as no painter has yet painted, whose models are nowhere to be found, yet are nature herself and life itself and the most glorious beauty man can conceive."[26]

El Greco, Dvorak says, "sought to paint the kind of things the saint beheld in her ecstasy."[27] In the *Burial of Count Orgaz* (1586-88), *Christ in the Garden of Gethsemane* (1608-14), the *Opening of the Fifth Seal* (1610-14), *Resurrection* (1597-1604), and *Toledo in a Storm* (1595-1600), to mention only those Dvorak does, El Greco fuses the formal qualities of antinatural color, figure, and space with the iconographic quality of the vision of the supernatural. These paintings do not represent the supernatural: they reveal it.

Sixteenth—century Mannerism, then, as Dvorak characterizes it, is primarily spiritual in its pictorial manifestation of the mystical knowledge of God and the world. Whether Dvorak regards this spirituality, with or without the formal qualities of antinatural color, space, and figure, as a real definition of "Mannerism," I do not know; that he so regards it is certainly not so obvious as some of his commentators and critics claim. What is obvious—and important to the elucidation of the concept of Mannerism—is that he differs from Friedlaender not over the definition or criteria of "Mannerism" but primarily over the meaning and criteria of "spirituality." Dvorak's use of "spirituality," unlike Friedlaender's, is, I think, vague precisely because it is obscure: how can immediate, emotional knowledge of the supernatural, whatever that is, become part of a painting? If Friedlaender's "spiritual" is interpretive in an explanatory sense, Dvorak's is at best interpretive in a purely invitational sense. That is, Dvorak's is not a hypothesis that helps to explain a picture: it is a recommendation to see it in a certain way.

I want now to turn to some recent discussions of Mannerism that are radically different from Friedlaender's or Dvorak's. But before I do, I must say something, even if in the baldest way, about one other philosophically important variant on the use of "Mannerism." In *From Leonardo to El Greco*,[28] Lionello Venturi writes on Mannerism as one aspect of European painting in the sixteenth century. On the whole, his account is based on Friedlaender's (and others') with a stress on anti-classicism, which Venturi traces to the neo-platonism of Ficino, and the pure formalism of the movement. The great reconciliation of the ideal with the real of classical art is rejected by Mannerism; nature is repudiated and the ideal is transformed into a cultivation of abstract forms for their own sake, in which imitation of the High Renaissance masters (especially in figures and motifs) and inventions that are purely imaginative supplant imitation of nature. Eventually this imitation and invention lead to mere repetition of forms (in the second generation of

Mannerism) with the consequent debilitation of the movement.

Venturi insists that either in its Italian development or as a European International Style, Mannerism is too varied and complex to yield a definition. Rather than an essence or common denominator, Venturi offers "salient characteristics." Hence, what makes his account philosophically significant is that the reasons he gives for particular works or artists being manneristic rest on a family of characteristics, with none of them seemingly necessary or sufficient. Pontormo and Rosso, for example, are Mannerists because of their antinatural treatment of figure and space; but Domenico Beccafumi's "sensitive handling of light [e.g., in his *Birth of the Virgin*, 1543] and his *sfumato* implemented by a dexterous use of lights and darks qualify him to rank as a mannerist."[29]

Venturi's most provocative claim, however, has to do with some of the major works of Tintoretto, which most art historians today would assign among the paradigms of Mannerism. To the contrary, Venturi argues that Tintoretto briefly flirts with Mannerism, then, like Titian and other Venetians, rejects it; consequently, his major works, such as the *Miracle of St. Mark* (1548), the great series in the Scuola di San Rocco (1564-88), or the *Last Supper* (1591-94) in San Giorgio Maggiore are not manneristic. They are unmanneristic, however, not because they fail to meet defining criteria but because their salient characteristics differ from those of Mannerism. These paintings, fundamentally incantatory and religious, stress content, not form. Light and shadow, space and movement, and "one of the richest palettes known to painting"[30] help create a new unity of form and matter, of ideal and real, that transcends Mannerism altogether.

The word Mannerism derives from the Italian *maniera*. Linguists and art historians trace *maniera* to Boccaccio's "manner" of doing or behaving (1353), Cennini's "style" of an individual artist or group of artists (1390), Ghiberti's "style" of an age (1450), Raphael's "three styles" of buildings in ancient Rome (1519), and Vasari's "style," used either with a qualifying term, such as "beautiful" or "German," or used absolutely, in the sense that an artist has style. Vasari's conception of *maniera* is regarded as the most important because of its role in sixteenth century art and criticim. Contemporary art historians debate Vasari's exact meaning of the absolute sense of *maniera* as well as the relation between this use and his other uses. Whatever the resolution of this issue may be, the term takes on the derogatory meaning of "stereotype" for Dolce (1557) and the even more pejorative sense of "fantastic idea" for Bellori (1672). Baldinucci coins *ammanierato*—"mannered"—again as an abusive term (1681). The substantive "mannerist" comes from Fréart de Chambray (1662) and is introduced into English by Dryden in his translation of Du Fresnoy's *De Arte Graphica* (1695). "Mannerism" (*Der Manierismus, Le maniérisme, Il manierismo*) as a style term designating a particular period of Italian art comes into general use only in the nineteenth century.[31]

"Mannerism" derives from *maniera*. In the same way, Mannerist art derives from the art of the *maniera*. The *maniera*, hence Mannerism, is a continuation of High Renaissance ideals; consequently it is not anti-classical in form or content. Such is the major thesis of a number of recent art historians. The first of these I wish to consider is C. H. Smyth. In "Mannerism and *maniera*,"[32] Smyth turns to the sixteenth—century conception of *maniera* as it was articulated by Dolce in his dialogue, *The Aretine (Dialogo della pittura, intitolato l'Aretino*, 1557) and by Vasari in his *Lives*, especially the Introduction to Part III (1550; 2nd ed., 1568), the two basic texts. Central in Dolce's dialogue is his contrast between Michelangelo and Raphael. He praises only Raphael because his paintings have *maniera*, "namely, bad practice where forms and faces almost always look alike."[33]

This uniformity which Dolce chastises, Smyth claims is the same ideal that Vasari praises: "*La maniera* became *la più bella* from the method of copying frequently the most beautiful things, combining them to make from what was most beautiful (whether hands, heads, bodies, or legs) the best figure possible, *and putting it into use in every work for all the figures.* . . ."[34] It is this ideal that reaches perfection in the sixteenth century.

Although Vasari and Dolce agree that *maniera* idealizes uniformity (the one liking it, the other not), neither, Smyth contends, understands what is behind this uniformity, that which can stand as fundamental in *maniera* painting: namely, "the more or less consistent application of principles that governed form and movement principles of posing figures at rest or in motion and of delineating, lighting, and grouping them."[35] It is these principles—conventions, habits, formulae—that characterize *maniera* painting and relate to *maniera* as a sixteenth century term.

Here is Smyth's list of these conventions: flattening of figures parallel to the picture plane; twisting of poses in two or three directions; flat light that intensifies the forced flatness of figures; juxtaposition of figures; angularity, especially of the arm across the chest or in the air; transformation of live figures into statues; attention to finish and details; and habitual tipping of the ground of the figures. Of these conventions regarding figure, composition, and space, figure is the most important.

What are the sources of these conventions? Primary is antique relief, especially extant Roman sarcophagi of the second to fourth centuries. *Maniera* painting, unlike painting *all'antica*, elaborates upon and modernizes the flatness of light and figure, the uniformity of poses, and so forth, of its models. Other sources are *Quattrocento* neo-Gothic, Michelangelo's *Battle of Cascina* and the Lazarus he contributes to Sebastiano del Piombo's *Raising of Lazarus*, and even Raphael, in *Parnassus*.

After "the gathering of the *maniera*," it begins in earnest in 1530 in Florence, then Rome, then Fontainebleau. Its best practitioners include Bronzino, Vasari, Salviati, Beccafumi, Polidoro, Perino, and Parmigianino, among others, but not Pontormo in the Certosa frescoes. During its heyday, in spite of its emphasis upon uniformity, it allows for variation and surprise, under another Vasarian rubric of license within the (antique-derived) rules. These variations range from the extremes of emotionless distance to high seriousness. In between, it "is in its element as decorative enrichment, encrusting walls, tapestries, and minor objects."[36] It finally disintegrates when uniformity becomes monotony and invention overelaboration. But in its prime, it creates works of art that can no longer be devalued.

Maniera in theory and practice is essentially an art of pose and gesture, modeled on antique relief. In the art and writings of Vasari, for instance, *maniera* represents no revolt against the High Renaissance, no expression of spiritual crisis. How, then, Smyth asks, can the modern conception of Mannerism as a formally anticlassical and expressively spiritual movement be reconciled with its source, the *maniera*? It cannot; consequently, "Mannerism" should apply only to the *maniera* painters and those who anticipated them. Thus, Pontormo's Visdomini altarpiece (1518) is manneristic but not, for example, his *Christ Before Pilate*, "however sensitive, refined, abstract, private, irrational, or eccentrically expressive."[37] This painting and similar ones (which for Friedlaender are among the paradigms of Mannerism) are best regarded, Smyth suggests, following Gombrich, as post-classic experimentations with High Renaissance forms, not as rejections of them. Rather than a division of painting in the period from about 1515 to 1590 into first and second generation Mannerism, he concludes, it would be better to retain the old term, "Late Renaissance," as a label for the whole period and restrict "Mannerism" to the *maniera* and its immediate antecedents.

John Shearman, in *"maniera* as an Aesthetic Ideal" and *Mannerism*,[38] goes further than Smyth in the rejection of Mannerism as an anticlassical style and in the identification of Mannerism with the *maniera*. For Shearman, Mannerism has its roots deep in the High Renaissance. "It became something different and individual by taking a part of the High Renaissance and subjecting that part to special development." Among its models are some of Michelangelo's *Ignudi* (1511-12) of the Sistine Ceiling, especially in their elegance, grace, and poise, and the unnatural beauty and harmony of color and form of Raphael's *St. Michael* (1517). Already anticipated by Leonardo, the refined style—which is the clue to the *maniera*, hence to Mannerism—is as much a theme in the full orchestration of the High Renaissance as the proto—Baroque. Mannerism begins and develops easily, as an art of articulate, sophisticated beauty, not out of spiritual crisis and despair. Its pervasive aesthetics of poise and grace rules out completely the traditionally attributed qualities of strain, brutality, violence, and overt passion. It is neither anticlassical nor a concentration on uniformity of pose and gesture, modeled on antique relief; both Friedlaender and Smyth, therefore, are in error in their conception of the Mannerist style.

"Mannerism" must be and can be defined. For without a true definition, Shearman contends, its use remains arbitrary and without controls in the historical account of sixteenth-century art. What is the proper meaning of "Mannerism"? What are the defining qualities of mannerist works? What group does the term cover? These are the central questions Shearman sets himself. All three answers lie in the sixteenth-century meaning of *"maniera."*

For when Lanzi first introduces the term *"manierismo"* (in 1792), which is our direct source of "Mannerism," it applies to painters and the qualities of their work that are much talked about, appreciated, and criticized in the sixteenth century.

What, then, is *maniera*? Although there is some variation, the evidence garnered from poetry, from the literature of manners, from certain writings of Dolce and Aretino, but most importantly from Vasari's *Lives*, points to the overwhelmingly absolute use of the term *maniera* as style which one has or lacks is Vasari's key term. He uses it to distinguish and to rank periods of Italian art; he singles it out as the only term of his famous five—*regola, ordine, misura, disegno* and *maniera*—that needs no definition, so well is it understood; and he means by it a certain kind of artistic accomplishment and refinement, with all that these encompass.

Vasari's and the sixteenth-century absolute sense of *"maniera"* descend from the French courtly literature of manners of the thirteenth to fifteenth centuries. Central in this tradition is the notion of *"savoir faire"*—of comporting oneself with civilized sophistication and manner. To behave with style is to be poised, elegant, refined, and effortless in a perfected performance. From these positive qualities, certain others, perennially regarded as negative, follow: To have style is to be unnatural, affected, self-conscious, and ostentatious. Also involved in this artificial code of behavior is the repudiation of revealed passion, evident effort, and rude naïveté.

Italian literature of manners, especially Castiglione's *Il Cortegiano* (1528) is basic to Vasari's *"maniera"* as well as to the whole of *maniera* art and criticism. Elegance, refinement, artificiality, effortless overcoming of difficulties (*"sprezzatura"*), virtuosity, and grace—all construed as positive qualities—are the obvious parallels between style in life and style in art. They are also the defining properties of the *maniera* in sixteenth-century art.

"Mannerism" has its linguistic and historic roots in the *maniera*. It was and should be once again a term reserved for an art "drenched in *maniera*."[40] The alternative, Shearman says, is the chaos of contemporary arbitrary definitions and the consequent distortion of sixteenth-century art.

Properly understood, Mannerism, in its overriding concern with the perfection of style, is fundamentally the "stylish style." As it develops, it embraces other aesthetic qualities, all compatible with those invested in *maniera*: variety, abundance, complexity, fantasy, obscurity, finish of detail, even the erotic, grotesque, esoteric, and pornographic. Although it is a style in which constituent parts of a work of art become as important as and sometimes more important than its whole, and in which content or subject is subordinate to form, Mannerism is not anticlassical but merely unclassical in its reversal of the normal relation of form and content. Perhaps, Shearman suggests, it is best understood as a super-sophisticated classicism because of its preoccupation with form as style.

Mannerism starts in Rome, not Florence. Its vital years of growth are 1520—27. "There was then in Rome, by chance, a brilliant group of young men, headed by Perino, Polidoro, Rosso, and Parmigianino, and it was in their hands that Mannerism was shaped into a style of universal significance." [41]

Perino del Vaga introduces it to Florence in 1522-23 with his cartoon, the *Martyrdom of the Ten Thousand*, which in spite of its subject exhibits a rarified Olympian ballet of *maniera* qualities to serve as a second great model (the first was Michaelangelo's *Battle of Cascina*) to the young painters. Apparently entered in competition for a commission along with Pontormo's design of the same subject, "full of passion, dynamic sequences of form, and explosive movements,"[42] Perino's entry is all refinement and invention. That Perino's manneristic work was chosen instead of the anticlassical contribution of Pontormo constitutes "a turning-point in Florentine art."[43] After his Volterra *Deposition* (1521) and his (newly discovered) *Dead Christ* (1526), done in Rome, Rosso becomes another leader of Mannerism, taking the *maniera* with him to Fontainebleau. The great Florentine period of Mannerism comes in the third through fifth decades of the century, with Bronzino, Vasari, Salviati, Cellini, and Giovanni Bologna. Even Michelangelo at about the same time, in his architecture, sculpture, and drawing, furthers the *maniera* with his inventions, especially his serpentine line.

Mannerism with "its self-conscious stylization [as] its common denominator of all Mannerist works of art"[44] exhibits itself in painting, sculpture, and architecture. It also includes gardens, fountains, and grottoes. Its virtuosity and hedonism accommodate as well the grotesque, the monstrous, and the pornographic—all for the sake of variety and amusement. Its accent on form rather than content, on style for its own sake, is also present in music and poetry. Mannerism then, for Shearman, is an International Style of the sixteenth century, covering all the arts.

Shearman raises many issues in his spirited account of Mannerism. Central is his definition of *"maniera"* as a sixteenth-century term for style and as a style term. That Mannerism is not anticlassical in form or expression follows from his definition, as do all the reasons he gives for various works or artists being or not being manneristic. Pontormo is never manneristic, Rosso's *Deposition* is not; nor are El Greco, Tintoretto, Pordenone, or Berruguete, whom he does not mention. Michelangelo is a Mannerist in some of his works—the *Victor*, for example—yet not for Friedlaender's reasons, but because of its "grace, complexity, variety, and difficulty."[45] So, too, with Giulio Romano's Palazzo del Té, whose exterior as well as interior are manneristic not because of their total rejection of classical principles but because of their wonderful assortment of variety and caprice, designed to delight rather than to depress.

As admirable as Shearman's consistency of application of his criteria of "*maniera*" is, and commendable as his attempt to force a revaluation of the second generation mannerists may be, we must ask: Is his definition of "*maniera*" correct? and, more important, I think, Does his account of Mannerism rest on a true definition of "Mannerism"?

I shall come to these questions presently when we have all the evidence before us. Just here, however, the basic issue between Friedlaender and Shearman can be stated: Is the *maniera*, whatever and whomever it includes a debilitation of the anticlassicism of Pontormo and Rosso or is it an entirely separate movement? Friedlaender rests his case on the *maniera* as an outgrowth of anticlassicism; Shearman, on the *maniera* as one flowering of the High Renaissance.

Can this disagreement be resolved by any true definition of "*maniera*"? Shearman thinks it can and must be. He is positive about "*maniera*" as the refined style. Smyth, we remember, is just as positive that "*maniera*" means ideal uniformity of pose and gesture, modeled on antique relief. Others, even among those who agree that "*maniera*" is predominantly an absolute term of style in the sixteenth century, differ from both Smyth and Shearman that "*maniera*" denotes only "the characteristic and indefinable feature of an artist's expression,"[46] thereby functioning in the same way as the later "*je ne sais quoi*" of the French theorists. That the disagreements over the meaning of "*maniera*" can be resolved by a true definition may be as much a delusion as the assumption that a true definition of "Mannerism" can settle the disagreements over that term.

Our final essay is S. J. Freedberg's "Observations on the Painting of the *maniera*."[47] As elusive as the *maniera* is, even in its chronology, Freedberg dates it from about 1540 to 1580 and centers it in Florence and Rome. Its pervasive strain is its artificiality of both form and content, which correctly invites its mannered quality as well as its sixteenth-century name.

In its theoretical aspect, "*maniera*" as sophistication and grace is first attributed by Vasari to the masters of the *maniera moderna*: Leonardo, Raphael, and Michelangelo achieve *bella maniera*, which is to function as the subsequent standard for all art. Thus, *maniera* as Vasari conceives it is a special quality which distinguishes the moderns from the *Quattrocento* but which Freedberg claims those masters would not have accepted as their unique and paramount contribution. For the modern Style, which we call the High Renaissance, is one that, like all classical styles, is founded on "a synthetic adjustment between aesthetic preference and actuality."[48] Vasari's "*maniera*" or "*bella maniera*," because of its emphasis upon achieved perfection in art to the neglect of art in relation to nature, is merely classicistic—an imitation of classical models rather than an acceptance of the classical ideal of the reconciliation of the aesthetic with the actual.

That *maniera* is classicistic, and hence both an adherence to and a betrayal of the High Renaissance, Freedberg continues, can be seen in its practice as well as in its theory. In form and content *maniera* painting divorces itself from nature to concentrate upon the aesthetic. Art becomes commentary on appearance instead of description of it. Abstraction and the reworking and transmutation of extant artistic form's replace classical idealization of nature. Plausibility gives way to aesthetic convincingness, achieved by the brilliant technique of hard delineation of line and lucid color, accenting the surfaces of things. Even *maniera*'s emphasis upon the plastic, where flesh becomes stone and stone becomes live, is a classicistically borrowed rendition of Michelangelo's sculpture.

In its allegiance to antecedent art as its sole source of inspiration, *maniera* painting is also an art of quotation. Its particular forms and in many cases its particular subjects are taken from High Renaissance or antique models. These quotations, severed from their contexts, become distorted and redirected so that their original meanings change in their new *maniera* settings. Inevitably, ambiguity and multivalence result, Freedberg points out, contributing to the overall elusiveness and artificiality so highly prized by the *maniera*. Even the mask—"the single most pregnant symbol"[49] of the *maniera*—is masked, as in Bronzino's Allegory, where it seems to reveal more of life than life's real face.

This penchant for visual quotation often combines with verbal quotation, especially in the *maniera* narrative fresco cycles which, because of their deliberate obscurity of sources or their transformations of them, constitute some of the most difficult rebuses in the history of art. All that remains clear is the ostensible decorative achievement—the reworking of all the materials into an outsize precious ornament, with, total disregard for the pre-existing architectural structure surrounding the frescoed wall.

In *maniera* religious art, the apparent contradiction between detached refinement and attached devotion, is resolved by its quality of aesthetic exaltation, which is the *maniera* equivalent of religious devotion, and which is generated by the vibrance of the forms and the tensions of the meanings. This art can be best compared to the traditional icon: "In both, the subject matter is rigidified, translated from history toward symbol; and the form in which it is presented is made crystalline and tends toward the abstract . . . and this form is the object of a precious working and elaboration."[50]

Maniera painting, thus, is an art of disjunction and multivalence. The High Renaissance fuses meanings of form and content. The immediate post-classical painting of some of Raphael's pupils and of Pontormo and Rosso fractures this unity either by emphasizing form or content to the exclusion of the other or by pitting one against the other. But *maniera* makes "an artistic principle of multiplicity and multivalence."[51] What, then, is the relation between the High Renaissance, the post-Raphaelesque Roman school, the expressionism of Pontormo and Rosso, and the *maniera*? How much of the period 1520—80 is Mannerism?

The pupils of Raphael, especially Perino and Polidoro, are classicistic and become, along with the Roman convert Parmigianino, the forerunners of the *maniera*. Pontormo and Rosso—"the fractious Florentines"—are experimental, even to the extreme of being anticlassical, but this is true only from 1520 to 1526, and even then they also strive for the *maniera* qualities of grace, finesse, and ornament. With these two reminders about the limited role of anticlassical revolt and the constant presence of *maniera*, Freedberg returns to the Friedlaender distinction between first generation or Early Mannerism and the *maniera*. Having characterized the various styles between 1540 and 1580, he proposes a proper use of "Mannerism" rather than a definition of it. Basic to his decision is his affirmative answer to the questions: Are the style or styles of Pontormo, Rosso, and others of the so-called first generation of Mannerism "sufficiently close in essential ways to that of the *maniera* to be connected with it, rather than distinguished from it by a different name"? and, Are the styles of both Early Mannerism and the *maniera* "sufficiently distinguishable in essential ways from that of the classical High Renaissance?"[52]

Mannerism thus, according to Freedberg, has its linguistic roots in the *maniera* but its artistic roots in the immediate post-classical period of the High Renaissance. The great difference between Early Mannerism and the *maniera* is the restrictive character of the latter. "Its specialized aestheticism is a limit on what we may call the humanity of art."[53] This criterion also serves to relate Tintoretto and El Greco to Mannerism; for both, like Pontormo and Rosso, transcend their *maniera* vocabulary to affirm the "profundity of overt human drama"[54] in art.

III

Other essays, especially some on the architecture of Mannerism and on Mannerism as an International Style, ought to be considered in any complete discussion.[55] Some reputable art historians of the sixteenth century deny that Mannerism is a separate style, preferring to treat its various manifestations as expressions of the late Renaissance under the general rubrics of Early, High, and late Renaissance art.[56] The arguments advanced by these historians both for the extension and for the elimination of the style term, I believe, add nothing to the logic of the concept of Mannerism since they revolve around the enlargement or rejection of the same sets of criteria employed by those historians whom we have detailed and who do regard Mannerism as a separate style, "with the same kind of reality (and no more) as the other style periods that are commonly acknowledged."[57]

On this assumption that Mannerism is a style in sixteenth-century art, I want now, in our concluding section, to return to our two central questions: How do the historians of Mannerism use the style concept of Mannerism? and, How does their use compare with what art historians say about the concept of style in art history?

Among our six historians, there is much agreement: on the sources, nature, and development of Mannerism and the *maniera* of the sixteenth century, especially in Florence and Rome. But there is as much disagreement over the place and date of the origin of Mannerism, over its specific relation to the High Renaissance, its chronology, its relation to the *maniera*, its paradigms, its range, and its causes.

Fundamental to all these major disagreements, I want to argue, are not the varying purportedly true definitions of "Mannerism," which Shearman claims are the main source of disagreement, but different sets of criteria for the correct use of "Mannerism." If we turn, as we must, from their quarrels about the sources, influences, paradigms, extent, and development of Mannerisim to their supporting reasons, we can find the clue to their disagreements as well as to the logic of the concept of Mannerism. Their style-giving reasons are central in the elucidation of the concept of Mannerism. Their answers to What is Mannerism? are to be found in their reasons for particular works or artists being manneristic.

"Mannerism," for each of our six historians, is a style term that functions as a name or label to designate certain sets of characteristics of certain works of art of the sixteenth century whose similarities and differences from previous and later works or from some contemporary works warrant their grouping as an independent unity or style.

Corresponding to these sets of characteristics "manneristic—making properties" are certain sets of criteria for the correct use of "Mannerism." Each historian has his own set which differs, sometimes radically, from the others. Only one, Shearman, states that his is a definitive set, and therefore a true definition of Mannerism, although it is possible to attribute such a set to Dvorak and to Smyth as well. However, if my account of Friedlaender is correct, he most certainly has no such set of criteria, only a complex necessary criterion regarding figure in space. And both Venturi and Freedberg disclaim definitions of "Mannerism."

Whatever the claims or disclaimers about definitive sets of criteria or even about necessary criteria for the correct use of "Mannerism" as a style term, we must now ask: Is there extant such a set or a necessary criterion? Can there be, if the concept of Mannerism is to retain its assigned role? Need there be, in order to provide a coherent account of Mannerism?

Affirmative answers to these three crucial questions rest on the asumption that Mannerism, indeed that all style terms are logically closed concepts, amenable to true definitions in terms of their necessary and sufficient criteria that correspond to their necessary and sufficient properties.

It is this assumption, I believe, that is false. That it is false can be seen in the actual functioning of the criteria for "Mannerism" as these criteria play their role in the style-giving reasons of the historians of Mannerism. In order to understand the logic of style concepts, we must turn from the debates about the nature of Mannerism to the full range of disagreement over why or whether a particular work or artist is or is not manneristic. There we find that Mannerism is not a closed concept; that it does its assigned job only on the assumption that there is no definitive set of criteria, no necessary criterion for its correct use. For example, Friedlaender, we recall, says that Michelangelo's *Victor* is manneristic because of the figure's "screw-like upward thrust, his long, stretched-out, athlete's leg, his small Lysippian head, and his regular, large—scale, somewhat empty features."[58] Shearman agrees that the work is manneristic but gives reasons which have nothing to do with anticlassical figure in space: the *Victor* is manneristic because of its "grace, complexity, variety, and difficulty,"[59] achieved mainly through Michelangelo's serpentine line that expresses completed rather than restless or disturbed action.

Again, for Friedlaender, Pontormo's *Christ Before Pilate* is a paradigm of Mannerism; for Smyth, it is a paradigm of sixteenth-century expressionism, not manneristic at all because it has no ideal uniformity of figure or pose.

And so it goes. Without repeating the evidence, I want to insist that unless it recognizes the indigenous vagueness of the concept, no reading of the vast array of disagreement among the historians over why or whether a particular work or artist is or is not an example or even a paradigm of Mannerism can do justice either to the disagreements or to Mannerism as an historical phenomenon.

As its use in style-giving reasons reveals, "Mannerism" is not closed, but vague in the sense that the criteria for its correct use are not complete or completable. To claim that the criteria are complete or could be—as for example, by stipulation, to render these criteria as a precise set—is to misunderstand and foreclose on their assigned role in the history of art.

What is this vagueness that I claim is the basic logical feature of the concept of Mannerism? Consider as an illuminating model an example from C. L. Stevenson: the concept of a cultured person.[60] I say of someone that he is a cultured person; I am asked why he is or why I say he is, and I reply: Because he is widely read and acquainted with the arts. My questioner counters: Nonsense. To be sure, he reads a lot, and he knows much about the arts, but he has no imaginative sensitivity; so he's a boor, not a cultured person at all.

In this exchange, both of us are working toward persuasive definitions of "a cultured person," definitions that rest on stressed criteria. These criteria are vague in two different senses: "Imaginative senitivity" is unclear and obscure in a way that "widely read" and "acquainted with the arts" are not. But the latter two are still vague in the sense that they provide no precise cut-off point or boundary in their application. Individual criteria, therefore, can be vague in meaning or application.

There is a third kind of vagueness in this example that Stevenson suggests but does not explore: the inadequacy or incompleteness of the set of criteria; "cultured" is vague in its extant or professed set of criteria, which differs from the vagueness of the individual criteria. Here vagueness contrasts with completeness, not with clarity or precision.

"Mannerism" is like "cultured." Its individual criteria may be, although they need not be, vague in their meaning or application. "Spiritual" is obscure in Dvorak's set of criteria. "Elongation" has no exact application in all cases:

where, for example, does "elongation" end and "verticality" begin in Friedlaender's set of criteria? Friedlaender's "spiritual", on the other hand, is not obscure; nor is his criterion of "spilling over the frame," which is as exact a criterion and no more vague in application than "pregnant: with child" is.

But "Mannerism," like "cultured," is vague in another sense as well: its set of criteria, whether its individual members are clear or not, exactly instanced or not, is incomplete and incompletable.

As we have amply shown, art historians use "Mannerism" to label, describe, interpret, and evaluate or revaluate certain works of art with certain specified characteristics in a specified region of space and time. It does its assigned job under certain criteria. For one historian (Friedlaender), it functions under a "decisive" criterion, which comprises a number of others, a, b, and c. For a second historian (Dvorak), it functions under similar criteria, a and b, but c has a different interpretation, so let us call it d. For a third historian (Venturi), it functions under a cluster or family of "salient" criteria, a, b, c, d, and f, where no one criterion is necessary, no collection of them is sufficient. For a fourth historian (Smyth), "Mannerism" functions under a general criterion, "*maniera*" (let us call it m), which in turn functions under the criterion of ideal uniformity of pose and gesture, n, and which is regarded as definitive for both "Mannerism" and "*maniera*". For a fifth historian (Shearman), it functions under the same general criterion, "*maniera*" which in turn functions under the criteria of refinement, artificiality, difficulty, and grace, o, p, q, and r, and which are also claimed to be definitive for both "*maniera*" and "Mannerism." Finally, for a sixth historian (Freedberg), it functions under two sets of criteria: "*maniera*" to which he adds the criterion of multiplicity and multivalence of meanings, s; and experimental or anticlassical expressionism, t.

In every case, we can ask whether these criteria are clear and are precisely applicable to the works specified as manneristic by the historians. If they are not clear or are questionable in their application, they are vague. But they are not vague in the way in which the individual sets of criteria—a, b, and d; "*maniera*" (as n; as o, p, q, and r; as s); or s and t—are vague; or even all these sets together are vague. For the vagueness of the sets, taken individually or collectively, is a vagueness of the incompleteness and incompletability of the set. Therefore the fundamental vagueness of "Mannerism" consists in the perennial possibility of intelligibly enlarging or exchanging the criteria for its correct use. Unless we acknowledge this vagueness of the concept of Mannerism, we cannot make sense of the different moves which our historians have successively made and which future historians may make as they choose different criteria, perhaps even other than formal and iconographical ones, that will enable them to present a new account of Mannerism.

"Mannerism" is not only irreducibly vague; it is also beneficially vague. For the concept, in its incompletability of criteria, which allows for new histories of Mannerism, offers new sources of illumination of the works of art themselves. These new ways of inviting us to look at works of art—explicable only if we assume the possibility of new or enlarged sets of criteria—are as integral a part of art history and the role of style concepts in it as the authentication and dating of works of art. The historian's interpretations of particular works of art or groupings of them are as important as any of his other procedures. Without the vagueness of "Mannerism," these new interpretations, so rich in their aesthetic implications, would cease to come into being. It is consequently simply not true that without a true or real definition of "Mannerism," its history remains chaotic. Indeed, with such a definition—a complete set of necessary and sufficient criteria—there would be no continuing history of Mannerism.

"Mannerism," then, if my argument is correct, has no definition, no set of necessary and sufficient criteria, or even any necessary criterion. It does not need such criteria in order to support its style-giving reasons. It cannot have such criteria if the historical role of "Mannerism" as an irreducibly and beneficially vague concept is to be preserved.

"Mannerism," we have said, functions under certain criteria, none necessary, none sufficient, none definitive. These individual criteria are sometimes clear and clearly instanced but are also often obscure and inexact in their application.

These individual criteria can be classified also as descriptive or interpretive. All are employed by our historians to mark out features of works of art which they label manneristic. But only some of them are descriptive in their use. I suggested in our discussion of Friedlaender that, as he uses the term "spiritually subjective," it functions as an interpretive term to integrate all the manneristic elements of a painting. It purports to explain the work rather than to describe one aspect of it. Because it rests on elements in the work—uncanonical space, antinatural figure, asymmetry, unnatural color—that are related under the category of the nonoptically subjective way of observing objects in space, Friedlaender's "spiritually subjective" is an hypothesis about what is central in a manneristic work. Dvorak's "spirituality" is also in part an interpretation of certain elements in certain works of art, especially the Toledo paintings of El Greco. But because he invests these works with an element that is not clearly present (namely, emotional certainty of religious beliefs), his criterion serves to invite us to see these paintings as spiritual in his sense rather than as an explanation of the elements to be seen in them.

Many criteria of "Mannerism" are interpretive rather than descriptive in their use. All that are claimed to be central, whether definitively or not, are interpretive, serving as explanatory hypotheses about mannerist works. But there are others, not put forth as central, which are also interpretive: "elusive" as against "violent," "empty features" as against "elongated ones", "menacing" as against "brutal," and so on.

This whole subject of the kinds of criteria or terms and utterances to be found in art history deserves thorough investigation. In *Hamlet and the Philosophy of Literary Criticism*, I have tried to show the fruitfulness of distinguishing among the various kinds of terms and utterances in the clarification of many disputes of literary critics.[61] I have no doubt that similar results could be obtained from a careful consideration of the terms and utterances of art history.

That "Mannerism" is irreducibly vague, it can now be summarily shown, does clarify many of the fundamental disagreements among the historians of Mannerism. Debates about the origins of Mannerism, its place and date of origin, its founders, its paradigms, its range and development, whether or why a particular work or artist or group is or is not manneristic, whether Mannerism is an International Style, encompassing not only painting and sculpture, but architecture, music, and literature as well—all of these, I submit, are not questions that yield true or false answers that ultimately depend upon definitive criteria of "Mannerism." On the contrary, all of them are explicable only in terms of the selected criteria from the inexhaustible, vague set of criteria of "Mannerism." Does Mannerism start in Rome, or in Florence; in 1520, or in 1530; with Pontormo, or with Perino? Is it inspired by Michelangelo, and by his *Battle of Cascina, Ignudi,"* or the *Victor*? Does it include Tintoretto? Does it include Pontormo? Is it anticlassical, unclassical, classicistic, or superclassical? Each of the professed answers revolves systematically around criteria that are garnered from an inexhaustible class of criteria.

The attempt to pin down the criteria of "Mannerism" to those of the *maniera* rests, I think, on a double illusion: that the *maniera* is clearly definable and that Mannerism is identical with the *maniera*. As we have seen, there is no agreement on the definition of the *maniera*; what is more devastating, even if there were, it would not follow from such a definition that mannerism as a style phenomenon descends from the linguistic rather than the artistic roots of the *maniera*. On this issue, Friedlaender and Freedberg exploit one range of possibilities among the criteria of "Mannerism" and Shearman, a different range. Whether Mannerism is to be restricted to its linguistic rather than its artistic origins depends on the historian's decision, not on an historical fact.

That the style concept of Mannerism is irreducibly vague contrasts sharply with the various statements about the concept of style in art history by Schapiro, Ackerman, Hauser, and Gombrich. This contrast, therefore, provides the answer to our second question: namely, How does the use of "Mannerism" compare with art historians' statements about the concept of style in art history? If my account of the role or logical grammar of "Mannerism" is correct, this follows: their doctrines that styles are constancies of form motives, form relations, and expressive qualities; or are stable yet flexible ensembles of characteristics; or are fictional ideals of necessary and sufficient properties; or are hypothetical blends of norms and forms—all these doctrines are inadequate in the same fundamental way. They leave out the irreducible vagueness of at least one style concept, and they do so because they overlook the range and significance of disagreement among art historians in their style-giving reasons.

With the exception of Hauser, whose definition of style as an ideal essence is itself a fiction, invented to satisfy the spurious need for necessary and sufficient criteria as a buttress for style-giving reasons, the various statements about style apply brilliantly to the historians of Mannerism, taken in isolation, independently of their disagreements with one another. Here especially, constancy and ensemble take root in the particular sets of criteria for the correct use of "Mannerism" offered by the individual historians. Both Schapiro and Ackerman give adequate descriptions of our six historians' different uses of "Mannerism." For each of these historians employs criteria that serve to mark out certain constancies of form elements, form relations, and expressive qualities or certain ensembles of convention of form and symbolism on the assumption that these constancies or ensembles are sufficiently stable and flexible to render Mannerism a separate style. Ackerman's additional claim that these ensembles are hypotheses—which Gombrich generalizes as a universal doctrine about style concepts, but which Ackerman restricts to the criteria rather than the style concept—is also sound because the individual sets of criteria for "Mannerism" do function as interpretive hypotheses about what is central, though not necessarily definitive, in mannerist works. It is, therefore, not the emphasis upon the hypothetical character of the criteria that is defective in the art historians' account of style; it is their omission of what is implied by this hypothetical character, namely, the perennial possibility, and thus irreducible vagueness, of competing sets of criteria as integral at least to Mannerism as a style concept. Ackerman's reading of Mannerism or any other legitimate style as a series of related statements away from an original statement of a problem is an especially revealing example of this deficiency. Is there, we must ask, a clearly statable problem of Mannerism? What is to count as an original statement of Mannerism, as the historians of Mannerism make abundantly evident, is itself at stake in the intrinsic debatability of the concept.

Gombrich's contention that all styles are hypothetical blends of norm and form requires special consideration. As it stands, it is ambiguous. If it means in the case of Mannerism that "Mannerism" is used by historians to describe and evaluate, it is certainly true but hardly exciting. If it means that the extant criteria of "Mannerism" comprise both descriptive and evaluative ones, it is true for some historians, e.g., Shearman's "refinement," but not true for others, e.g., Friedlaender's criteria which are descriptive or interpretive. If it means, as I think Gombrich intends it to mean, that *every* criterion for "Mannerism" is both normative and descriptive, then we have a thesis that is as exciting as it is false. For example, are all of Friedlaender's criteria reducible to an implicit preference for "the less than classical" that parallels Gombrich's reduction of Wölfflin's purportedly descriptive polarities to the normative or preferred classical versus "the less than classical"? Does Friedlaender simply exchange one principle of exclusion for another? To be sure, Friedlaender rejects Wölfflin's "sins to be avoided" but he does not offer a new set in their place. It may be argued, as Gombrich does, that this is exactly what Dvorak attempts with his criterion of "spirituality." But as we have seen, Friedlaender's "spiritually subjective" functions as an interpretive, not as an evaluative or even descriptive, criterion. Once it is introduced, he also employs it as a basis for a revaluation of Mannerism. Its introduction, however, blends description of artistic elements with an interpretation of them. Friedlaender offers an hypothesis about form—i.e., antinatural figure in unnatural space—in order to dissociate this form from a traditionally invested norm. This procedure is not to blend norm and form, any more than cleansing our eyes is to exchange one pair of glasses for another. Gombrich, it seems to me, confuses blending norm and form with neutralizing traditional blends in order to procure a new evaluation of form. To neutralize is not necessarily to evaluate or revaluate, although it may be motivated or succeeded by them.

In this paper I have tried mainly to show that at least one style concept is irreducibly vague; that this vagueness is the fundamental logical feature of the role of this concept, to be discerned best in the range of disagreements among the historians in their style-giving reasons; and consequently that it is false that all style concepts or the concept of style in art history are logically closed in the sense that they do have, must have, or require sets of necessary, sufficient, or definitive critera and their corresponding properties in order to provide a coherent history of art. Whether other style concepts, such as High Renaissance or Baroque or Gothic, are also irreducibly vague, although I believe that they are, I leave open. Whether all style concepts, including Impressionism, Cubism or Abstract Expressionism are irreducibly vague, although I think they are not, I also leave open. Furthermore, there are other issues—for example, the causal use of style—about which I have said little or nothing, even though they may be as important as the substantive use of style. But it seems to me that the latter problem is central in the clarification of the other issues of art history, and that is why I have concentrated on it.

One question remains: What is the relation between the openness of at least some genre concepts and the irreducible vagueness of at least one style concept? Is "Mannerism" like "tragedy," which is open in the sense of having no necessary or sufficient criteria and no undebatable criteria, or like "drama" or "novel," which are open in the sense of having no necessary or sufficient criteria but at least some undebatable ones, such as "plot" or "character"? "Mannerism," I have argued, has no necessary or sufficient criteria and no unchallengeable criteria, and thus is more like "tragedy" than like "drama" or "novel." But it differs from these genre concepts in at least two important respects. First, its assigned role does not require that it accommodate new cases with their new properties: its perennial flexibility does not extend to future works of art in the way that these genre concepts do. Rather its flexibility relates to past works of art that are historically bounded by space and time. Second, the disagreements about the correct use of "Mannerism" converge more on the exchange of sets of criteria than on their enlargement to cover new cases or on the rejection of putatively necessary criteria.

Because of these two differences, I am inclined to regard "Mannerism" as distinct from genre concepts and perhaps akin to the explanatory concept of centrality in the criticism of works of art. For the debates and disagreements over what is central or most important in a particular work of art seem to have the same vast array of irreducible vagueness about what is to count as Mannerism.[62] On this interpretation of "Mannerism," we have a striking vindication of Gombrich's hypothesis that style concepts function as hypotheses in art history because they attempt to formulate what is central or most important and distinctive in certain groupings of works of art.

Whether these two differences between "Mannerism" and genre concepts entail a radical distinction between openness and irreducible vagueness, I do not know. But I am confident that all efforts to render open concepts closed and vague concepts complete at once misunderstand those concepts entirely and foreclose on their historically assigned roles.

NOTES

Chapter Two, *Hamlet*: Philosophy the Intruder

1. Eliot, T. S. "Hamlet," *Selected Essays* (London 1932), p. 141.

2. All quotations from *Hamlet* are from *The New Shakespeare*, ed. John Dover Wilson (Cambridge, 1934). Hereafter, references to this work will appear in the text following the quoted material.

3. Campbell, Lily B. *Shakespeare's Tragic Heroes: Slaves of Passion* (New York, 1952), p. 38.

4. Campbell, p. 109.

5. Campbell, p. 132.

6. Campbell, p. 147.

7. Spurgeon, Caroline F. E. *Shakespeare's Imagery and What It Tells Us* (Boston, 1958), p. 9.

8. Spurgeon, p. 316.

9. Spurgeon, p. 318-319 (italics in original).

10. Clemen, Wolfgang H. *The Development of Shakespeare's Imagery* (London, 1951), p. 113.

11. Clemen, p. 111.

12. Clemen, p. 112.

13. Clemen, p. 112.

14. Fergusson, Francis. *The Idea of a Theater* (Princeton, 1949), p. 120.

15. Fergusson, p. 120.

16. Fergusson, p. 122.

17. Fergusson, pp. 127-128.

18. Fergusson, p. 139.

19. Fergusson, p. 127.

20. Stoll, E. E. *Hamlet: A Historical and Comparative Study* ("Research Publications of the University of Minnesota," VIII, No. 5 (1919), p. 63.

21. Wilson, John Dover. *The New Shakespeare, Hamlet* (Cambridge, 1934), pp. lx-lxi.

22. Coleridge, Samuel T. *Shakespearian Criticism*, ed. Thomas M. Raysor (2 vols.; London, 1960), I, 16.

23. Coleridge, II, p. 230.

24. Coleridge, I, p. 18 (italics in original).

25. Coleridge, II, 150.

26. Coleridge, II, 150.

27. Coleridge, I, p. 34.

28. Coleridge, I, p. 35.

29. Coleridge, II, pp. 154-155.

30. Wilson, John Dover. *What Happens in ℠Hamlet"?* (Cambridge, 1935), p. 229.

31. Bradley, A.C. *Shakespearian Tragedy* (New York, 1955), p. 40.

32. Tillyard, E.M.W. *Shakespeare's Problem Plays*, (London, 1957), p. 17.

33. Tillyard, pp. 26-27.

34. Coleridge, p. 28.

35. Coleridge, p. 31.

Chapter Three, *Othello*: A Tragedy of Perfection Flayed and Flawed

1. Weitz, Morris. "*Literature Without Philosophy; Antony and Cleopatra,"* Shakespeare Survey 28 (1975), 29-36.

2. Gardner, Helen. *The Noble Moor* (Annual Shakespeare Lecture of the British Academy, 1955), Proceedings of the British Academy, XLI, 189-205; this quotation, as well as the others from her essay, is from p. 189.

3. Muir, Kenneth. in *Shakespeare's Tragic Sequence* (London, 1972), ch. 5, provides a splendid survey of traditional and contemporary interpretations, including some of the variants on Othello as a tragedy of sexual jealousy.

Chapter Four, The Coinage of Man: *King Lear* & Camus's *L'Étranger*

1. All quotations are from the new Arden edition, edited by Kenneth Muir (1952).

2. Vintage edition, translated by Stuart Gilbert (1946), p.72. All quotations are from this edition.

Chapter Seven, Poetics

1. Bradley, A. C. *Shakespearean Tragedy*, p. 20.

2. Bradley. "Hegel's Theory of Tragedy," *Oxford Lectures on Poetry*, p. 86.

3. Campbell, Lily. *Shakespeare's Tragic Heroes*, Appendix A, p. 249.

4. Campbell, p. 15.

5. Wilson, John Dover. *What Happens in "Hamlet,"* p. 39.

6. Wilson, p. 50 (italics in original).

7. Alexander, Peter. *Hamlet: Father and Son*, p. 40.

8. Alexander, pp. 88-89.

9. Alexander, p. 183.

10. Alexander, p. 184.

11. Harrison, *Shakespeare's Tragedies*, p. 10.

12. Harrison, p. 16.

13. Harrison, p. 17.

14. Harrison, p. 21 (italics in original).

15. Harrison, p. 273.

16. Harrison, p. 110.

17. Charlton, H. B. *Shakespearian Tragedy* (Cambridge, 1948), p. 12.

18. Charlton, p. 93.

19. Tillyard, E. M. W. *Shakespeare's Problem Plays* (London, 1950), p. 14.

20. Tillyard, p. 14.

21. Tillyard, p. 28.

22. Tillyard, p. 31.

23. Besides the classical discussion of Lessing, the Schlegels, Goethe, Hegel, Schopenhauer and Nietzsche, there are, among others, discussions of the tragic in *Hamlet*: John Lawlor, *The Tragic Sense in Shakespeare* (London, 1960); Bertram, Joseph, *Conscience and the King*; James V. Cunningham, *Woe or Wonder*; William Rosen, *Shakespeare and the Craft of Tragedy* (Cambridge, 1960); Stirling Brents, *Unity in Shakespearean Tragedy*, (New York, 1956); Robert Speaight, *Nature in Shakespearean Tragedy* (London, 1955); John Vyvyan, *The Shakespearean Ethic* (London, 1959); Willard Farnham, *The Medieval Heritage of Elizabethan Tragedy*, (Oxford, 1956); and H. D. F. Kitto, *Form and Meaning in Drama* (London, 1956).

24. Besides Aristotle, Lessing, Goethe, the Schlegels, Hegel, Nietzsche, and Schopenhauer, other writers on the nature of tragedy include: J. W. Krutch, *The Modern Temper* (New York, 1929); F. L. Lucas, *Tragedy* (revised ed; London, 1957); D. D. Raphael, *The Paradox of Tragedy* (Bloomington, 1960); and T. R. Henn, *The Harvest of Tragedy* (London, 1956).

25. See: Una Ellis-Fermor, *The Frontiers of Drama* (London, 1948); and S. K. Langer, *Feeling and Form* (New York, 1953).

26. F. L. Lucas writes of *The Three Sisters*: "There is, for me, no more really tragic ending in all drama" (Lucas, p. 74).

27. Muir, Kenneth. *Shakespeare and the Tragic Pattern*, (Annual Shakespeare Lecture of the British Academy), 1958, p. 146.

28. Muir, p. 153.

29. Knights, L. C. "How Many Children Had Lady Macbeth?" *Explorations* (London, 1951).

30. Traversi, D. A. *An Approach to Shakespeare*.

Chapter Eight, Literature and Philosophy: Sense and Nonsense

1. Santayana, George. *Three Philosophical Poets: Lucretius. Dante. Goethe.* Cambridge, Mass.: 1910.

2. Sidney, Sir Philip. *Defense of Poesy.* In Hyder E. Rollins and Herschel Baker (eds.) *The Renaissance in England* (Boston. 1954), pp. 608-609.

3. Sidney, op. cit., p. 610.

4. Jonson, Ben. *Prologue to Epicoene*, 1609.

5. Cf. also Archibald MacLeish mentioning to Mark Van Doren that Katsimbalis recited to him with great effect a poem of Sfereis in Greek although he did not understand

a word of it. In *The Dialogues of Archibald MacLeish and Mark Van Doren* (New York, 1964), p. 200.

6. Despreaux, Nicolas Boileau. "L'Art poétique." In his *Oeuvres divers* (1st edition, Paris, 1674).

7. Pope, Alexander. *An Essay On Criticism* (London, 1713).

8. Johnson, Samuel. "Preface To Shakespeare." In *Rasselas. Poems and Selected Prose*, ed. Bertrand H. Bronson (New York, 1958), p. 241.

9. Wordsworth, William. *Selected Poetry*, ed. Mark Van Doren (New York, n.d.), p. 675.

10. Wordsworth, op. cit., pp. 684 and 693.

11. Wordsworth, op. cit., p. 688.

12. Coleridge, Samuel Taylor, *Biographia Literaria*, ed. J. Shawcross, revised by G. Watson (London, 1956), Chapter IV.

13. Coleridge, op. cit., Chapter XV

14. Coleridge, *Miscellaneous Criticism*, ed. T.M. Raysor (London, 1936), p. 277.

15. Hazlitt, William. "On Poetry in General." in *Hazlitt on Literature*, ed. J. Zeitlin (New York, 1913).

16. Shelley, Percy Bysshe, "A Defence of Poetry" In *Shelley's Prose*, ed. D.L. Clark (London, 1954).

17. Mill, John Stuart, "Thoughts on Poetry and Its Varieties." In *Dissertations and Discussions* (London, 1875).

18. Leopardi, Giacomo, *Zibaldone de pensieri*, quoted from René Wellek: *A History of Modern Criticism* 1750-1950, vol. 2 (New Haven and London, 1955), p. 276.

19. Arnold, Matthew. *Selected Criticism of Matthew Arnold*, ed. Christopher Ricks (New York and Scarborough. 1972), pp. 92-117.

20. Ricks, ed. pp. 368-369.

21. Ricks, ed. pp. 379-383.

22. Croce, Benedetto. *La Poesia* (Bari, 1936).

23. Richards, Ivor Armstrong. *Principles of Literary Criticism* (London) pp. 261-271

24. *Othello*, I, iii, 99-103.

25. *Othello*, V, ii, 304-305.

26. *Othello*, V, ii, 302-303.

27. *Othello*, V, ii, 304-305

28. Berlin, Isaiah. *The Hedgehog and the Fox* (1953), pp. 39-40.

Chapter Nine, Genre and Style

1. See, e.g., M. C. Bradbrook. "Fifty Years of the Criticism of Shakespeare's Style: a Retrospect," *Shakespeare Survey*, VII (1954): "There is no question relating to Shakespeare as a writer that does not involve his style . . . . Yet on this central problem comparatively little has been written" (p. 1).

2. First published in *Journal of Aesthetics and Art Criticism*, XV (1956).

3. Schapiro, Meyer, "Style," first published in A. L. Kroeber, ed., *Anthropology Today* (Chicago, University of Chicago Press, 1953); reprinted in M. Philipson, ed., *Aesthetics Today* (New York, Meridian, World Publishing Co., 1961). All references are to this reprint.

4. Schapiro, p. 83.

5. Schapiro, p. 83.

6. Schapiro, p. 81.

7. Ackerman, James S., "A Theory of Style," *Journal of Aesthetics and Art Criticism*, XXI (1962). Reprinted in M. C. Beardsley and H. M. Schueller, eds., *Aesthetic Inquiry* (Belmont, California, Dickenson Publishing Co., 1967). All references are to this reprint.

8. Ackerman, p. 56.

9. Ackerman.

10. Ackerman, p. 59.

11. Ackerman, p. 60.

12. Hauser, Arnold. *The Philosophy of Art History* (New York, Alfred A. Knopf, 1963) and *Mannerism*, 2 vols. (London, Routledge, Kegan Paul, 1965).

13. Hauser, *Mannerism*, I, 111.

14. Hauser, *Philosophy of Art History*, p. 209.

15. Hauser, *Mannerism*, I, 18-19.

16. Both essays are collected in E. H. Gombrich, *Norm and Form: Studies in the Art of the Renaissance* (London, Phaidon, 1966).

17. Kubler, George. *The Shape of Time* (New Haven, Yale University Press, 1962), p. 130.

18. Inaugural Lecture, 1914. Published in translation in 1925, under the full title "The Rise of the Anticlassical Style in Italian Painting in 1520." Reprinted in Walter Friedlaender, *Mannerism and Anti-Mannerism in Italian Painting* (New York, Schocken Books, 1965). All references are to this reprint.

19. Friedlaender, p. 6.

20. Friedlaender, pp. 23-24.

21. Friedlaender, p. 29.

22. Friedlaender, p. 31.

23. Friedlaender, p. 34.

24. The full title of the translated essay is "The Anti-Mannerist Style around 1590 and Its Relation to the Transcendental" (1930). Reprinted in Friedlaender. I quote from p. 48.

25. First delivered as a lecture in 1920 and published in Max Dvorak, *Kunstgeschichte als Geistesgeschichte*, 1953. Translated in *Magazine of Art*, XLVI (1953). All references are to this translation.

26. Dvorak, p. 21.

27. Dvorak, p. 21.

28. Venturi, Lionello. *From Leonardo to El Greco* (New York, World Publishing Co., 1956).

29. Venturi, p. 234.

30. Venturi, p. 216. On the history of *maniera*, see esp. Marco Treves, *"Maniera*, the history of a Word," *Marsyas*, I (1941); Sir Anthony Blunt, *Artistic Theory in Italy, 1450-1600* (London, 1940), ch. 7; and R. Klein and H. Zerner, eds., *Italian Art, 1500-1600* ("Sources and Documents in the History of Art Series," Englewood Cliffs, Prentice-Hall, Inc., 1966), esp. pp. 53-91.

32. Smyth, C. H. "Mannerism and *maniera*" in M. Meiss, ed., *The Renaissance and Mannerism (Studies in Western Art: Acts of the Twentieth international Congress of the History of Art*, Princeton, Princeton University Press, 1963), II, 174-199.

33. Quoted by Smyth, "Mannerism," p. 177.

34. Smyth, p. 177.

35. Smyth, p. 181.

36. Smyth, p. 194.

37. Smyth, p. 198.

38. Shearman, John. *"Maniera* as an Aesthetic Ideal" in Meiss, *The Renaissance and Mannerism*; and Shearman, *Mannerism* (Baltimore, Penguin Books, 1967).

39. Shearman, *"Maniera* as an Aesthetic Ideal," p. 213.

40. Shearman, *Mannerism*, p. 23.

41. Shearman, *"Maniera* as an Aesthetic Ideal," p. 215.

42. Shearman, p. 217.

43. Shearman, p. 217.

44. Shearman, *Mannerism*, p. 35.

45. Shearman, p. 84.

46. Briganti, Giuliano. *Italian Mannerism*, tr. M. Kunzle (Leipzig, Volkseiger Betrieb, 1962), p. 6. Cf. Blunt, ch. 7.

47. Freedberg, Sydney J. "Observations on the Painting of the "maniera", *The Art Bulletin*, XLVII (1965). Freedberg discusses Mannerism also in *Parmigianino* (Cambridge, Harvard University Press, 1950) and in *Painting of the High Renaissance in Rome and Florence*, 2 vols. (Cambridge, Harvard University Press, 1961).

48. Freedberg, "Observations," p. 188.

49. Freedberg, p. 187.

50. Freedberg, p. 194.

51. Freedberg, p. 194.

52. Freedberg, p. 195.

53. Freedberg, p. 195.

54. Freedberg, p. 196.

55. On Mannerist architecture, a concise study is Nikolaus Pevsner, *An Outline of European Architecture* (Baltimore, Penguin Books, 1951), ch. 5; on Mannerism as an International Style, see F. Wurtenberger, *Mannerism: the European Style of the Sixteenth Century*, trans. by M. Heron (New York, Holt, Rinehart, and Winston, 1963). Both contain good bibliographies on their subjects.

56. See, e.g., M. Salmi, "Tardo Rinascimento e primo Barocco, Manierismo, Barocco, Rococò: Concetti e termini," *Convegno intl*, Rome 1960 (Rome, Academia Nazionale dei

Lincei, 1962), pp. 305-17.

57. Shearman, *Mannerism*, p. 15.

58. Friedlaender, p. 13.

59. Shearman, *Mannerism*, p. 84.

60. Stevenson, C. L. "Persuasive Definitions," *Mind*, 47 (1938).

61. See esp. Part II.

62. On centrality as an explanatory concept, see my *Hamlet and the Philosophy of Literary Criticism*, ch. xv.

PUBLICATIONS BY MORRIS WEITZ

BOOKS:

Philosophy of the Arts. Cambridge: Harvard University Press, 1950. Reprinted by Russell and Russell, 1964.

Philosophy in Literature: Shakespeare, Voltaire, Tolstoy and Proust. Detroit: Wayne State University Press, 1963. (Hardcover and Paperback.)

Hamlet and the Philosophy of Literary Criticism. Chicago: University of Chicago Press, 1964. Published in England by Faber and Faber, 1965. Published as Meridian Paperback, 1966; as Faber and Faber paper-covered edition, 1972; and as Midway Reprint Edition, University of Chicago, 1974.

The Opening Mind: A Philosophical Study of Humanistic Concepts. Chicago: University of Chicago Press, 1977.

Theories of Concepts. London: Routledge and Kegan Paul, 1988

Hanslick, E. *The Beautiful in Music*, ed., Library of Liberal Arts, 1957.

Problems in Aesthetics, ed., New York: The Macmillan Co., 1959, Revised and enlarged, with new introductions, in Second Edition, 1970.

Twentieth Century Philosophy: The Analytic Tradition, ed., New York Free Press, 1966.

ARTICLES:

"Does Art Tell the Truth?" *Philosophy and Phenomenological Research*, 1943.

"Analysis and the Unity of Russell's Philosophy," *The Philosophy of Bertrand Russell*, "Library of Living Philosophers," vol. 5, 1944. Reprinted as Harper Torchback.

"The Logic of Art," *Philosophy and Phenomenological Research*, 1945.

"Philosophy and the Abuse of Language," *Journal of Philosophy*, 1947.

"Analysis and Real Definition," *Philosophical Studies*, 1950.

"Art, Language and Truth," in (eds.), Vivas and Krieger, *The Problem of Aesthetics*, 1951.

"Professor Ryle's Logical Behaviorism'," *Journal of Philosophy*, 1951.

"T. S. Eliot: Time as Mode of Salvation," *Sewanee Review*, 1952; reprinted in B. Bergonzi, ed., *T. S. Eliot: Four Quartets*, Macmillan Ltd., 1969.

"Criticism Without Evaluation," *Philosophical Review*, 1952; Reprinted in H.G. Duffield, *Problems in Criticism of the Arts*, Chandler Co., 1968.

"Oxford Philosophy," *Philosophical Review*, 1953.

"Art and Symbolism," *Review of Metaphysics*, 1954.

"Analytic statements," *Mind*, 1954, reprinted in *Analytic Statements* (Wadsworth) 1975.

"Truth in Literature," *Revue internationale de philosophie*, 1955. Reprinted in J. Hospers, (ed.) *Introductory Readings in Aesthetics*, Free Press, 1969.

"The Role of Theory in Aesthetics," *The Journal of Aesthetics and Art Criticism*, 1956. (Matchette Prize Essay). Reprinted in M. Rader, *A Modern Book of Aesthetics*; Morris Weitz, *Problems in Aesthetics*; A. Castell, *Introduction to Modern Philosophy*; Beck, *Perspectives in Philosophy*; J. Margolis, *Philosophy Looks at the Arts*; Smith, *Aesthetics and Language in Art*; Beardsley and Schueller, *Aesthetic Inquiry*; Duffield and Bilsky, *Tolstoy and His Critics*; H.G. Duffield, *Problems in Criticism of the Arts*; F. Coleman, *Contemporary Studies in Aesthetics*; Reprint in Bobbs-Merrill Series of Philosophy Reprints; G. Stein, *The Forum of Philosophy*, McGraw-Hill, 1972; W. Henckman, ed., *Asthetik, Wissenschaftliche Buchgesellschaft*, 1974; and *Problematica* (Stuttgart, 1975), among others.

"The Philosophy of Criticism," *Proceedings* of the III International Congress of Aesthetics, 1956.

"Aesthetics," *Chroniques de Philosophie*, 1958, (Written for UNESCO.)

"Reasons in Criticism," *Journal of Aesthetics and Art Criticism*; 1962. Reprinted in C. Barrett, (ed.) *Collected Papers in Aesthetics*, Blackwell, 1966; in Weitz, *Problems in Aesthetics*, second edition.

"The Form-Content Distinction," in. W. Kennick, ed., *Art and Philosophy*, St. Martin, 1964.

"Tragedy," *Encyclopedia of Philosophy*, Macmillan, 1967.

"Analysis, Philosophical," *Enc. of Phil.*, 1967.

"Marcel Proust," *Enc. of Phil.*, 1967.

"The Nature of Art," in D. Ecker and E. Eisner, eds. *Philosophies of Art Education*, Blaisdell, 1966.

"Knowledge in Art," *Proceedings*, Interamerican Congress of Philosophy, 1967.

"The Organic Theory," in Tillman and Cahn, eds., *Readings in Aesthetics*, Harper and Row, 1968.

"Purism and the Dance," in L. Jacobus, ed., *Aesthetics and the Arts*, McGraw-Hill, 1968.

"Genre and Style," *Proceedings*, RIV International Congress of Philosophy, 1968.

"Genre and Style," *Contemporary Philosophic Thought*, vol. 3., State University of New York Press, 1970.

"Professor Goodman on the Aesthetic," *Journal of Aesthetics and Art Criticism*, 1971.

"The Coinage of Man: *King Lear* and Camus' *Stranger*," Proceedings, Brockport Centre for Philosophic Exchange 1970; *Modern Language Review*, Jan. 1971.

"The Content of Form," *New Literary History*, vol. II, 2.

"Amy Warburg," *The Art Bulletin*, March, 1972 (Review essay of E.N. Gombrich, *Amy Warburg: An Intellectual Biography*).

"Open Concepts," *Revue Internationale de Philosophie*, 172, pp. 86-110.

"What is Aesthetic Education?," *Education Theatre Journal*.

"The Concept of Human Action," *Philosophic Exchange*.

"Wittgenstein's Aesthetic," *Language and Aesthetics*, University of Kansas Press, 1973.   Reprinted in *Aesthetics: A Critical Anthology*, New York: St. Martins, 1977.

"The Grounds of Sense: The Philosophy of Everett J. Nelson," *Philosophy and Phenomenological Research*, 1973.

"Interpretation and the Visual Arts," *Theoria*, 1973.

"Literature Without Philosophy: Antony and Cleopatra," *Shakespeare Survey*.

"Art: Who Needs It?" *Journal of Aesthetic Education*, 1976.

"Research on the Arts and in Aesthetics: Some Pitfalls, Some Possibilities," *Art and Aesthetics: an Agenda for the Future*, Cemrel and National Institute for Education,
        Reprinted: *Arts and Aesthetics: An Agenda for the Future*, ed., S. Madeja.1975 Cemrel; 1977; *The Journal of Aesthetic Education*, vol. II, No. 2, April 1977.

"Literature and Philosophy: Sense and Nonsense," *Yearbook of Comparative Criticism*, 1988.

"Ryle's Theories of Concepts," *Midwest Studies in Philosophy*, vol. 6, 1981.

"Descartes' Theory of Concepts," *Midwest Studies in Philosophy*, vol. 8, 1983.

"Making Sense of the Tractatus," *Midwest Studies in Philosophy*, vol. 8, 1983.

"On Criticism," *Sonus*, vol. 2 no. 1, 1981.

"But is it Art?," *Sonus*, vol. 10, no. I 1989.

REVIEWS:

About 70 or so, in *Philosophical Review, Ethics, Mind, Journal of Philosophy, American Scholar, Virginia Quarterly Review, Partisan Review,* etc.

INDEX OF PROPER NAMES